ACE ENDICO CONTINUES TO EVOLVE.

As our product lines and offerings grow and our warehouse expands, so do the opportunities of your culinary imagination. Ace Endico has always stood for quality and impeccable customer service, and our state-of-the-art facility has strengthened our capacity to be able to deliver, offering our chef and food professional customers even greater ways to express their culinary artistry.

We now offer a complete selection of gourmet specialty food ingredients, from pastry components, specialty meats and produce, quality oils and vinegars, the world's finest chocolate, and much more.

Our history, our present strength, our future company promise and ambitions have all inspired the collection of recipes offered in this cookbook. We hope this delicious collection prepared by Master Chef Edward G. Leonard and his talented and award-winning ACF Team inspires you. Our gift to you, let this worldly mix of cultures and flavors allow your culinary imagination fuel for years to come.

Bon Appetit!

Ace Endico Corporation 80 International Blvd Brewster, NY 10509
(845) 940-1501 / (914) 347-3131 / (212) 517-3035 / FAX (845) 940-1516

www. aceendico.com

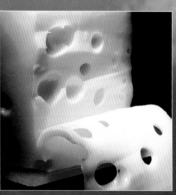

Cooking with America's Championship Team

ACF

Sizzling recipes from Chef Edward G. Leonard, CMC
and the American Championship Culinary Team

First published in the United States of America in 2009 by:

LTD Publishing, llc.• 7330 E. Sheridan St. • Scottsdale, AZ 85257 • (480) 990-7444

LTD Publishing, llc.
Author: Chef Edward G. Leonard, CMC
Project Chef: Jonathan Moosmiller, CEC
Art Direction/Design/Layout: Graham Walters, Rhino Design Group
Photography: John Ormond, Vaughn St. Imaging
Recipe Editor: Alice Thompson
Line Editor: Elin Jeffords

ISBN# 970-09815729-1-8

Printed & Bound in Korea
Overseas Printing Corporation.

Cooking with America's Championship Team

ACF

Sizzling recipes from Chef Edward G. Leonard, CMC
and the American Championship Culinary Team

The Legacy of American

Cuisine is in our hands.

Our humble but confident approach

along with a professional demeanor ensures

that we will be leaving our legacy in the

history of global competitions as we succeed

at our goals and achieve our objectives

representing the cuisine of our country and

the cooks and chefs who live it every day

they step in a kitchen.

—Chef Edward Leonard, CMC, WGMC

Ferdinand Metz, CMC

As I reflect on the past 40 years and the participation of American Culinary Teams in world class competitions, I cannot help but marvel at the incredible progress we all have made.

Having early on been relegated to just filling a spot on the international competition stage, ACF teams evolved over time to one of the most innovative and respected teams in the global arena.

How could this have happened and what drove these teams to achieve such an incredible success story? The answers are embodied in the words of legacy, leadership and commitment.

It takes competent and consummate professionals who understand that by building on a legacy of three Championships in the Hot Cuisine category does not diminish, but in fact highlights their own collective accomplishments.

It takes extraordinary leadership from a team manager to direct a group of individual chefs motivate and mold them into a cohesive team with an Esprit de Corps that accepts the difficult task of delicately balancing the respect for tradition, while not compromising the teams' quest for self expression. It is that spirit, that appreciates the risks of innovation, which in turn can yield extraordinary rewards.

It takes unwavering dedication to the common cause, not to individual ambitions. Championship teams are never appointed, but evolve based on the individual and collective commitment to pursue excellence on all fronts and at all times.

But it takes so much more. All team members know that there is no substitute for hard work, nor is there a leeway for substandard performance at any time. The problem with success is that it breeds exponential and sometimes unrealistic expectations, but it is this very burden that energizes the teams to overcome all obstacles, which would prevent them from reaching their goals. It also takes mental resiliency to deal with the highs and lows that are always part of any competition and it takes pride, confidence and courage to compete at any level, let alone on the world stage.

It has been said that it is not the destination sought, but the journey traveled, which is the true benefit of any competition. The experience and privilege of working within a group of highly dedicated chefs, free and able to share their knowledge cannot be measured by the number of medals and awards, as the ultimate prize is the enriching learning process that makes us better chefs. This notion is, however not clearly understood by all.

This book and its story of a few chefs shouldering the burden of a whole nation is an absolutely obligatory addition to every serious cook's library.

Finally, I salute all those American Teams that have been able to harness and devote their energies, talents and dedication in representing our great cuisine and country. They have lived and succeeded by their team credo: One for all and all for one.

Ferdinand Metz, CMC

Captain and Manager 1976 to 1988
Team member for over 20 years
April 8, 2009

Having witnessed the remarkable voyage of team USA, I can only say this was the greatest experience that I have had since becoming a member of the American Culinary Federation. Under the inspirational leadership of Chef Edward Leonard CMC, I have witnessed the cutting edge of American cuisine on the world stage. From the start of the first practice to the final layout in Germany in 2008 the development and execution of the wonderful dishes, menus, and recipes in this book will excite you beyond your culinary dreams. As president of the American Culinary Federation, and a former competitor I have never seen such dedication and devotion to our craft as demonstrated by these fine young men and women during their tenure on the team. Having tasted some of these wonderful dishes and having seen what I would call the greatest cold food displays at the Olympics and the World Cup, I can only say that this book reflects the dedication and devotion to excellence these great young people gave on behalf of our country and most of all the members of the American Culinary Federation.

So finally, let the book speak for itself and I am sure that you will be using these recipes for many years to come. You will be inspired by the phenomenal cold food displays and the wonderful menus they executed for all the members of the American dining public.

So, let's get cooking. As you try each recipe remember that the dedication and the hours they put into themselves the culinary delights and great dining experiences that makes this book a treasure to keep.

Bon appetite

John Kinsella CMC

American Culinary Federation,
national president

John Kinsella, CMC
American Culinary Federation
national president

Chef Leonard makes his rounds offering advice and encouragement as the National Team USA prepares for the cold food display.

A Team of Champions

This book reflects the dedication, hopes, hard work and aspirations of a group of chefs who took on the task of representing the American Culinary Federation and the United States at the Culinary Olympics in October of 2008.

The team journey includes many stories beyond the medals and awards won. There is also the sense of accomplishment, the disappointments, victories, friendships made, respect built and the resulting global admiration. The team of 2008, along with the 2004 and 2000 team, dedicates this book and our work of 12 years to all of the culinarians, apprentices, students and chefs in all areas of the profession as well as the members of the American Culinary Federation for their hard work and the contributions made daily to our great craft of cookery.

We started with a simple mission 12 years ago, to make a difference in the world of cuisine. With the achievements made and the lessons learned by the chefs of Team USA, I think all would agree we made a difference and inspired others to be better at their craft.

The 2008 Olympics in Erfurt, Germany was the end of a journey that will never be forgotten. The final destination was really the beginning for a new team and those chefs brave enough to start the journey all over again. The quest for excellence is a road that takes commitment, dedication and the ability to be pushed to the limit, it is one that never ends.

Only those who strive to achieve greatness can truly grasp how much this group of chefs gave of themselves. Their sacrifices, hard work and training helped realize the dream we all shared. The passion and love for food consumed us at all times and energized us for competing against the best chefs in the world with success to be proud of and disappointments to learn from.

The chefs of Team USA 2008 and our Team USA predecessors have made an impact on the industry that is felt daily within American cuisine by many culinarians the world over. They will become the leaders in our profession and take the philosophy of being the best possible along with them in everything they do. This will create a chain reaction and more dedicated chefs will strive to raise the bar and represent the cuisine of the United States every time they step into the kitchen.

We took the path less chosen; we did not follow but instead led, with a belief in the cuisine of today that will emerge as the standard for the future. Champions do not always win but they do exhibit the dedication, endurance and achievements that set them apart from the rest along with the ability to take a risk. That said, the 2008 Team and all those who came before are true champions.

Edward G. Leonard. CMC, WGMC
Manager ACF Culinary Team USA 2008

Edward G. Leonard, CMC, AAC — Team Manager

Chef Leonard's resume reads like a book. During his tenure as President, he is credited with bringing the American Culinary Federation into a prominent position by branding, strict ly focusing on quality, creating new logos and demonstrating a passion for cooking that helped ACF gain respect within the organization and globally and encouraged other culinary associations around the world to take the lead from ACF.

With Leonard leading team USA from 1998 to 2008 the accolades and medals garnered by the various USA teams have been many. The global community came to respect a team that was confident but humble and with the sole mission of making a difference and never fearing to try new endeavors in cuisine and put themselves on the line. When the ACF Culinary team USA won the hot food championship in 2004 the global culinary community knew that the cuisine of the USA was indeed at the pinnacle of excellence.

As his peers and colleagues will tell you, the man called "Chef" lives his passion for what he does every single day. Currently the assistant general manager and director of culinary operation at the Westchester Country Club, chef Leonard has also published 6 books in the past 5 years. His current release is "You Eat with Your Eyes"

He has earned over 50 gold medals in the USA and internationally for cookery. Honors from Sante magazine, Food Arts, The American Academy of Chefs, The Cordon d'Or and a honorary doctorate from Johnson and Wales university show the respect he has been afforded by many in the profession.

When asked his key to success, Chef Leonard replies simply, I have been fortunate enough to surround myself with extremely talented, loyal and passionate chefs, cooks and managers who love cuisine and love the challenge of raising the bar every day they step in a kitchen or on their property no matter what the venue. It is because of them I have had the opportunity to keep learning and gaining experiences that will last me a lifetime.

Edward G. Leonard, CMC, AAC
Team Manager

Richard Rosendale, CEC
Team Captain

Joachim Buchner, CMC

Daniel Scannell, CMC

Jamie P. Keating, CCC

Mellisa K. Root

Richard Rosendale, CEC — Team Captain

Richard Rosendale, CEC, opened Rosendales, a modern American restaurant, in Columbus, Ohio, in March 2007. Rosendale was formerly top chef at the award-winning Tavern Room at The Greenbrier in White Sulphur Springs, W. Va. He has competed in many national and international culinary competitions, amassing more than 35 medals. Rosendale was honored as the U.S.A.'s Chef of the Year™ for 2005 at the ACF national convention. He graduated first in his class in an ACF apprenticeship program in 1997 at Westmoreland Community College in Youngwood, Pa. In addition, he is a certified professional ice carver.

Joachim Buchner, CMC

Joachim Buchner, CMC, is executive chef at Chevy Chase Club in Chevy Chase, Md. Before joining the club, Buchner worked at the Dusseldorf Hilton in Germany. Buchner came to the United States in 1983. His experience working in small specialty restaurants and large established hotels led him to open restaurants for several new hotels.

In 1987 Buchner returned to Germany to complete German master chef certification. Three years later, he earned his certified master chef (CMC) designation. He has won numerous medals, awards and prizes, and has competed in many national and international culinary competitions, including the 2005 Salon Culinaire Mondial in Basel, Switzerland. Buchner was also member of ACF Culinary Team USA 2004.

Daniel Scannell, CMC

Daniel J. Scannell, CMC is currently the Chef at La Gorce Country Club in Miami Beach. Daniel has been a competing member of the ACF Culinary Team USA / National 2000, 2004 and 2008. In 2003 he became one of only 62 certified master chefs in the United States. In 2007 he was named Northeast Regional U.S.A.'S Chef of the Year™. Daniel also had the distinct honor of being the 144th Distinguished Visiting Chef at Daniel's Alma

Mater, Johnson & Wales University in Providence and received an Honorary Doctorate Degree in Culinary Arts from that same institution in May 2006. In May 2008, Daniel was granted Global Master Chef Certification from the World Association of Chefs Societies (WACS) at their world congress in Dubai, United Arab Emirates. Daniel lives on Miami Beach with his wife Pamela and daughter Ireland.

Jamie P. Keating, CCC

Jamie Keating is chef/owner of Gourmet Events, a catering company at RiverMill Event Center in Columbus, Ga. Keating has earned more than 25 national and international culinary medals, including three gold medals at the Internationale Kochkunst Ausstellung in Erfurt, Germany and two gold medals in the hot-food and cold-food categories at the 2005 Salon Culinaire Mondial in Basel, Switzerland.

Keating received his formal education from Paul Smith's College in New York. Additional education was at The Culinary Institute of America at Greystone, St. Helena, Calif. He apprenticed at Arpège (Michelin three stars) and Le Cordon Bleu School of Culinary Arts in Paris, France.

Melissa K. Root

Mellisa K. Root is a pastry chef at Payard Pâtisserie & Bistro at Caesars Palace in Las Vegas. Throughout her career, Root has earned numerous medals in many national competitions, as well as gold and silver medals at the American Culinary Classic held at the 2007 National Restaurant Association Restaurant, Hotel-Motel Show.

Root has continued working with many of the nation's top culinary and pastry-arts experts, including François Payard; Laurent Branlard; Darrin Aoyama, and CEPC; Charles Carroll, CEC, AAC. Formerly, she was the pastry chef at the acclaimed River Oaks Country Club in Houston. Root attended the baking and pastry-arts program at the California Culinary Academy in San Francisco.

2008 ACF Culinary Regional Team USA

(left to right)

Mellisa K. Root

Timothy Prefontaine, CSC

Joseph M. Leonardi

Michael Matarazzo, team captain

Drew B. Garms

Edward G. Leonard, CMC, AAC,
    team manager

2008 AAC Culinary Regional Team USA

(left to right)

Jill Bosich, CEC, CCE, AAC - AAC
    Team Manager

Christopher Desens, CEC, AAC

Daryl L. Shular, CCC

Scott Fetty

Randy J. Torres

Loan Co

2008 ACF Culinary Youth Team USA

(left to right)

Mike Palazzola

John Gelineau

Wayne Sieve

Mike Bush

Kevin Taylor

Steven Jilleba, CMC, CCE, AAC,
    team manager

Not pictured:

Paul Kampff, CEC, team coach

Kevin Storm, CEC, team coach

Craig Meyer, CEC, team coordinator

Team Behind the Team

Some of many members of the team behind the team since 1998.

Chef Harmut Handke, CMC,
coach and advisor

Chef Peter Timmons, CMC,
coach and advisor

Chef Daniel Huglier, CMC,
coach and advisor

Pastry Chef Gilles Renissence,
coach and advisor

Chef Victor Gielesse, CMC,
coach and advisor

Keith Coughenour, CEC,
coach

Garrett Sanborn, CEC,
design team, coach and advisor

Debbie Kelder,
travel agent

Jean St Hillare,
chief Steward for 7 years

James Decker, CEC,
national team sous chef 2004

Shawn Hanlin, CEC,
team sous chef 2008

Robert James, CCM,
executive director of Westchester Country Club

Mariana Delgado Gambini, CPC
Pastry Chef, Westchester Country Club

Mr. Michael Feil, CCM
General Manager, Westchester County Club

Mr. William Minard, CCM
GM, COO, Scarsdale Golf Club

John Kinsella, CMC
ACF President

Chef Joe Aiello, CEC
ACF National Treasure

The many apprentices since 1998 that traveled and worked with us

Behind every successful endeavor are the people who through their hard work and generosity make the impossible happen.

Working without accolades and spotlight, their contributions made it all possible. Accepting no medals and with no trophies to display, they gave of themselves to make others succeed.

This, in my view, is a humble gesture of much importance at a time when too often self-satisfaction takes the stage. There is no thank you big enough to show the appreciation we have for the team behind the team.

Our efforts would not have been possible without the donations of money and supplies, hours of shared expertise and talent, the hard work of packing, cleaning, cooking meals as well as the day-to-day support of the culinary team. Transportation, creating the custom tables showcasing the cold food displays and all the other logistics that went in to achieving results was a huge challenge — one met with passion and the fortitude to provide everything needed for the competing chefs.

Through the long days and exhausting nights, amidst all the challenges, the team behind the ACF Culinary Team USA was always able to rise to the task at hand.

Ferdinand Metz, CMC — Pioneer of American cuisine and our mentor, with the 1976 to 1988 teams. Ferdinand was our coach and advisor from 2000 to 2008 and shared his knowledge and love of food, which inspired us all.

Brad Barnes, CMC — Brad was architect and designer for over 20 tables. He worked hard to achieve elegant tables that showcased the team's food. He also managed all shipping, packing and important details for the team. He was also there to offer feedback on our food and give us a different perspective to consider.

Charles Carroll, CEC — Carroll is one of the few chefs who have been at this game since 1988. He was a member on city teams and regional teams and a member of the national team in 2000. His service did not stop there. He coached the 3rd place regional team in 2004 and served as the cold food coach for the 2008 national team. He hosted many sessions for teams at his club and was always there with us.

Chef Thomas Vaccaro — Tom is a pastry chef of a special breed. He could have been a national team member but instead chose to mentor young, upcoming pastry chefs and have them take the spotlight. In short, without Chef Tom's coaching and roll-up-the- sleeves attitude, we would not have achieved the success we did over the years in the pastry category.

Chef Jonathan Moosmiller, CEC — The team sous chef and host chef for the 2004 and 2008 teams, Jonathan supported us with ordering food, cleaning up the kitchen and helping provide all items needed to make the team members feel at home.

Chef Steve Jilleba — Steve was instrumental in gaining the team much needed sponsorship, coaching and assistance in the past 10 years. He also took on the task of coaching the youth teams in 2004 and 2008 with great success. He was there for us whenever he was needed.

Edwin Brown — At international events Mr. Brown is always there to meet and greet. The ultimate gentleman and ambassador, he is known and respected by so many in the USA and across the globe. His help in securing kitchens, hotel rooms, and whatever we needed was invaluable to the team.

1956 U.S. Culinary Team
Fred Wohlkopf
Paul Laesecke, captain
Paul Debes
Paul Leuppe
Otto Spielbichler

1960 U.S. Culinary Team
Paul Laesecke, manager
Charles Finance, captain
Tony Ackermann
Charles Daniel
Edmond Kasper

1964 U. S. Culinary Team
John Monbaron, manager
Willi Rossel, captain
Richard Mack
Otto Schlecker
Hubert Schmieder

1968 U.S. Culinary Team
Jack Sullivan, manager
Richard Mack, captain
Ferdinand Metz
Gerhard Schmid
Casey Sinkeldam

1972 U.S. Culinary Team
Jack Sullivan, manager
Bernard Urban, captain
Milos Cihelka
Franz Eckert
Gerhard Grimeissen

1976 U.S. Culinary Team
Richard Bosnjak, manager
Ferdinand Metz, captain
Bruno Ellmer
Gerhard Grimeissen
Gerhard Schmid

1980 U.S. Culinary Team
Ferdinand Metz, manager
Klaus Friedenreich, captain
Gerhard Grimeissen
Klaus Loos
Richard Schneider

1984 U.S. Culinary Team
Ferdinand Metz, manager
Richard Schneider, captain
Marcus Bosiger
Daniel Hugelier
L. Timothy Ryan

1988 U.S. Culinary Team
Ferdinand Metz, manager
L. Timothy Ryan, captain
Mark Erickson
Hartmut Handke
Daniel Hugelier
Christopher Northmore

1992 Culinary Team U.S.A.
Keith Keogh, CEC, AAC, manager
Keith Coughenour, CC, captain
Martha Crawford, CWPC
Lawrence McFadden, CC
Franz Popperl, CEC, CCE
Michael Russell, CMC

1996 Team USA National
Keith Keogh, CEC, AAC, manager
Christian Clayton
Keith Coughenour, CC
Daniel Dumont
Lawrence McFadden, CWC
William Wolf

2000 ACF Culinary Team USA National
Edward Leonard, CMC, AAC, manager
Alfonso Contrisciani, CMC, captain
Darrin Aoyama
Charles Carroll, CEC
Derin Moore, CWC
Daniel Scannell, CEC

2004 ACF Culinary Team USA National
Edward Leonard, CMC, AAC, captain
Joachim Buchner, CMC
Patricia Nash
Richard Rosendale, CC
Daniel Scannell, CMC
Russell Scott, CMC

2008 ACF Culinary National Team USA
Edward Leonard, CMC, AAC, manager
Richard Rosendale, CEC, captain
Joachim Buchner, CMC
Jamie Keating, CCC
Mellisa K. Root
Daniel Scannell, CMC

The Journey to Erfurt

Before a journey begins there is much planning and preparation. The success of the journey depends on this. From preliminary meetings to practice, to traveling globally competing against great chefs from other countries, the trials and tribulations of the journey began.

In a boardroom at the Westchester Country Club the planning and discussion of culinary philosophy began to shape the team of 2008. Relying on the success of the past team and current trends in American cuisine, we set out to review how we could achieve our goals and objectives. We ensured each member's commitment to the team's objectives over the next four years.

The team spent many hours on R&D within our own properties and determined whether the concepts developed could become reality. The real challenge started when we all came together and began to form a synergy among the various talents.

Over the three years, the work schedule for the team was intense, with 40-60 days of travel for competitions and commitments, 60-70 days travel for practice and over 800 hours between R&D work and practice sessions. The team would also compete is Basel, Switzerland and Luxembourg, garnering straight gold medals in both competitions prior to the IKA event in 2008. Many trips to Erfurt were made to ensure all the resources needed to succeed so far from home would be in place.

The team agreed on one thing; that we wanted to showcase the new cooking techniques and presentational style used in contemporary cuisine and cook food as we do everyday in our own operations. We wanted to make a statement with everything we did and make sure our food was true to ourselves. From the presentations to the utilization of sous vide and slow cooking methods, we displayed a diverse range of food in both the cold and hot competitions. Though we fell short of winning the IKA event, we were proud of the three gold and one silver awarded to us and achieving the goal of winning back-to-back gold medals at IKA in 2004 and 2008, which had not been done since 1984 and 1988.

The journey to Erfurt was grueling. We gave and then gave some more. We walked away with accolades, medals, achievements and some disappointments. We gained friendships for life, education of the highest level and the experience of a lifetime. We learned new ways of working that will remain an important part of us. The new influences and the discipline learned have made us different and better chefs. That new chef is one of pride — confident yet humble — a chef that will try to make a difference everyday and is willing to take on the obligation of training others who desire the opportunity to be the best.

It is a proud time in a chef's career when he or she represents the cuisine of the ACF and USA. It is an honor to gain the respect of those around the globe who now recognize that the passion and talent of American chefs is up there with the best of them.

It is said that the USA and those who live here are not liked or respected globally, especially in Europe. In the global culinary arena this is far from the truth. Those who cook and share the heat of the kitchen are proud to call American chefs colleagues and friends and have a deep respect for their talent and commitment as we do theirs.

Excitement builds as chefs from around the world gather before the opening ceremonies of the Culinary Olympics.

The ceremonial lighting of the torch represents the start of the Culinary Olympics.

"Every time we cook in the global arena we apply our craft and are committed to displaying the cuisine of America at the highest standard there is" —Chef Edward G Leonard, CMC

Winning Traits 2000 to 2008

The chefs of Team USA formed a cohesive group that was humble but confident and showed professionalism of the highest order while working towards our common goals and objectives. Teamwork was placed ahead of individual ambition and pride. No team member or person was better than the next when we practiced or went into battle. The regional teams supported the national teams and assisted in every way possible. Those from the national team also helped coach the youth team or regional teams and no request was off limits. The goal was simple. If all of us were to be successful, all of us had to work together. As with any endeavor, the rewards went far beyond the medals and the trophies. It is the friendships we made, the education and self-improvement gained as well as the ability to go forward and accomplish even more then the medals or accolades show.

Accomplishments of ACF Culinary Team USA over the past 12 years of competition.

Year	Event	Team	Hot Food	Cold Food	Overall
2000	Basel Swiss	National	3 Gold	Silver	Cold Championship
	Scothop	National	3 Gold	Gold	
	IKA 2000	National	4 Gold	Silver	Cold Championship
		Regional	3 Gold	Bronze	
		Youth	2 Gold	Silver	
	Culinary Classic	National	3 Gold	Gold	World Championship
2004	Luxembourg	National	Gold	Silver	
	IKA 2004	National	1 Gold/ 2 Silver	Gold	World Hot Championship/ Third Over All
		Regional	3 Gold		Third place in the world
		Youth	Bronze	Gold	
	Luxembourg	National	Gold	Gold	
	Basel	National	Gold	Gold	
	Culinary Classic	National	2 Gold/ Silver	Gold	Third Place Finish
2008	IKA 2008	National	2 Gold/ Silver	Gold	Sixth Place
		ACF Regional	3 Gold		World Champions
		AAC Regional	3 Gold		Third Place in the world
		Youth	Gold	Gold/Silver	
	Total Medals Garnered	45 Gold medals 8 Silver 1 Bronze 5 Championships			

All the hard work pays off as the judges discuss the ACF National Team cold food presentaion.

Cooking with America's Championship Team

ACF

Competition Cooking

Hot food, first plate: Poached Halibut and Lobster Mousse, New England Clam Chowder Croquette, Smoked Bacon Foam & Celery Jelly, Saffron & Butter Poached Potatoes, Warm Pork Belly.

Hot food, Main Course: Braised Petit Shank & Palm Heart, Lamb Rib Eye Crépinette, Pequillo Pepper & Potato Caponata, Broccoli Puree & Pressed Greens, Crispy Goat Cheese Fritter, Natural Jus.

Hot food, Dessert: Apple Layers & Warm Gingerbread, Seasonal Terrine, Apple Mousse, Apple Sorbet, Spiced Cookie and Jelly.

ACF 2008 National team cold food table.

ACF 2008 National team cold food table.

Left: Savory Vanilla Carrot Mousse &
Citrus Fruit, Purple Haze Chevre,
Nuts & Grapes. (Buchner)

Right: Barbequed Lamb Tenderloin, Braised
Lamb Breast & Potato Mosaic, Roasted
Vegetables. (Buchner)

Left: Quail Duet Roasted Breast & Foie Gras
Filled Leg, Vegetable Salad. (Buchner)

Right: Lobster Terrine & Smoked Salmon,
White Asparagus Panna Cotta. (Buchner)

Left: Poached Halibut & Lobster Mousse, New
England Clam Chowder Croquette, Slow
Cooked Clams & Smoked Bacon Foam,
Poached Potatoes & Warm Pork Belly.
(Buchner)

Right: Pickled Rack of Rabbit, Vegetables en
Gelée, Red Currant & Bitter Lettuces, Toasted
Barley Salad . (Buchner)

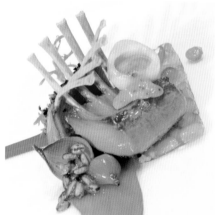

Left: Pork Belly Slowly Cooked In It's Own
Pouch, Mushroom Polenta, Border of
Aromatic Vegetables, Black Truffle
Sauce & Gremolata. (Scannell)

Right: Salmon & Halibut Duet in a
Pickled Radish Wrap, Bloody-Mary Celery &
Red Radish Salad, Cream Cheese, Bagel Chips
& Vodka Tomato Spheres. (Scannell)

Left: Cured Salmon, Pickled Red Onion & Caviars, served cold. (Keating)

Right: Skate Wing Filled with Peas & Truffles, Bacon Vinaigrette, served cold (Keating)

Left: Palm Hearts Stuffed with Slow Cooked Veal & Gremolata, served warm (Keating)

Right: Carrot Tear on Carrot Cake Base with Pistachio Goat Cheese, served cold (Keating)

Left: Trio of Foie Gras Mousse in Port Wine Gelee, served cold (Keating)

Right: Chorizo & Fried Egg Yolk, Wild Mushrooms, served warm (Keating)

Left: Stuffed Sardines on Potato with Aioli, served warm (Keating)

Right: Lobster "Frankfurter", served warm (Keating)

Poached Sirloin Layered with Mushroom "Daube" Coated in Mustard Cream, Pressed Oxtail, Truffle & Wild Mushroom Terrine, Loin & Herbed Stuffing Wrapped in Leeks & Portobello, Rows of Tarragon & Beef Consommé Tubes Around Marrow, Panna Cotta, Asparagus, Potato, Tomato & Boucherone, Mushroom & Foie Gras Rillette, Blue Cheese & Vegetable Salad, Thyme-Scented Mushroom Vinaigrette, Herb Emulsion. (Rosendale)

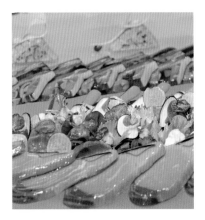

Clockwise from upper left: 1. Poached Stuffed Chicken Supreme, Salted Ox Tongue, Truffles & Sauce Supreme, Pressed Steamed Greens, Soft Poached Quail Egg & Golden Potatoes. 2. Persillade Crusted Corned Lamb Chop, Vegetables "Piccadilly", Carrot & Pea Flan, Stuffed Boiled Onion, Three Mustard Sauce. 3. Cedar Salmon Pave, Vegetable & Rice Crusted Smoked Shrimp, "Two Finger" Poi Stuffed Cabbage, Carrot Spheres & Shaved Coconut. 4. Steamed Alaskan King Crab, Open Ravioli, Saffron Pasta & Creamed Fennel, Salpicon of Crab, Truffles & Peas, Zucchini Ribbons, Curly Peppers & Drawn Butter. (Scannell)

Tofu Stuffed Carrot, Hominy & Kidney Bean Boudin, Individual Winter Vegetable Terrine, Warm Wakame Gelee, Half Dried Little Tomatoes, Pickled Sea Vegetables, Fried Pearl Onion's & Hot Mustard Sauce, Silken Tofu Cheese Cake, Potato Boats, Soy Glazed Tapioca & Soba Sticks, Ginger Tofu Meringues & Pickled Cabbage, Gingered Carrot Coulis, Vegetable Crisps. (Scannell)

Chocolate show piece.

Pistachio Custard,& Vanilla Mousse, Raspberry Gelee, & Chocolate Obsession Cake, White Chocolate Mousse, Toasted Marshmallow & Linzer Cookie Stack, Raspberry Coulis & Chambord Foam. (Scannell)

Lemon & Bing Cherry Cake, Warm Cherry Crumble with Kirschwasser & Cherry Swirl Cream, Cherry Gelee, Lemoncello Ice & Sour Cherry Reduction. (Root)

Clockwise from upper left: 1. Lemon & Bing Cherry Cake, Warm Cherry Crumble with Kirschwasser & Cherry Swirl Cream, Cherry Gelee, Limoncello Ice & Sour Cherry Reduction. 2. Salted Caramel Pastry Cream, Vanilla Bean Mousse & Apple Spice Cake Terrine, Warm Cranberry Gingerbread, Apple & Hazelnut Slice, Apple Cider & Vanilla Bean Syrup. 3. Trio of Macaroons, Fresh Fruit & Champagne Gelee, Citrus Berry Foam. 4. Milk Chocolate Mousse Cake, Passion Fruit & Apricot Curd Coconut & Mango "Martini" with Passion Fruit Tapioca, Bittersweet Chocolate Sauce. (Root)

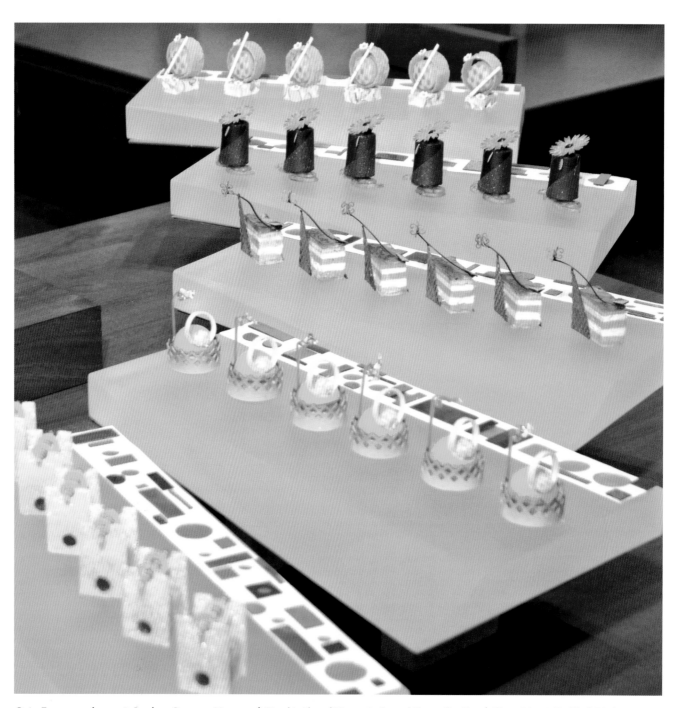

Petite Fours, top to bottom: 1. Raspberry Rosewater Macaroon & Pistachio Almond Nougat. 2. Caramel Orange Bon Bon & Citrus Crisp. 3. Vanilla & Mocha Buttercream in Almond Cake with Caramelized Almonds. 4. Brandy Bon Bon Liqueur, Pineapple Curd & Coconut Cream. 5. Lemon & Red Currant Pate de Fruit.

Cooking with America's Championship Team

A C F

Recipes

Alligator and White Bean Chili with Ancho Corn Fritters

Chef Jamie P. Keating, CCC (photo page 23)

Serves 4

Chili:

1 pound alligator tail meat, diced

Salt and freshly ground pepper

2 tablespoons vegetable oil

3/4 cup diced yellow onion

1/2 cup diced carrot

1 small celery stock, diced

1 garlic clove, minced

2 cups cooked white beans

1 quart chicken stock

Chile powder

Ground cumin

1 cup peeled, seeded and diced tomato

2 tablespoons chopped cilantro

Ancho Corn Fritters:

1 cup all-purpose flour

1 1/2 teaspoons baking powder

2 tablespoons sugar

Pinch kosher salt

1 large egg, beaten

1/2 cup milk

2 tablespoons melted unsalted butter

1 cup blanched corn kernels

1 tablespoon ancho chile paste

Oil for deep frying

To Make the Chili:

- Season the alligator meat with salt and pepper. Heat the oil in a Dutch oven until very hot and sear the meat on all sides. Add the onion, carrot, celery and garlic and continue to cook, stirring, for 5 minutes.
- Add the beans and stock to the pan. Season the stew with chile powder and cumin and cook until the meat is tender. Add the tomatoes and cilantro and cook until heated through. Season with salt and pepper.

To Make the Ancho Corn Fritters:

- Sift the flour, baking powder, sugar and salt into a medium mixing bowl. In another bowl, whisk together the egg, milk and melted butter. Stir the dry ingredients into the wet, then fold in the corn and chile paste.
- Heat the oil until very hot and drop spoonfuls of the batter into the oil and fry until golden brown. Serve with the chili.

Chefs Keating and Leonard discuss even the smallest detail while selecting samples for the cold food display.

Alligator and White Bean Chili with Ancho Corn Fritters (pg 22)

Butternut Squash "Consommé" with Butternut Squash Flan (pg 24)

Cream of Parsley Root Soup with Crab Leg and Parsley Foam (pg 24)

Chicken and Sausage Gumbo (pg 25)

Butternut Squash "Consommé" with Butternut Squash Flan

Chef Wayne Sieve (photo page 23)
Serves 4

Consommé and Flans:

4 butternut squash, peeled,
　　halved and seeds scraped out
4 cups vegetable stock
1/2 cup maple syrup
2 large egg yolks
1/2 cup heavy cream
Salt and freshly ground pepper
1 teaspoon curry powder

Garnish:

2 slices smoked bacon, finely diced
1 zucchini
3 cups vegetable stock
　　(reserved from cooking squash)
1 carrot
Salt and freshly ground pepper

Finish and Serve:

Micro greens

To Make the Consommé and Flans:

- Chop the squash and place it in a large saucepan with the stock and maple syrup. Simmer until the squash is very tender. Strain the mixture, reserving the squash and the stock separately.
- Pass the squash through a food mill or ricer. Place the puree in a strainer set over a bowl and let sit until all liquid has drained out of the squash. Reserve the liquid and solids separately.
- Preheat the oven to 350°F. Combine 1/2 cup of the squash solids and 3/4 cup of the reserved vegetable stock in a blender and process until smooth. Pour into a bowl and add the yolks and cream. Whisk until incorporated and season with salt and pepper. Add in another 1/3 cup of the squash solids and the curry powder.
- Spray 4 small ramekins with nonstick spray and divide the mixture between the ramekins. Bake until set, about 20 minutes.

To Make the Garnish:

- Place the bacon in a small pan and cook until it has rendered its fat. Remove the bacon from the pan and drain on paper towels.
- Cut the zucchini into the desired shape; cook in the vegetable stock until tender; remove with a slotted spoon and add to the liquid that drained out of the squash (the consommé). Cut the carrot into the desired shape; cook in the vegetable stock until tender; remove with a slotted spoon and add to the consommé.

To Finish and Serve:

- Unmold a warm flan into each of 4 bowls. Spoon hot consommé and vegetables around each and top flans with bacon and micro greens.

Cream of Parsley Root Soup with Crab Leg and Parsley Foam

Chef Joachim Buchner, CMC (photo page 23)
Serves 6

Soup:

1/4 cup unsalted butter
2 cups peeled, diced parsley root
1/2 cup diced onion
1/2 cup peeled, diced celery root
1/4 cup all-purpose flour
1 quart vegetable or chicken stock
Salt and freshly ground white pepper
3/4 cup heavy cream

Crab:

1 tablespoon unsalted butter
2 tablespoons white wine
1/2 cup sliced Alaskan king crabmeat

Parsley Foam:

2 cups flat-leaf parsley leaves
1 cup vegetable stock
Sea salt and freshly ground black pepper
1 teaspoon granulated lecithin

Finish and Serve:

12 fried flat-leaf parsley leaves

To Make the Soup:

- Melt the butter in a large saucepan over medium heat. Add the parsley root, onion, and celery root and sauté until soft; do not let the vegetables brown. Sprinkle the flour over the top of the vegetables and continue to cook, stirring, for 1 to 2 minutes. Stir in the stock and bring to a boil.
- Season the soup with salt and pepper. Transfer to a blender and process until smooth. Strain the soup and stir in the cream. Reheat the soup and keep it hot (not boiling) for serving. Adjust the seasoning just before serving if necessary.

To Make the Crab:

- Preheat the oven to 300°F. In a small ovenproof skillet, melt the butter over medium heat. Add the white wine and the crabmeat. Place the skillet in the oven and warm for 3 minutes.

To Make the Parsley Foam:

- Combine the parsley and stock in a blender and blend until smooth. Strain the mixture, discard the solids, and transfer the broth to a small saucepan. Heat the broth and season with salt and pepper. Add the lecithin, remove from the heat and let stand for 5 minutes. To serve, use a hand-held blender to foam the liquid.

To Finish and Serve:

- Ladle the soup into bowls and place some crabmeat into each. Spoon some parsley foam onto each serving and garnish with fried parsley leaves

Chicken and Sausage Gumbo

Chef Jonathan P. Moosmiller, CEC (photo page 23)

Serves 4

Gumbo:

1 cup canola oil

2 andouille sausages,
    sliced 1/4-inch thick

5 boneless, skinless chicken thighs,
    cut into 1/2-inch pieces

1 cup all-purpose flour

1 small onion, diced

1 green bell pepper, diced

4 stalks celery, diced

5 fresh okra pods, tops trimmed and
    discarded, pods thinly sliced

3 quarts chicken stock

1 teaspoon of your favorite
    Cajun spice mix

1/8 teaspoon cayenne, or to taste

Kosher salt and freshly
    cracked black pepper

Finish and Serve:

2 cups chicken stock

1 cup long-grain rice

Salt to taste

4 scallions, thinly sliced

Hot sauce for serving

To Make the Gumbo:

- Place a 6-quart cast-iron pot over medium heat and allow to heat for 10 minutes. Add ½ cup of the canola oil. As soon as the oil begins to smoke, add the andouille. Cook, stirring occasionally, until the sausage is evenly browned. Using a slotted spoon, remove the browned sausage and reserve. Add the chicken to the pot and brown. Remove with a slotted spoon and reserve.

- Add the remaining 1/2 cup oil and the flour to the pot. Stir with a wooden spoon until the flour and oil are combined completely to form a roux. Continue to cook the roux, stirring constantly, until it becomes the color of dark chocolate, about 20 minutes. Once the desired color is achieved, add the onion, bell pepper, celery and okra to the pot. Reduce the heat to low and continue to cook for another 10 minutes. Add 1 quart of the chicken stock and stir until smooth, then add in remaining chicken stock along with the reserved sausage and chicken. Stir in the Cajun spice and cayenne. Raise the heat to medium and bring to a simmer, stirring frequently. Simmer for 20 minutes. Season with salt and fresh cracked pepper.

To Finish and Serve:

- In a 1-quart saucepan, bring the 2 cups of chicken stock to a simmer. Stir in rice and salt. Reduce heat to low, cover and simmer until rice is cooked and all liquid is absorbed. Place a scoop or mold of hot rice into each warmed serving bowl. Add desired amount of gumbo and garnish with scallions. Serve immediately with your favorite hot sauce on the side.

Gently Poached Salmon Mousse and Spiced Miso Broth with a Garnish of Curly Peppers and Curried Tofu

Chef Daniel J. Scannell, CMC
Serves 4

Dashi:

4 pieces cut konbu seaweed

4 cups bonito flakes

1 gallon and 5 cups cold water

Miso Soup:

5 cups dashi

1 teaspoon tamari

1 teaspoon honey

2 ounces yellow miso

1 tablespoon chopped ginger

1 cup sliced mushrooms

1 jalapeño, seeded and thinly sliced

2 tablespoons bonito flakes

Poached Salmon Mousse:

10 ounces cleaned diced salmon, free of
    any blood line

2 tablespoons cornstarch

2 tablespoons milled cooked Yukon
    gold potatoes

1/4 cup vermouth or sake

1 egg white

1/2 cup heavy cream

1/2 teaspoon kosher salt

1/2 teaspoon ground white pepper

1 gallon simmering dashi

Finish and Serve:

4 (1/4-inch) slices curried tofu, seared
    and diced

1 tablespoon sliced green scallions

4 tablespoons curly peppers

To Make the Dashi:

- Rinse the konbu under cool running water and place it in a large stock pot. Add the bonito flakes and cold water and bring just to a simmer, being careful not to let the mixture come to a boil. Remove from the heat and let stand 5 minutes. Remove and discard konbu and place the pot back over medium heat. When the bonito flakes sink to the bottom, strain the dashi through a strainer lined with cheesecloth.

To Make the Miso Soup:

- In a small saucepan, combine 1 cup of the dashi, the tamari and honey. Bring to a simmer and remove from the heat. Set aside. In another saucepan, whisk together the remaining 4 cups dashi, miso, and ginger and simmer the mixture for 10 minutes. Strain out and discard the ginger. Combine both mixtures. Add the mushrooms, jalapeño and bonito.

For the Poached Salmon Mousse:

- Combine all the ingredients except the dashi in a food processor and pulse until you have a mousse. Press the mousse through a tamis. Fit a piping bag with a plain 1/8-inch tip and fill it with the mousse. Bring the dashi to a boil and adjust the heat so it just barely simmers. Squeeze the piping bag and pipe the mousse in a circular motion into the simmering dashi, making long fish noodles. Cook for approximately 2 minutes. Carefully remove the noodles from the stock with a fine-mesh spider.

To Finish and Serve:

- Warm 4 soup bowls and place some tofu in each. Add miso soup and salmon noodles. Sprinkle with scallions and curly peppers.

With the skills of a seasoned pro, chef Scannell arranges pieces for transportation to the competition.

Matzo Ball Soup with Stuffed Turkey Wing and Vegetables

Chef Daniel J. Scannell, CMC
Serves 4

Matzo Ball Soup:

1 cup matzo meal

1/4 cup vegetable oil

6 large eggs, lightly beaten

1 teaspoon kosher salt

1/4 teaspoon ground white pepper

1 quart seasoned chicken stock

1 bay leaf

About 20 parsley stems, tied

4 ounces diced blanched carrots

4 ounces diced blanched celery

12 blanched pearl onions

2 tablespoons chopped parsley leaves

4 ounces chopped shredded chicken

Stuffed Turkey Wings:

1/2 pound ground turkey

1/2 cup pumpernickel bread, soaked in
  water and squeezed dry

1 large egg, beaten

1 teaspoon Dijon mustard

2 tablespoons chopped parsley leaves

1 tablespoon toasted caraway seeds

1 teaspoon crushed red pepper flakes

1 cup heavy cream

1 teaspoon kosher salt

1/2 teaspoon freshly ground pepper

Turkey or chicken stock for poaching

4 deboned, trimmed fresh turkey wings

Finish and Serve:

Extra-virgin olive oil for drizzling

To Make the Matzo Ball Soup:

- Mix together the matzo meal, vegetable oil, eggs, salt and white pepper; cover and refrigerate for 30 minutes.
- In an 8-quart stock pot, bring the chicken stock, bay leaf and parsley stems to a rolling boil. Using a 1-ounce scoop, drop the matzo mixture into the boiling stock. Reduce the heat and simmer the matzo balls for approximately 30 minutes. Add carrots, celery, onions, parsley leaves and shredded chicken.

To Make the Stuffed Turkey Wings:

- Combine all the ingredients except the stock and turkey wings in a food processor and pulse to make a mousse. Pour stock to a depth of 3 inches in a large stock pot. Poach a small amount of the mousse in the stock; taste and adjust seasonings if needed.
- Fill each wing with the mousse mixture. Wrap each wing in cheesecloth. Have the stock at a bare simmer and poach the wings until they reach 165°F. on an instant-read thermometer. Allow the wings to cool in the stock overnight.
- Remove the turkey wings from the stock, unwrap, and discard the cheesecloth. Smoke the wings over wood smoke until they are light-brown in color.

To Finish and Serve:

- Divide the matzo balls and soup between warmed bowls. Slice the turkey wings and add a few slices to each bowl. Drizzle with oil and serve.

Oysters Rockefeller Soup with Roasted Fennel and Onion

Chef Timothy R. Prefontaine, CSC
Serves 4

Soup:

3 strips bacon, diced
1/2 cup diced fennel
1 tablespoon chopped garlic
1 1/2 tablespoons chopped shallot
2 tablespoons white wine
2 tablespoons unsalted butter
2 tablespoons all-purpose flour
2 cups chicken stock
1 cup heavy cream
3/4 cup fresh oysters
2 cups fresh spinach leaves
1/4 cup Pernod
Sea salt and ground white pepper

Garnishes:

1 cup diced fennel
1/2 cup diced onion
2 teaspoons olive oil
Salt and freshly ground pepper
1/2 cup chopped spinach
1/4 cup cooked couscous
1/2 cup red bell pepper juice
Pinch sugar
4 fresh oysters
1/2 cup seasoned flour
2 large eggs, beaten
Fresh bread crumbs for coating
Canola or peanut oil for deep frying

To Make the Soup:

- Heat the bacon in a medium saucepan over medium heat. Add the fennel, garlic and shallot and cook until the vegetables are tender and a little brown fond starts to build up on the bottom of the pan. Deglaze the pan with the white wine. Add the butter; when melted, stir in the flour. Add the stock and cream and bring to a simmer. Add the oysters and cook for 2 minutes.
- Puree the soup in a blender and pass it through a fine-mesh strainer. Puree half of the soup again with the spinach leaves and Pernod and strain again. Season the soups with salt and pepper. Set the two soups aside separately.

To Make the Garnishes:

- Preheat the oven to 375°F. Toss fennel and onion with olive oil and season with salt and pepper. Roast in a small baking dish until tender. Fold in the spinach and couscous. Set aside.
- Place the pepper juice in a small saucepan and simmer until thick. Stir in the sugar and a pinch of salt.
- Dredge the oysters in the seasoned flour, dip in the eggs, then coat with bread crumbs. Heat the oil in a medium saucepan, fry the oysters, and keep them hot until serving.

To Finish and Serve:

- Warm 4 serving bowls and place a small amount of the fennel and couscous mixture in each. Top with a fried oyster. Place a serving of the spinach soup in a measuring cup with a pouring spout and a serving of the other soup in another measuring cup. Take a cup in each hand and slowly pour each soup into half the bowl, pouring at the same time. Drizzle with the reduced pepper juice and serve.

CHEF'S NOTES

- To make red bell pepper juice, remove seeds and stems from red bell peppers, cut into large pieces, and run through a vegetable juicer.

ACF Regional chefs, Root, Leonardi and Prefontaine wait patiently during closing ceremony to hear the overall results.

Parmesan Consommé, Fresh Asparagus, 55-Minute Egg, Pasta, Truffle and Parmesan Crackling

Chef Richard Rosendale, CEC
Serves 4

Consommé:

2 pounds Parmesan rinds, broken into 1-inch pieces
2 1/2 quarts chicken stock
8 large egg whites
Splash white wine

Cheese Crackling:

1/4 cup grated Parmesan

Eggs and Garnish:

4 large eggs
8 asparagus spears
1 cup cooked penne pasta

Finsih and Serve:

4 slices black truffle
Chervil sprigs
1 tablespoon extra-virgin olive oil
Sea salt and cracked black pepper

To Make the Consommé:

- Place the Parmesan rinds and stock in a saucepan. Bring to a simmer, adjust the heat and cook for 15 minutes. Cover and set aside for 20 minutes, then strain through a fine-mesh strainer. Chill the Parmesan stock down over an ice-water bath.
- Whisk the egg whites until they hold very soft peaks. Whisk the chilled stock, wine and whites together and place over low heat. Bring the mixture to a very slow simmer; as the egg whites coagulate they will rise to the surface of the broth, leaving behind a crystal-clear consommé. Carefully ladle out the consommé, leaving the egg whites in the pan. Strain the consommé through a strainer lined with a coffee filter.

To Make the Cheese Crackling:

- Sprinkle the Parmesan over the bottom of a nonstick skillet. Place over medium heat and cook until the cheese is melted and comes together to form a thin layer on the surface of the skillet. Remove the cheese from the pan and place it on a cutting board. Let the cheese set up for about 5 minutes and then cut it into small pieces.

To Make the Eggs and Garnish:

- For the eggs, you will need a heating immersion circulator; set the water bath for 64°C. When the bath reaches 64°, place the eggs, still in their shells, very gently in the water bath (you may want to cook a few extra eggs just in case you break one or two). Let the eggs cook for exactly 55 minutes, then remove from the bath.
- If you are not going to serve the eggs right away, peel them and immerse them in cold water to stop the cooking; you can reheat the eggs later by pouring some very hot (but not boiling) water over the eggs and letting them sit in the water for 6 minutes.
- Meanwhile, cut the asparagus into bite-size pieces and blanch in boiling water for 2 minutes. Drain, chill in ice water, and drain again. Slice the penne into bite-size pieces and set aside as well.

To Finish and Serve:

- When ready to serve, place a warm, peeled egg in each soup bowl, being careful not to break it, and add the asparagus, pasta and hot Parmesan consommé. Sprinkle some of the cheese crackling over the soup, place a truffle slice and chervil over each egg and drizzle a little olive oil over each. Sprinkle with sea salt and cracked pepper.

CHEF'S NOTES

- To cook the egg for this soup, you will need a heating immersion circulator, which we use for sous vide cooking. This piece of equipment is very accurate, and using it to cook the eggs takes this soup from ordinary to sublime.

Pork Shoulder and Chorizo Chili with Cheddar Spoonbread

Chef Drew Garms
Serves 4

Chili:
1/4 **cup** vegetable oil
1 **pound** pork shoulder, cut into
    1-inch cubes
1/2 **pound** Mexican chorizo, sliced
1 **cup** diced onion
1 **cup** diced roasted, peeled red bell
    pepper
1 **cup** roasted, peeled Anaheim chiles
1 minced jalapeño
2 **tablespoons** minced shallot
1 **tablespoon** minced garlic
3 **tablespoons** chile powder
1 1/2 **teaspoons** ground cumin
1 1/2 **teaspoons** ground coriander
1/4 **cup** beer
4 **cups** diced tomatoes
2 **cups** chicken stock
1 **cup** roasted corn kernels
1 **cup** cooked, rinsed black beans
2 **tablespoons** chopped cilantro
Salt and freshly ground pepper

Spoonbread:
2 **cups** chicken stock
6 **tablespoons** unsalted butter
2 **tablespoons** sugar
1 **tablespoon** salt
1/2 **pound** cornmeal
1 **cup** egg yolks
1 **cup** milk
1 **tablespoon** baking powder
1 **cup** grated Cheddar cheese

Avocado Butter:
1 ripe avocado, peeled and pitted
1/4 **cup** unsalted butter, softened
1 **tablespoon** lime juice
Pinch cayenne
Pinch ground cumin
Salt and freshly ground pepper

To Make the Chili:
- Heat the oil in a large heavy pot and sear the pork until golden brown. Remove the pork from the pot and set it aside, leaving the fat in the pot. Add the chorizo and cook until it is browned. Remove the chorizo and add the onion, bell pepper, chiles and jalapeño; cook until the onion is just translucent. Stir in the shallot, garlic, chile powder, cumin and coriander. Lower the heat and cook gently, stirring, for about 5 minutes, being careful not to burn the spices.
- Deglaze the pot with the beer. Stir in the diced tomatoes, stock and reserved pork. Bring to a simmer, cover the pot, and braise until the pork is very tender. Stir in the corn, beans and reserved chorizo and heat through. Remove from the heat, stir in the cilantro, and season the chili with salt and pepper. Cool the chili quickly over an ice bath and then fill small oven-proof serving bowls or crocks two-thirds full with the chili.

To Make the Spoonbread:
- In a large saucepan, bring the stock, butter, sugar and salt to a boil. When the butter has melted, whisk in the cornmeal and cook, stirring, until the mixture is thick and glossy. Transfer the mixture to the bowl of a mixer fitted with the paddle attachment and beat on low until the mixture is cool.
- Beat in the egg yolks a little at a time. Slowly beat in the milk. Beat in the baking powder and stir in the cheese.

To Make the Avocado Butter:
- Combine all the ingredients in a food processor and pulse until combined. Chill until serving.

To Finish and Serve:
- Preheat the oven to 350°F. Cover the tops of the chili in the crocks with a thin layer of spoonbread. Bake until the spoonbread is golden brown and the chili is hot. Serve with a small dollop of the avocado butter on top.

Roasted Cauliflower Soup with Cocoa Jelly, White Chocolate Custard and Caviar

Chef Jonathan P. Moosmiller, CEC
Serves 4

Cocoa Jelly:

1 cup water

2 teaspoons unflavored Knox
gelatin powder

3 tablespoons quality cocoa powder

2 teaspoons glucose

1/2 teaspoon agar agar

White Chocolate Custard:

6 ounces heavy cream

1 sprig of thyme

1 large egg

1 large egg yolk

Sea salt

20 white chocolate chips

Soup:

1 head cauliflower

1/4 cup extra-virgin olive oil

2 tablespoons unsalted butter

1 ounce minced shallot

Sea salt and ground white pepper

Grated nutmeg

4 cups milk

3 ounces crème fraîche

1 large egg

6 ounces fine panko bread crumbs

Oil for deep frying

Finish and Serve:

2 ounces osetra caviar

To Make the Cocoa Jelly:

- Place 1/2 cup of the water in a small bowl and sprinkle with 1 teaspoon of the gelatin powder; allow the gelatin to bloom for 10 minutes.
- In a small stainless-steel saucepan, combine the remaining water and remaining gelatin powder with the cocoa and glucose and bring the mixture to a boil over medium heat. Add the agar agar and bloomed gelatin and whisk vigorously; continue to boil for 1 minute. Strain the liquid through a fine sieve into a shallow flat-bottom pan. Refrigerate until set. Use a round cutter to punch out disks of the jelly and refrigerate until serving.

To Make the White Chocolate Custard:

- Place the cream and thyme in a small stainless-steel saucepan and scald over medium heat. Remove from heat, cover the pan tightly, and allow to steep for 10 minutes.
- Combine the egg and egg yolk in a small bowl and whisk well. Whisking constantly, pour the hot cream into the egg. Season with salt. Spray 4 glass ramekins with cooking spray and place them into a small baking dish. Place 5 white chocolate chips in the bottom of each ramekin. Strain the custard through a fine-mesh sieve and divide evenly between the 4 ramekins. Add warm water to the baking dish to come about one-third up the sides of the ramekins. Place the baking dish in the oven and bake until the custards are set, about 25 minutes. Keep warm until serving.

To Make the Soup:

- Using a paring knife, remove 20 small florets from the cauliflower head and set aside. Cut the remaining head into uniform pieces.
- Place a 2-quart stainless-steel saucepan over medium heat and add the olive oil and butter. When the butter has melted, add the cauliflower pieces (not the florets) and the shallot and season lightly with salt, pepper and nutmeg. Continue to cook, stirring occasionally, until the cauliflower is soft and becomes lightly caramelized. Add the milk and bring to a simmer; simmer for 15 minutes. Remove from the heat and puree in a blender. Add the crème fraîche and puree again until silky smooth. Adjust the seasoning with more salt, pepper and nutmeg if needed.
- Meanwhile, place the egg in a small bowl and whip well with a whisk. Place the panko in another bowl. Dip the reserved florets in the egg and then coat in the panko. Fry the breaded florets in 350°F. oil until golden brown. Drain on paper towels. Sprinkle lightly with salt and reserve in a warm place until serving.

To Finish and Serve:

- Place one disk of cocoa jelly in the bottom of each of 4 heated serving bowls. Unmold the custards from the ramekins and place one on top of each cocoa disk. Using 2 spoons, form 4 equal quenelles of caviar and place one on top of each custard. Place 5 of the fried florets around each custard. Gently pour soup into each bowl and serve immediately.

Smoked Gouda, Peppered Bacon and Mushroom Soup

Chef Chris Desens, CEC
Serves 4

Soup:

1 strip peppered bacon, julienned

1 strip peppered bacon, diced

3 tablespoons unsalted butter

1/4 cup diced yellow onion

1/4 cup diced celery

2 cups trimmed, sliced mushrooms
(cremini, shiitake or
white button)

1/2 teaspoon minced garlic

1/4 cup all-purpose flour

2 tablespoons Madeira

2 tablespoons sherry

2 cups chicken stock

1 cup heavy cream

1 cup grated smoked Gouda

1/8 teaspoon fresh thyme leaves

1 bay leaf

Salt and freshly ground pepper

Croutons:

Clarified butter

Diced crustless bread

Fresh thyme leaves

Shiitake Bacon:

1/4 cup thinly sliced shiitake
mushroom caps

1 teaspoon mushroom soy

1 teaspoon olive oil

BEVERAGE RECOMMENDATION

Amontillado sherry or 2005 Brandborg
"Northern Reach" Pinot Noir

To Make the Soup:

- Cook the julienned bacon in large pot until crisp; remove with a slotted spoon, drain and reserve for garnish.
- Add the diced bacon to the pot and cook until nearly crisp. Add the butter, onion, celery and mushrooms and cook until the mushrooms release their liquid. Add the garlic and cook 1 more minute. Stir in the flour and make a roux. Stir in the Madeira and sherry. Whisk in the chicken stock.
- In a separate pot, heat the cream and cheese together and stir until the cheese melts. Puree the mixture in a blender and fold it into the soup base. Add the thyme and bay leaf and season to taste with salt and pepper. Continue to cook until all the flour taste disappears. Remove the bay leaf before serving.

To Make the Croutons:

- Heat the clarified butter in a skillet and the add bread cubes and thyme. Toast over medium heat until golden brown and crisp.

To Make the Shiitake Bacon:

- Preheat the oven to 250°F. Combine the mushrooms, soy and olive oil and toss to coat. Lay the mushroom pieces out on a baking rack and bake until crisp.

To Finish and Serve:

- Ladle the soup into bowls and garnish with the reserved julienned bacon, the croutons and the shiitake bacon.

CHEF'S NOTES

- This soup is a nice variation on a classic and works well on a variety of menus.

Terrine of Rabbit and Mushrooms in Chilled Carrot Soup

Chef Michael Matarazzo
Serves 4

Rabbit Terrine:

8 ounces chicken leg meat

1 large egg white

1 cup heavy cream

1/4 teaspoon fresh minced sage leaves

1 tablespoon Madeira

1/2 teaspoon kosher salt

1/4 teaspoon ground black pepper

1 teaspoon unsalted butter

1/4 cup trimmed, finely diced
    chanterelle mushrooms

2 rabbit loins

2 thin slices prosciutto

Carrot Crisps and Soup:

8 thin slices carrot, cut lengthwise and
    each about 1/8-inch thick

1 cup simple syrup

1 quart fresh carrot juice, chilled

Sea salt

Finish and Serve:

12 carrot leaves

Extra-virgin olive oil

To Make the Rabbit Terrine:

- Put the chicken meat in a food processor and pulse until smooth. With the motor running, add the egg white. Slowly pour in the cream and process until the mixture is smooth and homogenous. Transfer the chicken mixture to a small mixing bowl and fold in the sage, Madeira, salt and pepper.

- In a small skillet, melt the butter and sauté the mushrooms until tender. Cool completely, then add to the chicken mixture. Transfer the mixture to a pastry bag; pipe about 1 ounce of the mixture onto a piece of plastic wrap. Then using a small offset spatula, spread the mixture out to form a rectangle about 3 inches by 5 inches and about 1/4-inch thick. Place the rabbit loins side by side into the middle of the mixture, pressing into it slightly. Using the plastic wrap, wrap the chicken mixture around the loins, enclosing them completely. Twist the ends of the plastic tightly to create a cylinder and tie them with butcher's string. Use a small needle to pop any air pockets in the terrine. Place the terrine into a 150°F. water bath for about 12 minutes; remove and cool in an ice-water bath.

- Shingle the slices of prosciutto onto a new piece of plastic wrap. Unwrap the cooled terrine and place it on the prosciutto. Wrap the prosciutto around the terrine and wrap the whole again tightly in plastic wrap. Refrigerate for at least 2 hours so that the prosciutto sticks to itself.

To Make the Carrot Crisps and Soup:

- Blanch the slices of carrot in boiling salted water for about 20 seconds and immediately cool them in an ice-water bath. Dip the slices into the simple syrup and lay them on a baking sheet lined with a Silpat; make sure they don't touch. Place in a food dehydrator and dehydrate until very crisp, about 2 hours.

- Season the carrot juice with sea salt and keep chilled.

To Finish and Serve:

- Unwrap the rabbit terrine and slice it into ¾-inch-thick medallions. Place 2 medallions side by side in the middle of each serving bowl. Pour the carrot juice into the bowls and garnish each with carrot leaves, a drizzle of olive oil and 2 carrot crisps.

*ACF Regional team cold food
display wins another Gold.*

Tomato Consommé and Lebanese Couscous

Chef Jamie P. Keating, CCC
Serves 4

Tomato Water:

4 vine-ripe tomatoes
1 garlic clove
1 tablespoon Madeira
Pinch kosher salt

Couscous:

1 tablespoon extra-virgin olive oil, plus
    more for drizzling on the couscous
2 teaspoons chopped shallot
1/2 teaspoon chopped garlic
3 ounces Lebanese couscous
9 ounces chicken stock
2 teaspoons chopped fresh basil
Kosher salt and ground pepper

Pickled Vegetables:

8 breakfast radishes
8 red pearl onions
8 baby cucumbers
1 cup cider vinegar
1/2 cup water
2 tablespoons sugar
Pinch kosher salt

Tomatoes:

8 grape tomatoes, peeled and halved
8 yellow teardrop tomatoes, peeled
8 red teardrop tomatoes, peeled
Pinch sea salt
1 tablespoon extra-virgin olive oil

Finish and Serve:

Micro celery
Cilantro leaves

**BEVERAGE
RECOMMENDATION**

Chilled Silk Vodka

To Make the Tomato Water:

- Puree the tomatoes, garlic and Madeira in a blender. Line a strainer with cheesecloth, place the strainer over a bowl to catch the liquid, and pour the puree into the strainer. Place bowl and strainer in the refrigerator and let drain overnight.
- Discard the solids in the strainer. Season the tomato water with salt.

To Make the Couscous:

- Heat the oil in a saucepan and sauté the shallot and garlic. Add the couscous and cook until lightly toasted. Add stock and simmer until the couscous is cooked but still firm. Spread the couscous over a sheet pan to cool, then stir in the basil, season with salt and pepper, and drizzle with olive oil.

To Make the Pickled Vegetables:

- Place the radishes, onions, and cucumbers in a bowl. In a small saucepan, combine the vinegar, water, sugar and salt and bring to a boil. Stir until the sugar and salt dissolve. Pour over the vegetables.

To Make the Tomatoes:

- Combine all the ingredients and toss lightly.

To Finish and Serve:

- Place couscous in serving bowls. Top with tomatoes and pour in tomato water. Garnish with micro celery and cilantro leaves and serve with the pickled vegetables.

Citrus-Poached Cold-Water Lobster with Pickled Cucumber, Organic Field Greens and Kumquat-Truffle Vinaigrette

Chef Daryl Shular (photo page 45)
Serves 4

Citrus-Poached Lobster:

2 cups orange juice

1/2 cup lemon juice

1/2 cup white wine vinegar

2 cups water

1 sprig fresh thyme

1 bay leaf

1/2 teaspoon red pepper flakes

Salt and freshly ground pepper

4 lobster tails

Pickled Cucumber:

1/2 cup water

1/4 cup sugar

1/4 teaspoon red pepper flakes

1/2 cup Sauterne vinegar or other white-wine vinegar

1/4 ounce salt

1 European (seedless) cucumber, peeled

Kumquat-Truffle Vinaigrette:

1 pound kumquats, sliced

1/2 ounce black truffle peelings, chopped

1/2 ounce chopped garlic

1/2 ounce chopped shallots

1/2 ounce chopped basil

1 cup orange juice

1 1/2 cups grapeseed oil

Salt and freshly ground pepper

Finish and Serve:

Organic field greens

To Make the Citrus-Poached Lobster:

- In a large saucepan over high heat, combine all the ingredients except the lobster and bring to boil. Lower the heat until the mixture just simmers, then add the lobster tails and cook slowly for 6 to 8 minutes. Once tails are cooked through, remove them from the poaching liquid and chill in an ice bath. (To maximize flavor, shock the lobster in chilled poaching liquid.)

To Make the Pickled Cucumber:

- Combine all the ingredients except the cucumber in small saucepan and bring to a simmer. Stir to dissolve the salt and sugar and remove from the heat. Cool completely.
- Remove any small seeds in the cucumber and cut it into 1/4-inch dice. Add cucumber to the liquid and marinate for 1 1/2 to 2 hours.

For the Kumquat-Truffle Vinaigrette:

- Stir together all the ingredients except the salt and pepper. Season with salt and pepper and refrigerate until serving.

To Finish and Serve:

- Slice the lobster tails and lay one tail on each plate. Surround with field greens and pickled cucumber. Drizzle with the vinaigrette.

Citrus-Poached Cold-Water Lobster with Pickled Cucumber, Organic Field Greens and Kumquat-Truffle Vinaigrette (pg 44)

Baked Pears Stuffed with Saga Blue Cheese (pg 46)

Endive, Plump Apricots, Candied Walnuts, Blue Cheese and Orange Hazelnut Vinaigrette (pg 46)

Contemporary Tuna Niçoise with Frisée and Saffron Potato (pg 47)

Baked Pears Stuffed with Saga Blue Cheese

Chef Drew Garms (photo page 45)
Serves 4

Pears:

4 tablespoons cold unsalted butter

2 pears, split and cored

1/4 cup sugar

1/2 cup pear brandy

Few drops of lemon juice

1 vanilla bean, split

4 1-inch cubes Saga blue cheese

Streusel:

2 tablespoons sugar

2 tablespoons almond flour

2 tablespoons all-purpose flour

1 tablespoon oatmeal

Pinch of salt

2 tablespoons cold unsalted butter, diced

Finish and Serve:

8 ounces baby lettuce

Aged balsamic vinegar

Olive oil

Salt and freshly ground pepper

To Make the Pears:

• In a large skillet, melt 2 tablespoons of the butter. Place the pears in the skillet cut-sides down and cook until caramelized on the bottom. Add the remaining butter and the sugar to the skillet and cook until the sugar starts to brown. Turn the pears over and add the brandy, lemon juice and vanilla bean. Baste each pear with a liquid in the pan. Continue cooking until the pears begin to soften but are still quite firm. Remove the pears from the skillet with a slotted spoon, place a cube of cheese in the center of each and set aside.

• Continue cooking the caramel in the pan until it is thick enough to coat the back of a spoon. Set aside.

To Make the Streusel:

• Combine all the ingredients except the butter in the bowl of an electric mixer. Add the butter and mix with the paddle attachment just until the streusel is well mixed and holds together. (Do not over mix.)

To Finish and Serve:

• Preheat the oven to 350°F. Cover the tops of the stuffed pears with the streusel and bake until streusel is golden brown and pear is soft.

• Toss the lettuce with the balsamic, olive oil, and salt and pepper. Arrange a handful of lettuce on each plate with a warm pear half. Drizzle the plate with some pear caramel.

Endive, Plump Apricots, Candied Walnuts, Blue Cheese and Orange Hazelnut Vinaigrette

Chef Richard Rosendale, CEC (photo page 45)
Serves 4

Candied Walnuts:

1 large egg white

2 tablespoons sugar

1 cup walnut halves

Pinch salt

Salad and Vinaigrette:

2 cups orange juice

1/4 cup white-wine vinegar

2 tablespoons honey

1 cup hazelnut oil

1 cup olive oil

Salt and freshly ground pepper

3 heads Belgium endive

Lemon juice

2 heads frisée

1/2 cup dried apricots, steeped in hot water until softened

1/2 cup crumbled blue cheese

To Make the Candied Walnuts:

• Preheat the oven to 325°F. In a medium bowl, whip together the egg white and sugar until the mixture forms soft peaks. Add the walnuts and salt and toss. Spread on a sheet pan lined with a Silpat and bake for 12 minutes.

To Make the Salad and Vinaigrette:

• Place the orange juice in a small saucepan and reduce to 1 cup. Combine the orange concentrate, vinegar and honey in a food processor. With the motor running, slowly pour the hazelnut oil and olive oil through the feed tube. Season with salt and pepper.

• Trim the bottoms of the endive and slice the heads into 1-inch pieces. Rinse in a large bowl of cold water that has a little lemon juice squeezed into it to prevent the endive from browning. Cut the frisée into bite-size pieces.

• Drain the endive, pat dry, and toss in a large bowl with the frisée and some of the orange vinaigrette. Divide between serving plates and garnish each with apricots, blue cheese and candied walnuts.

Contemporary Tuna Niçoise with Frisée and Saffron Potato

Chef Richard Rosendale, CEC (photo page 45)
Serves 4

Tomato Coulis:

1 tablespoon olive oil

1/4 cup finely diced onion

l/4 cup finely diced fennel

1 tablespoon minced shallot

1 teaspoon minced garlic

1 tablespoon tomato puree

1/2 cup white wine

1 pound tomatoes, peeled and chopped

1 tablespoon extra-virgin olive oil

Salt and freshly ground pepper

Tuna Terrine:

3 tuna palates (see Chef's Notes)

1 tablespoon aged balsamic vinegar

Coarse sea salt and freshly
    ground pepper

1 shallot, minced

1/2 cup white wine

5 sprigs fresh thyme

1 crushed garlic clove

12 mussels

5 bronze gelatin sheets

1 cup tomato coulis

1 hard-cooked egg, chopped

Leaves from 8 sprigs fresh parsley,
    chopped

Leaves from 1 sprig fresh basil, chopped

Saffron Potato:

1 Idaho potato

2 tablespoons saffron threads

1 sprig fresh thyme

1 teaspoon salt

5 grinds black pepper

Finish and Serve:

2 bunches frisée

Olive oil

Juice of 1 lemon

Salt and freshly ground pepper

1 bunch French beans

1 sprig basil leaves

To Make the Tomato Coulis:

- In a heavy saucepan, heat the olive oil. Add the onion and fennel and cook without browning the vegetables for 6 minutes. Add the shallot and the garlic and cook 1 more minute. Stir in the tomato puree, then stir in the wine. Cover the top of the pan with parchment and lower the heat. Cook, covered, until the vegetables are very soft.
- Stir in the tomatoes and simmer 20 minutes, uncovered. Transfer the sauce to a powerful blender (or blend it in small batches) and process until smooth. Strain through a fine-mesh sieve. Stir in the extra-virgin olive oil and season with salt and pepper.

To Make the Tuna Terrine:

- Slice the tuna into rectangular pieces to fit the mold you are using. Freeze the tuna pieces until slightly frozen and very cold. Sear each side on a very hot grill just until it has grill marks, about 1 minute per side; the tuna should still be very rare. Brush the tuna with the balsamic vinegar, season with sea salt and pepper and refrigerate until chilled.
- Place the shallot, white wine, thyme and garlic in a large saucepan, cover and bring to a boil. Add the mussels, cover again, and cook until the mussels open. Strain and reserve the liquid. Remove the mussels from the shells and dice the meat; reserve for garnish.
- Bloom the gelatin in ice water, then place it in a saucepan with the mussel juice and heat until dissolved. Add the tomato coulis. Add the egg, parsley, basil, and the reserved diced mussels. Season with salt and pepper.
- Spay a terrine mold with cooking spray and line with plastic wrap. Place a layer of the tuna in the terrine and then pour some of the coulis mixture on top. Repeat the process twice more and then place a tuna palate on top to securely cover the top of the terrine.
- Cover the top with plastic, weight the terrine, and refrigerate overnight or until the gelatin is fully set.

To Make the Saffron Potato:

- Place all the ingredients in a vacuum bag, seal the bag, and cook in a 85° Celsius water bath for 1 hour and 20 minutes. After cooking, cool the potato while still in the bag in a ice bath to stop the cooking process.

To Finish and Serve:

- Slice the terrine and place on serving plates. Toss the frisée with olive oil, lemon juice and salt and pepper. Garnish the plates with slices of the saffron potato, the French beans, basil leaves and the frisée.

CHEF'S NOTES

- The slices of tuna we use at Rosendales are rectangles that measure about 3 x 6 inches and are about 1/4-inch thick, and these fit perfectly into our terrines. Whatever shape you cut your tuna, just make sure it fits in your mold perfectly.

Crispy Asparagus with a Salad of Potato, Egg, Truffle and Frisée

Chef Edward G. Leonard, CMC
Serves 4

Salad:

2 Yukon gold potatoes, peeled

1 cup chicken stock

1 teaspoon unsalted butter

Pinch sea salt

4 large eggs, hard cooked and peeled

1 small black truffle, sliced

2 heads frisée, washed and all
   dark-green fronds removed

2 tablespoons extra-virgin olive oil

Juice of 1 lemon

Crispy Asparagus:

12 stalks medium green asparagus,
   peeled and blanched

1 cup seasoned flour

3 large eggs, whipped

2 cups panko bread crumbs,
   finely ground

Oil for deep frying

Salt

Finish and Serve:

Black Hawaiian sea salt

Dried tomato chips

Tomato confit

To Make the Salad:

- Slice the potatoes into 1/4-inch-thick disks. Using a round cutter, cut 12 round circles from the disks. Save the potato scraps for another use. Place the 12 circles in a saucepan and add the stock, butter and sea salt. Place over medium heat and bring to a simmer. Adjust the heat and simmer until the potatoes are just cooked through. Remove the potatoes from the liquid and allow to cool.
- Using an egg slicer, slice each egg. Take one full slice of egg and place on each potato circle. Reserve the remaining egg slices for another use. Top the egg slices with a truffle slice.
- Place the frisée in a small bowl. Add oil, lemon juice and remaining truffle slices and toss lightly.

To Make the Crispy Asparagus:

- Pat the asparagus dry with paper towels and toss in the seasoned flour. Place the eggs and panko separately in 2 shallow bowls. Dip each stalk into the eggs and then roll in the panko.
- Just before serving, heat the oil in a deep fryer to 350°F. Fry the asparagus until golden brown and crisp. Drain on paper towels and sprinkle with salt.

To Finish and Serve:

- Place 3 asparagus stalks on the left side of each of 4 serving plates. Shingle 3 of the potato-egg stacks next to the asparagus on each plate and sprinkle with black sea salt. Divide the frisée between the plates and garnish each with tomato crisps and tomato confit. Serve immediately.

*Chefs Leonard and Rosendale feel the heat as
plating begins in the hot kitchen.*

Fried Green Tomato Salad

Chef Jamie P. Keating, CCC

Serves 4

Pickled Onions:

1 medium red onion, peeled and
    sliced 1/4-inch thick

1 cup white-wine vinegar

1/4 cup sugar

1 tablespoon salt

2 cups water

Pimento Coulis:

1 teaspoon oil or butter

1 garlic clove, chopped

1/2 cup heavy cream

1/2 cup diced pimento

Salt and ground white pepper

Basil-Bacon Dressing:

3 strips bacon, cooked and
    finely chopped

1/4 cup mayonnaise

1/4 cup sour cream

1/4 cup diced and caramelized onion

1 tablespoon buttermilk

1 teaspoon white vinegar

1/4 teaspoon basil puree

1/8 teaspoon roasted garlic

1/8 teaspoon salt

Green Tomatoes:

2 cups all-purpose flour, seasoned

3 large eggs, lightly beaten

4 cups cornflakes, finely ground

2 green tomatoes, sliced 1/4-inch thick

Finish and Serve:

Oil for deep frying

Kosher salt

2 ounces mâche lettuces

8 angel hair pasta noodles, fried and
    coated with chili dust

Flavored oils for plating (optional)

To Make the Picked Onions:

- Combine all the ingredients in a 2-quart saucepan and bring to a simmer. Remove from the heat and place the bottom of the pan in an ice-water bath to cool. Keep cool until serving.

To Make the Pimento Coulis:

- Heat the oil or butter in a small saucepan and sauté the garlic. Add the cream and bring to a simmer. Add the pimento, then blend the mixture until smooth. Season with salt and white pepper.

To Make Basil-Bacon Dressing:

- Mix all the ingredients in a medium bowl. Taste the dressing and adjust the seasoning if necessary.

To Make the Green Tomatoes:

- Have the seasoned flour, eggs and ground cornflakes each in a separate shallow bowl. Dredge the tomato slices first in the flour, then in the egg, and finally in the cornflakes. Place on a sheet pan lined with parchment and refrigerate.

To Finish and Serve:

- Heat the oil in a large pot to 350°F and fry the tomato slices until golden brown. Place on a sheet pan lined with paper towels to drain. Sprinkle with kosher salt. Stack tomatoes with pickled onions on serving plates.
- Toss the mâche with some of the basil-bacon dressing and top the tomato stacks with some of the greens. Hold each stack together by skewering it with a fried noodle. Decorate the plates with pimento cream and flavored oils.

Lobster-Filled Sea Scallops and Warm Potato Salad with Black Truffles and Herb Salad

Chef Joachim Buchner, CMC
Serves 4

Potato Salad:

12 medium fingerling potatoes, cooked and peeled

3 tablespoons clarified butter

Salt and freshly ground pepper

1 teaspoon sugar

2 small shallots, thinly sliced

1 tablespoon sliced scallion

1 plum tomato, peeled and diced

1/2 cup extra-virgin olive oil

1/4 cup white-wine vinegar

4 slices bacon, cooked crispy and cut into large dice

Lobster-Filled Sea Scallops:

1/2 cup cooked lobster meat

2 tablespoons mayonnaise

1 chive, thinly sliced

1 teaspoon lemon juice, plus more for deglazing the pan

Dijon mustard

Pinch sugar

Salt and freshly ground pepper

1 tablespoon Ritz cracker crumbs

8 large sea scallops

3 tablespoons clarified butter

White wine

1 tablespoon cold unsalted butter

Chopped flat-leaf parsley

Herb Salad:

8 chives, cut into 2-inch lengths

Leaves from 2 sprigs fresh tarragon

1 small head frisée lettuce, broken into small sprigs

1/2 cup mixed micro greens

Celery greens

Lemon juice

Extra-virgin olive oil

Sea salt and freshly ground pepper

Finish and Serve:

8 slices black truffle

To Make the Potato Salad:

- Cut the fingerling potatoes in half. Heat the clarified butter in a large skillet, add the potatoes, and sauté until golden. Transfer the potatoes to a mixing bowl and season with salt, pepper, and sugar. Toss very gently with the shallots, scallion, tomato, olive oil and vinegar. Add the crispy bacon. Keep warm until serving.

To Make the Lobster-Filled Sea Scallops:

- In a mixing bowl, toss together the cooked lobster meat, mayonnaise, chive, lemon juice, Dijon mustard, and sugar. Season with salt and pepper. Fold in the cracker crumbs. Cut a pocket into the side of each sea scallops and fill it with some of the lobster mixture.
- When ready to serve, season the scallops with salt and pepper. Heat the clarified butter in a large skillet and sauté the scallops for 1 minute on each side. Reduce the heat, deglaze the pan with a splash of wine and some lemon juice. Add the cold butter and chopped parsley. Baste the scallops with the sauce in the pan and cook until heated through. Remove from the pan and keep hot.

To Make the Herb Salad:

- In a bowl, combine the chives, tarragon, frisée, micro greens and celery greens. Toss with lemon juice, olive oil, and season with salt and pepper.

To Finish and Serve:

- Place some of the potato salad on each plate. Top with 2 filled scallops, herb salad and 2 truffle slices.

Pickled Watermelon with Seasoned Cucumber

Chef Joseph M. Leonardi
Serves 4 or more

Pickled Watermelon:

1 vanilla bean

1 cup champagne vinegar

1/2 cup sugar

4 juniper berries

1 star anise pod

1 bay leaf

4 slabs peeled seedless watermelon

Frozen Goat Cheese Cream:

1 teaspoon lemon juice

3 ounces sugar

Freshly ground pepper

2 sprigs fresh thyme

4 ounces goat cheese

2 tablespoons mascarpone cheese

Citrus Foam:

1/2 cup fresh lemon juice

1/2 cup fresh orange juice

1/4 cup fresh lime juice

1 1/2 ounces sugar

1/2 teaspoon salt

1/2 teaspoon TIC stabilizer foam

Cider Vinaigrette:

1 cup apple cider

6 tablespoons cider vinegar

1 tablespoon honey

1 1/2 cups vegetable oil

Salt and ground white pepper

2 tablespoons chopped tarragon leaves

Seasoned Cucumber:

1 European cucumber

Juice of 1 lemon

1/4 cup olive oil

Grey salt and freshly ground pepper

3 tablespoons chopped flat-leaf parsley

2 tablespoons snipped fresh dill

Watermelon-Cucumber Shooters:

1 1/2 cups peeled, diced cucumber

3 1/2 cups diced watermelon

1/2 cup simple syrup

Finish and Serve:

Micro greens

Sliced kumquats or other citrus

To Make the Pickled Watermelon:

- Split the vanilla bean in half and scrape out all the seeds; save the bean for garnish. Place the vanilla seeds, vinegar, sugar, juniper, star anise, bay leaf and 1/4 cup water in a saucepan and bring to a boil. Simmer for 5 minutes and cool. Place the watermelon in the brine and leave until the melon has absorbed some brine and the desired taste is achieved.

To Make the Frozen Goat Cheese Cream:

- Place the lemon juice, sugar, pepper and thyme in a saucepan along with 1 cup water and bring to a boil. Add both cheeses and whisk to incorporate. Strain through a strainer lined with cheesecloth and cool. Process the mixture in an ice-cream machine and freeze until firm.

To Make the Citrus Foam:

- In a blender, combine the lemon juice, orange juice and lime juice and pulse until combined. Stir together the sugar, salt and TIC. Add to the blender and blend on high speed. Transfer the mixture to a saucepan and bring to a boil. Remove and cool. When needed, pour the mixture into a canister and charge with gas.

To Make the Cider Vinaigrette:

- Place the cider in a saucepan and simmer until it is reduced by half. Place in a bowl and whisk in the vinegar and honey. Slowly whisk in the oil to form an emulsion. Season to taste with salt and white pepper and whisk in the tarragon.

To Make the Seasoned Cucumber:

- Slice the cucumber into 3-inch-long sections, then use a mandolin to cut the sections long-ways into 1/8-inch-thick slices. Cut again in half lengthwise, then take 5 slices and overlap them on a serving plate. Drizzle with lemon juice and olive oil. Sprinkle with salt, pepper, parsley and dill. Refrigerate until chilled.

To Make the Watermelon-Cucumber Shooters:

- Place the cucumber, watermelon and simple syrup in a blender and blend until smooth. Add the 1 cup ice cubes and blend again.

To Finish and Serve:

- Place a slab of watermelon on top of the cucumber slices on the plates. Top the watermelon with the micro greens and kumquats. Place a quenelle of frozen goat cheese cream on each plate, along with a small glass of the watermelon-cucumber shooter and a vanilla bean. Drizzle the plates with cider vinaigrette and decorate with citrus foam.

Port Wine Poached Pear Salad with Gorgonzola Panna Cotta

Chef John T. Gelineau
Serves 4

Pears:

2 pears, peeled

2 cups port wine

1/4 cup sugar

1 tablespoon grated orange zest

1 cinnamon stick

5 star anise pods

3 whole cloves

5 black peppercorns

Panna Cotta:

1 cup heavy cream

4 ounces Gorgonzola cheese

5 sheets gelatin

1/2 teaspoon salt

Toast:

1 slice white bread

1 tablespoon olive oil

Salt and freshly ground pepper

1 teaspoon chopped fresh thyme

Salad:

1 celery stalk

8 grapes, halved

2 tablespoons dried cranberries

1 tablespoon cooked diced bacon

3 tablespoons red-wine vinegar

1 tablespoon minced shallot

1 teaspoon honey

1 teaspoon sugar

1 teaspoon Dijon mustard

1 teaspoon chopped parsley

1 teaspoon chopped fresh tarragon

1 teaspoon chopped fresh chives

1/4 cup olive oil

8 ounces baby greens

Salt and freshly ground pepper

To Make the Pears:

- Using a melon baller, remove the core and seeds of the pears from the bottom. Slice the pears into disks. In a small saucepan, combine the wine, sugar and zest. Tie the cinnamon, star anise, cloves and peppercorns in a piece of cheesecloth and add them to the pot. Add the pear slices and simmer the mixture for 15 minutes. Remove the pears with a slotted spoon and cool them.

To Make the Panna Cotta:

- In a saucepan, combine the cream and cheese and heat slowly, stirring occasionally, until the cheese is fully melted. Stir in the gelatin until melted. Stir in the salt and pour the mixture into 2-ounce molds. Refrigerate until chilled, then remove from the molds and reserve.

To Make the Toast:

- Preheat the oven to 350°F. Roll the bread slice through a pasta machine set to the number 4 setting. Cut the flattened bread into four triangles. Brush with oil and sprinkle with salt, pepper and thyme. Lay each piece over a rolling pin so it curves and bake on a sheet pan for 8 minutes. Cool and reserve.

To Make the Salad:

- With a mandoline, julienne the celery lengthwise into strips as long as the stalk. Place the strips in a bowl of ice water so they will curl up.
- In a small bowl, combine the grapes, cranberries and bacon. In another bowl, whisk together the vinegar, shallot, honey, sugar, mustard, parsley, tarragon and chives. Slowly whisk in the oil.

To Finish and Serve:

- Place 3 pear slices on each plate. On one side of each plate, place a toast topped with a panna cotta. Toss greens with some of the vinaigrette and season with salt and pepper. Place a mound of the greens on top of the pears. Drain the curled celery and toss it with the grape-cranberry mixture. Toss again with some of the vinaigrette and divide between the plates.

Roasted Golden Beet and Pink Grapefruit Salad with Pink Peppercorn Vinaigrette

Chef Daryl Shular
Serves 4

Salad:

2 small golden beets,
    peeled and cut into batons
Vegetable oil
Salt and freshly ground white pepper
Segments from 1 pink grapefruit
2 ounces red radishes, thinly sliced
6 ounces baby carrots,
    peeled and blanched
4 ounces green beans,
    trimmed and blanched
6 ounces cherry tomatoes (optional)
4 ounces asparagus,
    trimmed and blanched
6 ounces mixed spring greens
2 ounces zucchini,
    thinly sliced and blanched
4 ounces fennel, thinly sliced
1/2 ounce garlic, minced
1/4 cup extra-virgin olive oil

Pink Peppercorn Vinaigrette:

1/2 ounce pink peppercorns,
    crushed and sifted
1/4 teaspoon Dijon mustard
1/2 teaspoon chopped garlic
1/4 cup champagne vinegar
1/2 cup extra-virgin olive oil
1/2 ounce chopped parsley
Salt

To Make the Salad:

- Preheat the oven to 375°F. Toss the beets with a little vegetable oil and salt and pepper. Place on a sheet pan and roast until tender and lightly browned. Set aside.
- In a stainless-steel bowl, combine all the remaining ingredients. Toss and season to taste with salt and pepper. Refrigerate until serving.

To Make the Pink Peppercorn Vinaigrette:

- In a stainless-steel bowl, whisk together the peppercorns, mustard, garlic and vinegar. Slowly whisk in the olive oil until the mixture is emulsified. Whisk in the parsley and salt to taste and refrigerate until serving.

To Finish and Serve:

- Divide salad between plates. Top with roasted beets and drizzle with vinaigrette.

*Chef Shular makes a final wipe down
before turning over to the judges.*

Salsify Salad and Roasted Squab Breast with Huckleberry Vinaigrette

Chef Joachim Buchner, CMC
Serves 4

Huckleberry Vinaigrette:

1/2 cup huckleberries

1/4 cup orange juice

1/4 cup champagne vinegar

1 teaspoon sugar

Pinch xanthan gum

1/2 cup vegetable oil

Salt and freshly ground pepper

Salsify:

Acidulated water (25% lemon juice)
for holding the salsify

16 pieces salsify, peeled and cut into 3"
sticks

2 cups water

1/2 cup lemon juice

1 teaspoon salt

3 whole peppercorns

1 shallot, thinly sliced

Squab:

Vegetable oil

2 bone-in squab breasts

Salt and freshly ground pepper

2 tablespoons unsalted butter

1 sprig fresh rosemary

1/2 onion, sliced

2 garlic cloves, sliced

Finish and Serve:

3 cups mixed baby greens and herbs

To Make the Huckleberry Vinaigrette:

- In a blender, combine the huckleberries, orange juice, vinegar, sugar and xanthan gum. Blend on high speed for 30 seconds. Reduce the speed to slow and slowly pour in the oil; you should have an emulsified dressing. Season with salt and pepper and transfer to a bowl.

To Make the Salsify:

- Place the acidulated water in a stainless-steel or plastic container. Keep the peeled and cut salsify covered in the water until ready to cook.
- To cook the salsify, in a stainless-steel pot, combine the salsify, water, lemon juice, salt, peppercorns and shallot. Bring to a boil, add the drained salsify, and simmer until salsify is tender. Remove the salsify from the cooking liquid, and pat dry. Toss the salsify in the huckleberry vinaigrette and let marinate for 3 hours.

To Make the Squab:

- Preheat the oven to 350°F. Heat the oil in a large skillet over high heat. Season the squab with salt and pepper and sear each breast on all sides until lightly browned. Reduce the heat to medium and add the butter and rosemary to the skillet. When the butter has melted, add the onion and garlic and cook, basting the breasts with the butter in the pan, until the onion is tender. Transfer the skillet to the oven and roast until the squab is cooked through. Remove from the oven and let rest in a warm place for 10 minutes before carving.

To Finish and Serve:

- Place salsify on serving plates. Slice the squab as desired and divide between the plates along with the onion from the skillet. Top with mixed greens and drizzle with more vinaigrette.

CHEF'S NOTES

- Keeping the uncooked salsify in the acidulated water prevents it from discoloring.

Spring Asparagus Salad

Chef Scott A. Fetty
Serves 4

Chopped Asparagus:

4 stalks green asparagus, peeled, blanched and trimmed

4 stalks white asparagus, peeled, blanched and trimmed

1 teaspoon finely diced red onion

1 teaspoon minced tarragon

1/4 teaspoon minced capers

1/4 cup mayonnaise

1 tablespoon orange juice

Sea salt and cracked black pepper

Salad:

12 stalks green asparagus, peeled, blanched and trimmed

12 stalks white asparagus, peeled, blanched and trimmed

Sea salt and cracked black pepper

Roasted almond oil

2 Mineola tangelos, zested and segmented

1 pint petite radishes, julienned

1/4 cup lemon-flavored olive oil

3 ounces Meyer lemon juice

1 English cucumber, peeled (optional) and thinly sliced

Baby Bibb lettuce leaves

4 teaspoons radish sprouts

4 ounces chopped asparagus salad (see recipe above)

Meyer Lemon Crème Fraîche:

1 cup crème fraîche

2 Meyer lemons, zested and juiced

Honey

Rice vinegar

Ground white pepper

BEVERAGE RECOMMENDATION

A crisp Washington State Sauvignon Blanc, or an aperitif of limoncello and sparkling water

For the Chopped Asparagus:

- Combine all ingredients except the salt and pepper and marinate for 15 minutes. Season to taste with salt and pepper. Place a little of the salad at one side of each of 4 chilled serving plates.

For the Salad:

- Season the asparagus spears with salt, pepper, almond oil and tangelo zest and divide between the four plates.
- Toss the tangelo segments and the radishes with lemon olive oil and lemon juice and place some on each plate. Shingle two pieces of cucumber on top of the asparagus stalks. Garnish the top with some of the lettuce leaves which have been tossed in lemon olive oil. Arrange the radish sprouts and some chopped asparagus on top.

For the Meyer Lemon Crème Fraîche:

- Stir together the crème fraîche, lemon zest and lemon juice. Season to taste with honey, rice vinegar and white pepper. Drizzle each plate with a little of the mixture and a little more almond oil.

CHEF'S NOTES

- Crème fraîche, Meyer lemons, lemon-flavored olive oil, and roasted almond oil can be found in most specialty stores or ordered online.

Terrine of Fruits and Foie Gras

Chef Jamie P. Keating, CCC
Serves 4

Terrine:

6 ounces Grade A foie gras trimmings

2 teaspoons kosher salt, plus
more to taste

1 teaspoon cracked black pepper

1/2 liter (about 2 cups) white Port wine

1 quart chicken stock

1 ounce Great Lakes Powdered Gelatin

10 ounces white grape juice

Thinly sliced strawberries

1 Gala apple, diced, poached in red
wine and cooled

12 blackberries

1/2 mango, peeled, pitted and cut into
thin strips

1/4 cup Champagne grapes

Crackers:

1 pound 5 ounces high-gluten flour,
sifted

1/2 teaspoon fennel powder

1/2 cup unsalted butter, at room temperature

1 large egg

1/2 cup water

Salt

Finish and Serve:

Tender leaves from 2 bunches frisée

1 cup baby arugula

Fresh fruit for garnish

2 tablespoons mint oil

BEVERAGE RECOMMENDATION

King Estate Oregon Pinot Gris

To Make the Terrine:

- Sprinkle the foie gras with the 2 teaspoons salt and the cracked pepper. Marinate in the Port for 2 hours. Drain, wrap the foie gras in cheesecloth forming a torchon (cylinder); tie the ends with butchers' twine. Poach the torchon in simmering chicken stock for about 90 seconds, then cool in a bowl of ice water.
- Meanwhile, bloom the gelatin in the grape juice in a small stainless-steel bowl. Cover and let sit for 30 minutes. Place the bottom of the bowl with the gelatin in it over hot water. Stir until the gelatin is completely dissolved.
- Pass the cooled foie gras through a fine tamis and shape into a very thin cylinder. Arrange the fruits around the foie gras in a terrine. Have the gelatin at 76°F and pour it into the terrine. Chill until set, at least several hours.

To Make the Crackers:

- In food processor, blend pulse together the flour, fennel and butter. Add the egg, water and salt and pulse until combined. Knead the dough well, wrap in plastic wrap and chill.
- Preheat the oven to 200°F. Using a pasta machine, roll out the dough with the machine at the #1 setting. Cut into triangular strips and bake on parchment-lined baking sheets for 40 minutes.

To Finish and Serve:

- Slice the terrine and serve plated with the crackers, frisée, arugula, fruit and mint oil.

Warm Noodle Salad with Curried Beef Skewers

Chef Kevin Taylor
Serves 4

Sauce:

2 tablespoons Vietnamese fish sauce

2 tablespoons lime juice

1/4 cup warm water

4 teaspoons minced garlic

2 teaspoons minced ginger

2 teaspoons spicy red chile paste

3 tablespoons sugar

1 1/2 teaspoons salt

Beef Skewers:

3 tablespoons green curry paste

1 tablespoon canola oil

12 ounces filet mignon,
    cut into bite-size cubes

Noodle Salad:

2 cups cooked vermicelli rice noodles

1/4 cup bean sprouts

1/4 cup thinly sliced cucumber

2 tablespoons julienned carrot

2 tablespoons thinly sliced scallion

2 tablespoons sliced Thai basil leaves

2 tablespoons cilantro leaves

4 hot Thai chiles (optional)

Finish and Serve:

1/2 cup thinly sliced iceberg lettuce

2 tablespoons chopped toasted peanuts

BEVERAGE RECOMMENDATION

Vietnamese iced coffee

To Make the Sauce:

- Whisk together all the sauce ingredients in a medium bowl, whisking until the sugar and salt have dissolved. Refrigerate until ready to serve.

To Make the Beef Skewers:

- Whisk together the curry paste and oil. Add the beef and toss to coat. Refrigerate at least 3 hours.
- When ready to cook, skewer the beef and grill to the desired doneness, 5 to 7 minutes for medium-rare.

To Make the Noodle Salad:

- Place a mound of noodles on each plate; you can reheat the noodles in the microwave if you wish. Top the noodles with the sprouts, cucumber, carrot, scallion, basil, cilantro, and chiles (whole or sliced).

To Finish and Serve:

- Place some sliced lettuce on each plate and top each with a quarter of the beef. Sprinkle the noodle salad with chopped peanuts and pour the chilled sauce over the noodles and vegetables and serve.

CHEF'S NOTES

- This is a great summer dish, very fresh and light. If you have trouble finding some of the specialty ingredients, like Thai basil and Thai chiles, try an Asian grocery store.

Chef Taylor adds some finishing touches before platting.

Artichokes Three Ways

Chef Jonathan P. Moosmiller, CEC
Serves 4

Braised Artichokes:

2 large artichokes
2 cups water
1 lemon, halved
2 tablespoons extra-virgin olive oil
2 shallots, diced
3 garlic cloves, sliced
2 cups diced tomatoes
1/4 cup drained capers
1 cup white wine
1/2 cup tomato puree
5 basil leaves, cut into chiffonade
Salt and freshly ground pepper

Fried Artichoke:

1 large artichoke
Cornstarch
Oil for deep frying
Kosher salt

Stuffed Artichokes:

1 cup white wine
Juice of 2 lemons
3 sprigs fresh thyme
3 garlic cloves, crushed
1 bay leaf
2 large artichokes
3/4 cup mayonnaise
1/4 teaspoon Worcestershire sauce
1 teaspoon chopped flat-leaf parsley
Juice and zest of 1 lemon
1 cup lump crabmeat
Kosher salt and freshly ground pepper
2 cups panko bread crumbs toasted in
   clarified butter

To Make the Braised Artichokes:

- Remove the tough outer leaves of the artichokes. Using a serrated knife, cut off all of the leaves just above the base of each artichoke. Peel the tough skin from the stem of each and then use a spoon to scoop out and discard the choke from the base of each. Cut each cleaned artichoke into quarters and place the quarters in a bowl. Add the water and squeeze the lemon juice into the bowl.
- Heat a small saucepan over medium heat for 2 minutes. Add the oil, shallots and garlic and cook, stirring frequently, until the shallots are translucent. Add the diced tomatoes and capers and cook for 2 minutes. Add the wine and cook for an additional 2 minutes. Add the tomato puree, basil and the drained artichoke quarters. Bring to a boil, reduce the heat and simmer until the artichokes are tender, about 15 minutes. Season with salt and pepper and keep warm until serving.

To Make the Fried Artichoke:

- Using a sharp knife, split the artichoke in half lengthwise. Using a mandolin, slice the artichoke into thin slices approximately 1/16-inch thick. Place the slices in a bowl, sprinkle with cornstarch, and toss lightly to just coat the slices.
- Heat the oil in a deep-fat fryer to 325° F. Add the sliced artichokes one at a time to the oil and fry until they are lightly golden and crispy. Drain on paper towels and season lightly with salt.

To Make the Stuffed Artichokes:

- In a large saucepan, combine the wine, juice of 2 lemons, thyme, garlic and bay leaf. Set aside.
- Trim and clean the artichokes by peeling off and discarding the first 3 to 4 rows of outer leaves. Snip the sharp tips off the remaining leaves with kitchen shears. Peel the stems and bases of the artichokes carefully with a vegetable peeler. Place the clean artichokes in the saucepan and add enough cold water to cover. Bring to a simmer over medium heat; cover and simmer until the artichokes are tender, about 30 minutes. Remove the artichokes from the liquid and cool.
- While the artichokes are cooling, place the mayonnaise in a medium bowl. Whisk in the Worcestershire, parsley, and juice and zest of 1 lemon. Fold in the crabmeat. Season the mixture with salt and pepper.
- Once the artichokes are cool enough to handle, preheat the oven to 400° F. Split the artichokes in half lengthwise and remove the choke with a spoon. Fill the cavity of each artichoke with the crabmeat mixture. Cover each artichoke half with the toasted panko and place in a baking dish. Bake until golden brown and heated through.

To Finish and Serve:

- Warm 4 serving plates. Place 2 braised artichoke quarters on each plate along with 1/2 cup of the braising liquid. Gently place one of the stuffed artichokes halves on each plate with 2 pieces of the fried artichoke. Serve immediately.

Black Pepper Fettuccine with Morels and Country Ham Tossed in Goat Cheese Cream

Chef Chris Desens, CEC
Serves 4

Black Pepper Fettuccine:

1 cup all-purpose flour

1 large egg

3 large egg yolks

1 teaspoon olive oil

1/2 teaspoon coarsely ground
black pepper

Sauce and Vegetables:

2 tablespoons olive oil

1 tablespoon minced shallot

1 cup morel mushrooms, cleaned

1/4 cup white wine

2 cups heavy cream

1/4 cup diced country ham

2 tablespoons roasted garlic

1 tablespoon grated lemon zest

1/2 cup goat cheese

2 tablespoons julienned fresh
basil leaves

1 tablespoon chopped parsley

1 tablespoon snipped fresh chives

2 teaspoons chopped fresh tarragon

1/4 cup unsalted butter

Salt and freshly ground pepper

Garnish (optional):

Dried tomato chips

BEVERAGE RECOMMENDATION

Chianti, Brunello di Montalcino

To Make the Black Pepper Fettuccine:

- Combine all the ingredients and knead well. Rest the dough for half an hour, then roll out in a pasta maker and cut into fettuccine.

To Make the Sauce and Vegetables:

- Heat the oil in a large pan and sauté the shallot and morels. Add the wine and cook until reduced. Add all the remaining ingredients except the butter, salt and pepper and continue to simmer until the mixture thickens. Whisk in the butter and season with salt and pepper.

To Finish and Serve:

- Cook 8 ounces of the fettuccine in boiling salted water, drain, and add to the pan with the sauce and vegetables. Toss well and cook until heated through. Taste, adjust seasoning if necessary, and serve garnished with a tomato chip.

CHEF'S NOTES

- This is an appetizer we feature every spring when Missouri morel season hits, and it draws inspiration from great Missouri producers of country ham and goat cheese. It can easily be presented as an entrée as well.

*Chef Dessens skillfully arranges
a platter display for the ACC cold
food presentaion.*

Braised Endive Gratin with Beets and Apples

Chef Edward G. Leonard, CMC
Serves 4

Braised Endive Gratin:

8 heads red endive

2 tablespoons unsalted butter

1 teaspoon light-brown sugar

1 1/2 cups chicken stock

Kosher salt and fresh cracked pepper

4 puff pasty circles, each
    4 inches in diameter

1 large egg, whipped lightly

1 cup heavy cream, whipped to
    medium peaks

2 large egg yolks, whipped until foamy

Beets and Apples:

3 Granny Smith apples

1 tablespoon unsalted butter

1/2 teaspoon brown sugar

1/4 cup apple jack brandy

16 red beet cubes, each about
    1/2 inch square

1 cup apple juice

Finish and Serve:

Kosher salt and fresh cracked pepper

8 dried beet chips

To Make the Braised Endive Gratin:

- Trim the root end of each endive and split the heads in half lengthwise. Place a large sauté pan over medium heat and add the butter. Once the butter begins to bubble, add the endive cut-side down and sprinkle with the brown sugar. Cook until the endive is golden brown. Add the stock and season lightly with salt and pepper. Reduce the heat to low and cover the pan tightly. Continue to cook over low heat until the endive is cooked through. Remove from the heat and reserve.

- Preheat the oven to 400°F. Place the puff pastry on a sheet pan lined with parchment paper. Brush the circles lightly with the whipped egg. Place a wire rack over the pastry and bake until golden brown, about 10 minutes. Remove from the oven and allow to cool. Remove the wire rack and set the circles aside.

- Gently fold the whipped cream and egg yolks together and season the mixture with salt and pepper; set aside until serving.

To Make the Beets and Apples:

- Peel and core the apples and slice each into 12 wedges. Place a large sauté pan over medium heat and add the butter. Once the butter begins to bubble, add the apple wedges. Sprinkle in the brown sugar and continue to cook until the apples brown on all sides. Deglaze the pan with the brandy and continue to cook until the liquid is reduced to a syrup. Remove from the heat and reserve at room temperature.

- In a small stainless-steel saucepan, combine the beets and apple juice. Simmer over medium heat until the beets are tender. Remove from the heat and reserve until serving.

To Finish and Serve:

- Preheat the broiler. Place the endive halves on the puff pastry circles and cover them with the egg yolk mixture. Broil until lightly browned. Place one tart in the middle of each warmed serving plate. Gently reheat the apple wedges over medium heat and place 2 wedges at 12, 3, 6 and 9 o'clock on each plate.

- Reheat the beets in their liquid; drain, discard the liquid and season the beets lightly with salt and pepper. Place a beet cube between each of the apple piles on each plate. Garnish the plates with beet chips and serve immediately.

Cannelloni of Smoked Salmon with Celery and Cucumber Salad and Osetra Caviar

Chef Edward G. Leonard, CMC
Serves 4

Cannelloni:

1 cup cooked, riced potato

1 cup milk

1 tablespoon melted butter

1 large egg

5 tablespoons all-purpose flour

Clarified butter

4 tablespoons crème fraîche

12 ounces smoked salmon

Celery and Cucumber Salad:

2 cucumbers, peeled and juiced

6 teaspoons gelatin powder

12 ounces celery, peeled and
thinly sliced

1 teaspoon chiffonade of
flat-leaf parsley

Juice of 1/2 lemon

2 tablespoons extra-virgin olive oil

Kosher salt and fresh cracked pepper

Finish and Serve:

1 ounce osetra caviar

4 teaspoons crème fraîche

Red sea salt

Fried celery leaves

To Make the Cannelloni:

- In a medium mixing bowl, combine the potato, milk, melted butter and egg and whisk until smooth. Add the flour and stir until combined. Place a 10-inch nonstick sauté pan over medium heat and allow the pan to heat for 2 minutes. Add 1 teaspoon of clarified butter to the pan. Pour in 1/4 cup of the batter; swirl the pan so the batter forms a thin layer covering the entire pan. Cook until lightly golden brown, then flip the crêpe and cook the other side until golden. Repeat until you have 4 crêpes.

- Cut each crêpe into a rectangle that it is 3 x 7 inches. Place 1 tablespoon of crème fraîche on each and spread evenly. Place a single even layer of smoked salmon on top of each crêpe and roll each up so that the smoked salmon is encased inside. Wrap each roll with plastic wrap and refrigerate overnight.

To Make the Celery and Cucumber Salad:

- Place 1/2 cup of the cucumber juice in a stainless-steel bowl. Sprinkle the gelatin over the juice and allow it to bloom for 20 minutes. Place the bowl over simmering water and stir until the gelatin has melted. Remove from the heat, add the remaining juice and stir to combine. Pour the liquid into a level container so that it reaches a depth of ¼ inch. Refrigerate until the liquid is set.

- Place the sliced celery in a mixing bowl and add the parsley, lemon juice and oil and toss to coat. Season with salt and pepper, cover, and refrigerate.

To Finish and Serve:

- Divide the celery mixture into 4 equal portions and place one portion in the center of each serving plate. Use a sharp knife to cut the cucumber gelée into 1/4-inch cubes. Place 6 cubes on either side of the celery on each plate.

- Unwrap each salmon cannelloni and place one on each plate on top of the celery. Using a spoon, place a dollop of caviar on top of each cannelloni. Using 2 spoons, form small quenelles of crème fraîche and place one next to each cannelloni. Sprinkle the crème fraîche with red sea salt, garnish each plate with fried celery leaves and serve.

Carpaccio of Pig Ears, Hog Jowl Cobbler, and Blueberry and Apple Compotes

Chef Michael Matarazzo
Serves 4

Pig Ear Carpaccio:

2 tablespoons olive oil

1/2 cup finely diced onion

1/4 cup finely diced celery

1/4 cup thinly sliced leek

1 tablespoon minced shallot

1/4 cup apple brandy

1/4 cup dry white wine

1 1/2 pounds fresh pigs' ears, cleaned

2 quarts veal stock

4 sprigs fresh thyme

3 fresh sage leaves

1 bay leaf

20 black peppercorns

Kosher salt and freshly ground pepper

Braised Hog Jowl:

2 tablespoons olive oil

1/4 cup finely diced onion

1/4 cup finely diced peeled apple

1/4 cup finely diced celery

1 tablespoon minced shallot

2 tablespoons apple brandy

2 tablespoons white wine

1/2 pound fresh smoked hog jowl

3 sprigs fresh thyme

2 fresh sage leaves

1 bay leaf

15 black peppercorns

3 cups chicken stock

Salt and freshly ground pepper to taste

Foie Gras Streusel:

1/4 cup foie gras butter

1/4 cup all-purpose flour

1 tablespoon granulated sugar

1/2 teaspoon kosher salt

To Make the Pig Ear Carpaccio:

- Preheat the oven to 350°F. Line a square terrine mold with plastic wrap.
- Heat a large ovenproof pan over medium heat and add the oil. Add the onion, celery and leek and cook until the onion is translucent. Add the shallot and cook briefly. Deglaze with the brandy and simmer until almost dry. Deglaze again with the white wine and simmer until almost dry.
- Add the pigs' ears, stock, thyme, sage, bay leaf and peppercorns. Bring to a simmer, cover the pan securely with foil, and bake until the ears are very tender (if you squeeze the thickest part of an ear with your fingers they should go right through the flesh), about 3 hours.
- Remove the ears and set aside. Strain and reserve the liquid. Place the ears one at a time in the terrine, dipping each ear into the warm cooking liquid before placing it into the bottom of the terrine. Season each layer with salt and pepper. Fold the ears as needed to fit them snuggly in the terrine. Wrap the terrine in plastic wrap and press down on the surface to remove any air bubbles. Place the terrine in the freezer until frozen solid.

To Make the Braised Hog Jowl:

- Preheat the oven to 375°F. In a small rondeau, heat the oil over medium heat. Add the onion, apple, celery and shallot and cook until softened. Deglaze with the brandy and wine and simmer until almost dry. Add the jowl, thyme, sage, bay leaf and peppercorns. Pour in the chicken stock; the jowl should be covered by about 2/3 with stock. Bring to a simmer, cover the pan securely with foil, and bake until the jowl is very tender, about 3 hours.
- Remove the jowl and set it aside. Strain the cooking liquid through a chinois or fine-mesh strainer, discard the herbs, and place the liquid in a saucepan. Simmer until the liquid is reduced to a glaze. Season with salt and pepper. Cut the jowl into ½-inch cubes, add them to the glaze and set aside.

To Make the Foie Gras Streusel:

- Combine all the ingredients in the bowl of an electric mixer fitted with the paddle attachment. Mix until the mixture forms walnut-size clumps. Set aside.

To Finish and Serve:

- Preheat the oven to 375°F. Assemble individual cobblers by placing 1 cube of the braised jowl in the center of each lady apple half (see page ???). Cover the top of the apples with a generous mound of foie gras streusel and bake until the streusel is golden brown.
- Meanwhile, use a brush to paint a long straight line of the blueberry sauce across the middle of each serving plate. Slice the frozen pig ear terrine lengthwise on a meat slicer as thin as possible and about 4 inches in length. Place a slice in the center of each plate, angling it over the sauce to form an "X" on the plate.
- Place a warm cobbler in the center of the "X." Place 2 small mounds of the blueberry compote opposite each other in two quadrants of the "X." Mound apple compote in the other 2 quadrants and serve.

CHEF'S NOTES

- Chef Matarazzo serves this dish with Apple Halves (see page 224), Apple Compote (see page 224) and Blueberry Compote and Sauce (see page 225).

Crispy Vegetable Torte with Fried Goat Cheese and Roasted Tomatoes

Chef Edward G. Leonard, CMC
Serves 4

Fried Goat Cheese:

12-ounce log goat cheese

1 cup all-purpose flour

Kosher salt and freshly
    cracked black pepper

2 large eggs

2 cups fine panko

Roasted Tomatoes:

4 Roma tomatoes, peeled

1 tablespoon extra-virgin olive oil

Kosher salt and freshly
    cracked black pepper

Herbed Crème Fraîche:

1/2 cup crème fraîche

1 tablespoon snipped chives

1 teaspoon extra-virgin olive oil

Kosher salt and freshly
    cracked black pepper

To Finish and Serve:

Oil for deep frying

Kosher salt

4 large slices dried eggplant

8 slices dried zucchini

8 slices dried red beet

8 slices dried golden beet

4 teaspoons pesto sauce

1/4 cup fried parsley leaves

To Make the Fried Goat Cheese:

- Using a small knife, slice the log of goat cheese into 12 equal pieces. Place the flour in a small bowl and season lightly with salt and pepper. Crack the eggs into a separate small bowl and whip well. Place the panko in a third small bowl. Place the pieces of goat cheese into the bowl with the flour and toss gently until all pieces are coated evenly. Remove from the flour and shake off any excess. Place the slices into the whipped eggs and turn to coat. Let excess egg drip back into the bowl and coat the slices evenly in the panko. Place the breaded slices on a plate and set aside until serving.

To Make the Roasted Tomatoes:

- Preheat the oven to 275°F. Using a sharp knife, cut the peeled tomatoes into quarters and remove and discard the seeds. Place the quarters in a small bowl and toss with the olive oil and salt and pepper. Place the quarters on a sheet pan lined with a Silpat, making sure that none are touching. Roast the tomatoes for 1 hour. Allow to cool and reserve until serving.

To Make the Herbed Crème Fraîche:

- In a small bowl, combine the crème fraîche, chives and oil. Season with salt and pepper and refrigerate until serving.

To Finish and Serve:

- Heat the oil to 350°F. and fry the goat cheese slices until golden brown. Drain on paper towels and season lightly with salt. Reserve in a warm place while plating the rest of the dish.
- Place 4 room-temperature serving plates on a work surface. Make stacks of the vegetables and goat cheese by layering them in this order: slice eggplant, slice zucchini, slice goat cheese, tomato quarter, 2 red beet slices, slice goat cheese, tomato quarter, slice zucchini, slice goat cheese, tomato quarter, 2 slices golden beet, tomato quarter. Decorate the plates with the crème fraîche and pesto. Garnish with the fried parsley and serve.

Crispy Brandade Cakes with Manila Clams

Chef Edward G. Leonard, CMC
Serves 4

Brandade Cakes:

1 cup cooked, hot riced potato

2 tablespoons warmed heavy cream

1 tablespoon unsalted butter

1/2 pound smoked cod, flaked

2 tablespoons brunoise of
    cooked potato

Kosher salt and fresh cracked pepper

2 cups all-purpose flour

4 large eggs, cracked and
    whipped lightly

4 cups fine panko

Oil for deep frying

Clam Sauce:

2 tablespoons unsalted butter

1/4 cup sliced leek, white part only

1 tablespoon minced shallot

1 teaspoon sherry

1 teaspoon champagne vinegar

2 teaspoons white wine

1/2 cup clam broth

40 manila clams, purged

1/4 cup heavy cream

Potatoes and Spinach:

2 Idaho potatoes, peeled

1 tablespoon unsalted butter

1 cup chicken stock

1 sprig fresh thyme

2 tablespoons extra-virgin olive oil

1 shallot, sliced

2 garlic cloves, sliced

12 ounces spinach, stems removed,
    leaves well rinsed

Kosher salt and fresh cracked pepper

Finish and Serve:

2 ounces osetra caviar

8 dried leek strips

To Make the Brandade Cakes:

- In a stainless-steel bowl, combine the potato, cream, butter, smoked cod and bruniose of potato and fold gently until combine. Season with salt and pepper. Divide the mixture into 8 equal portions. Gently form each portion into a cylinder-shaped cake. Refrigerate the cakes for 15 minutes.
- Gently dust each cake with flour and coat each in the whipped eggs. Roll in the panko to coat. Just before serving, fry the cakes in 350°F. oil until golden brown.

To Make the Clam Sauce:

- Place a medium stainless-steel saucepan over medium heat and melt the butter. Add the leek and shallot and cook, stirring occasionally, until the shallot in translucent. Add the sherry, vinegar, wine and clam broth and bring to a simmer. Add the clams, cover the pan, and cook until the clams open. Remove the clams from the pan and remove the meats from the shells. Discard the shells; reserve the clam meats.
- Reduce the liquid in the pan until there is just 1/4 cup remaining. Add the cream and remove from the heat. Strain the sauce through a fine-mesh sieve and set aside until serving.

To Make the Potatoes and Spinach:

- Using a knife, cut 8 planks from the potatoes, each approximately 1 1/2 inches by 2 1/2 inches. Reserve the potato scraps for another use. Place the potato planks in a small saucepan and add the butter, stock and thyme. Cover the pan with a parchment-paper lid; bring the stock to a simmer over medium heat and cook until the potatoes are tender. Reserve the potatoes and cooking liquid separately.
- Just before serving, place a large sauté pan over medium heat and add the oil. Add the shallot and garlic and cook, stirring, until the shallot is translucent. Add the spinach and sauté until wilted, about 3 minutes. Season to taste with salt and pepper.

To Finish and Serve:

- Put the potato planks back into their cooking liquid and place over medium heat until warmed through. Place 2 of the planks onto each of 4 warmed serving plates, placing one in the center of each plate and one to the left of the first. Place 2 of the fried brandade cakes on each plate, placing one at 12 o'clock and one at 6 o'clock. Divide the spinach into 4 equal portions and place a portion on each plate to the right of the brandade that is at 12 o'clock. Spoon 1/2 ounce of the caviar onto the center potato plank on each plate.
- Put the clam meats in the sauce and gently heat through. Spoon a portion of the clams and sauce onto the second potato plank and the sautéed spinach. Garnish each plate with 2 dried leek strips and serve immediately.

Calamari Portuguese Fisherman's Style

Chef Daniel J. Scannell, CMC (photo page 83)
Serves 4

¼ **cup** extra-virgin olive oil

4 **ounces** piquillo pepper sauce,
plus more for serving

1 **cup** sliced red cherry peppers with
juice

2 **tablespoons** fresh marinara sauce

2 **tablespoons** chopped parsley

Oil for deep frying

1 **pound** calamari rings,
rinsed and patted dry

1 **cup** all-purpose flour

2 **tablespoons** grated Parmesan

Black olives

4 **slices** grilled bread

- In a large bowl, combine the olive oil, piquillo pepper sauce, cherry peppers, marinara and parsley and mix well. Set aside.
- Heat the oil in a fryer or deep, heavy pot to 350°F. Working in batches, dust the squid with flour and deep fry until golden brown. Remove from the oil with a slotted spoon and drain.
- Place the squid in the bowl with the pepper sauce and toss well. Divide between serving plates and sprinkle with the Parmesan and olives. Serve hot with grilled bread and drizzle with more pepper sauce.

Foie Gras and Pineapple Napoleon with Truffle Carmel

Chef Richard Rosendale, CEC (photo page 83)
Serves 4

Pineapples Slices:

1 golden pineapple, peeled and cored

3 **tablespoons** sugar

3 **tablespoons** unsalted butter

1 vanilla bean, split

Foie Gras Mousse:

12 **ounces** foie gras

1 **tablespoon** port

1 **teaspoon** Madeira

1 **teaspoon** salt, plus more to taste

Pinch ground nutmeg

Truffle-Foie Gras Caramel:

1/2 **cup** sugar

1 **tablespoon** glucose

1/4 **cup** water

1/4 **cup** heavy cream

1 **tablespoon** foie gras trimmings

1 **teaspoon** minced truffle

Finish and Serve:

Four 1/16-inch-thick slices pineapple,
dried in a dehydrator until very crisp

4 vanilla beans, dried in a dehydrator
until very crisp

Basil leaves for garnish

For the Pineapple Slices:

- Cut the pineapple into ¼-inch-thick slices. In a medium sauté pan, cook the pineapple slices in the sugar and butter until caramelized. Add the vanilla bean and continue to cook, basting the pineapple, until it is very tender and completely browned. Let the pineapple slices cool.

For the Foie Gras Mousse:

- Marinate the foie gras in the port, Madeira, salt and nutmeg for 3 hours.
- Place the foie gras in a vacuum bag and seal. Place the bag in a thermal bath at 62.5°C for 3 minutes. Remove the bag from the bath, cut the bag open and transfer the foie gras to a stainless-steel bowl set over another bowl of ice. Stir to emulsify.
- Pass the foie gras through a tamis, season, and then place in a piping bag. Pipe the foie gras over half the pineapple slices and spread smooth. Cover the foie gras with the remaining slices and press lightly to compact the mousse.

To Make the Truffle-Foie Gras Caramel:

- Combine the sugar, glucose and water in a small saucepan and place over medium heat. Simmer until the mixture begins to turn a dark amber color. Whisking constantly, slowly whisk in the cream. Lower the heat and cook the mixture for an additional 6 minutes. Add the foie gras trimmings and stir until they dissolve. Strain the caramel through a sieve and then stir in the truffle.

To Finish and Serve:

- Swipe some of the truffle caramel on each plate, then place a wedge of the pineapple and foie gras on each plate. Garnish with the dehydrated pineapple chips, the vanilla pods, and basil.

Calamari Portuguese Fisherman's Style (pg 82)

Foie Gras and Pineapple Napoleon with Truffle Carmel (pg 82)

Gratinée of Foie Gras with Apple, Beets and Salsify (pg 84)

Herb Poached Sable with Saffron Angel Hair Pasta (pg 85)

Gratinée of Foie Gras with Apple, Beets and Salsify

Chef Edward G. Leonard. CMC (photo page 83)
Serves 4

Foie Gras:

1 tablespoon unsalted butter

1/4 cup brunoise of Serrano ham

3/4 cup brunoise of assorted wild
mushrooms

2 tablespoons panko bread crumbs

1 tablespoon softened butter

1 tablespoon fines herbes

1 tablespoon veal jus

1 1/2 teaspoons heavy cream

4 slices grade A foie gras, each 1/2-inch
thick

Salt and freshly ground pepper

Sauce:

1/2 tablespoon foie gras fat

1/2 shallot, minced

3/4 cup veal jus

2 tablespoons Madeira

1/4 cup apple cider

Salt and freshly ground pepper

Apple, Beet and Salsify Salad:

1 teaspoon unsalted butter

1/2 cup blanched sliced salsify

1/2 cup roasted diced beets

1/2 cup roasted diced apples

Salt and freshly ground pepper

Finish and Serve:

Fried salsify

To Make the Foie Gras:

- Place a medium sauté pan over medium heat and melt the butter. Add the ham and cook until it becomes crispy. Add the mushrooms and cook, stirring often, until the mushrooms are cooked through. Remove from the heat and stir in the panko, softened butter, fines herbes, veal jus and cream. Set aside.

- Place a nonstick sauté pan over medium-high heat for 2 minutes. Season the foie gras with salt and pepper and place into the preheated pan. Cook until gold brown on the bottom, about 2 minutes. Flip the slices and cook the other side until gold brown. Remove from the pan and place on a metal baking sheet. Divide the ham and mushroom mixture evenly between the browned slices of foie gras and set aside until serving.

To Make the Sauce:

- Place a 1-quart saucepan over medium heat. Add the foie gras fat and shallot and sauté until the shallot is lightly caramelized. Add the veal jus, Madeira and cider and simmer until reduced and syrupy. Season with salt and pepper. Strain the sauce through a fine-mesh sieve and set aside until serving.

To Make the Apple, Beet and Salsify:

- Place a medium skillet over medium heat and melt the butter. Add the salsify, beets and apples and sauté until heated through. Season with salt and pepper.

To Finish and Serve:

- Place the foie gras slices under a preheated broiler and broil until the tops are golden brown. Place one slice of foie gras in the center of each of 4 warmed serving plates. Surround the slices with the apple mixture and drizzle the sauce around the plates. Garnish each plate with a piece of fried salsify and serve immediately.

Herb Poached Sable with Saffron Angel Hair Pasta

Chef John T. Gelineau (photo page 83)
Serves 4

Pasta:
4 1/2 ounces all-purpose flour
3 large egg yolks
1/2 whole large egg
1 tablespoon milk infused with saffron
1 tablespoon olive oil

Tomato Jam:
1 tomato, peeled, seeded and finely
diced (concassé)
2 tablespoons tarragon vinegar
1 tablespoon minced shallot
1 tablespoon chopped fresh tarragon
1 tablespoon sugar
1 tablespoon tomato juice

Cucumbers:
28 thin slices cucumber
1 tablespoon rice-wine vinegar
1 teaspoon chopped fresh dill
Salt and freshly ground pepper

Garnish:
2 ounces julienned fennel
2 ounces julienned red bell pepper
1 teaspoon fennel fronds
1 teaspoon olive oil
Pinch sugar
Salt and freshly ground pepper

Sable:
4 2-ounce portions sable fillet
1 teaspoon chopped parsley
1 teaspoon chopped fresh chervil
1 teaspoon chopped fresh chives
1 teaspoon chopped fresh tarragon
1 teaspoon salt
1/2 cup white wine
1/2 cup fish stock
1 tablespoon minced shallot
2 sprigs fresh thyme

Butter Sauce:
1/2 cup unsalted butter
2 tablespoons capers
1 tablespoon minced shallot
1 teaspoon minced garlic
1 tablespoon lemon juice
1 tablespoon chopped parsley
Salt and freshly ground pepper

To Make the Pasta:
- Mix the flour, yolks, egg, milk, and oil together in a mixing bowl. Knead the dough well, then roll through a pasta roller and cut into angel hair. Set aside until ready to cook.

To Make the Tomato Jam:
- In a small saucepan, combine all the ingredients and simmer until thickened. Cool and reserve.

To Make the Cucumbers:
- Lay out four piles of seven cucumber slices eachon parchment squares. Season with vinegar, dill, and salt and pepper. Reserve for service.

To Make the Garnish:
- Toss the fennel, bell pepper, fennel fronds, oil, sugar and salt and pepper together.

To Make the Sable:
- Coat the fish with the chopped herbs and salt. Bring the wine, stock, shallot and thyme to a simmer in a pan large enough to hold the fish in a single layer. Add the fish and poach until cooked through.

To Make the Butter Sauce:
- Melt the butter in a small saucepan and continue to cook until it just starts to brown. Add the capers, shallot, and garlic and sauté until fragrant. Remove from the heat and stir in the lemon juice, parsley and salt and pepper.

To Finish and Serve:
- Using a ring mold, lay out a circle of the cucumbers slices on each plate. Place a piece of fish on top of each circle of cucumbers and top each piece with some of the garnish. Cook the pasta in salted water, season it lightly, and use a fork to twirl balls of strands together. Spoon tomato jam on plates and top the jam with a pasta ball. Finish the plates with the butter sauce.

Lamb-Stuffed Piquillo Peppers, Saffron Risotto and Basil Oil

Chef Richard Rosendale, CEC
Serves 4

Lamb Jus:

1 tablespoon olive oil

1 cup lamb trimmings

1/4 cup sliced onion

1/4 cup sliced carrot

1/4 cup sliced shallot

2 unpeeled garlic cloves

1/2 cup white wine

3 quarts chicken stock

1 sprig fresh thyme

6 black peppercorns, crushed

Peppers:

2 cups cooked lamb shoulder

1 tablespoon bread crumbs

2 tablespoons grated Parmesan

1 teaspoon mixed chopped fresh
rosemary, thyme and parsley

1/4 cup diced piquillo pepper

1/4 cup lamb jus, plus more for
brushing the peppers

4 roasted, peeled whole piquillo peppers

Salt and freshly ground pepper

Saffron Risotto:

1 tablespoon olive oil

1 tablespoon minced white onion

1/4 cup dry white wine

1 cup Arborio rice

Pinch saffron threads

2 1/2 to 3 cups chicken stock

2 tablespoons unsalted butter

2 tablespoons grated Parmesan

Salt and freshly ground pepper

Basil Oil:

1 cup fresh basil leaves

1/4 cup canola oil

Salt

Finish and Serve:

4 slices Manchego

4 fried basil leaves

To Make the Lamb Jus:

- Heat the oil in a heavy saucepan and brown the lamb trimmings. Let the lamb caramelize completely on all sides, then add the onion, carrot, shallot and garlic. Cook the vegetables for 5 minutes more. Add the wine and simmer until syrupy. Add the stock 1 cup at a time, each time reducing until the stock has thickened to a syrup. Repeat this 6 times. With the final addition of stock, cover the lamb and vegetables and simmer 20 minutes; add more stock or water if needed to cover the solids.
- Remove the pan from the heat and skim excess fat off the surface of the sauce. Add the thyme and crushed peppercorns, cover the pot, and steep for 20 minutes. Strain and cool the sauce; reheat before serving and season with salt and pepper. If a thicker consistency is required, simmer the sauce until the desired consistency is achieved.

To Make the Peppers:

- Make a filling by shredding the cooked lamb shoulder and placing it in a medium bowl. Stir in the bread crumbs, Parmesan, herbs, diced piquillo pepper and lamb jus. Divide the mixture into 4 equal portions and use it to fill the 4 peppers. Press the filled peppers in the palm of your hand to make sure they are nice and compact.
- Preheat the oven to 350°F. Place the peppers on a baking dish, brush with a little lamb jus, and bake until heated through.

To Make the Saffron Risotto:

- Heat the oil in a heavy bottom pot. Add the onion and sweat for about 2 minutes. Stir in the white wine. Stir in the rice and saffron. Add a ladle of the chicken stock, and cook, stirring, until the pan is almost dry. Adjust heat to medium-low and continue to add stock a ladle at a time, adding more only when the last has almost evaporated and stirring almost constantly. When the rice grains are cooked but still a little crunchy in the center, remove the pan from the heat and stir in the butter and cheese. Season with salt and pepper.

To Make the Basil Oil:

- Blanch the basil leaves in boiling water for 30 seconds, then plunge them into ice water to stop the cooking. Drain, squeeze the leaves to remove excess water, and place them in a blender. Puree the oil and the basil together along with some salt. Pour the oil through a strainer lined with cheesecloth and let the mixture hang until all the oil has strained out; it could take as long as 24 hours to extract all the oil.

To Finish and Serve:

- Place a portion of the risotto on each plate and place a pepper on each portion. Drizzle a little of the basil oil over the peppers and top each with a slice of Manchego. Garnish each with a fried basil leaf and serve. You can also add more of the lamb jus if desired.

Lobster Brûlée with Veal Sweetbreads

Chef Jamie P. Keating, CCC
Serves 4

Sweetbreads:

3 cups buttermilk

1/2 yellow onion, julienned

1 bay leaf

2 black peppercorns

1 medium veal sweetbread

1/2 cup reduced veal stock

1 tablespoon canola oil

1/4 cup brunoise of carrot

1/2 cup bruniose of onion

1/4 cup brunoise of celery root

1 cup peeled, diced butternut squash

1 tablespoon all-purpose flour

2 tablespoons unsalted butter

Chopped fresh oregano leaves

Salt and freshly ground pepper

Lobster Brûlée:

4 ounces scallops

8 ounces raw lobster meat

1 large egg

1 cup heavy cream

Pinch kosher salt

Pinch cayenne

4 teaspoons sugar in the raw

Celery Stalk:

1 head cauliflower, blanched

1 cup heavy cream

Pinch prepared horseradish

Kosher salt

4 celery stalks, peeled and blanched

Finish and Serve:

2 vanilla beans

4 shelled lobster claws,
    poached in butter

BEVERAGE RECOMMENDATION

Castle Rock Pinot Noir,
Columbia Valley, California

To Make the Sweetbreads:

- Combine the buttermilk, onion, bay leaf and peppercorns in a large bowl. Add the sweetbread and refrigerate for at least 6 hours.
- Remove the sweetbread from the buttermilk. Bring the veal stock to a boil, add the sweetbread, and poach for 2 minutes. Remove it from the stock and shock in an ice water bath. Reserve the stock for later use. Break the sweetbread into small pieces and set aside.
- Heat the oil in a large saucepan and sauté the brunoise of carrot, onion and celery root and the butternut squash until softened. Stir in the flour. Stir in 1/4 cup of the reserved veal stock. Add the sweetbreads and stew for 20 minutes, stirring continuously. Remove the pan from the heat and stir in the butter. Stir in oregano, salt and pepper to taste.

To Make the Lobster Brûlée:

- Preheat the oven to 325°F. In a food processor, blend together the scallop and lobster meat. Add the egg and cream and pulse until smooth. Stir in the salt and cayenne. Divide the mixture between 4-ounce ramekins and bake in a water bath for 12 minutes.
- Allow to cool at room temperature. Just before serving, sprinkle the tops of the custards with sugar and caramelize.

To Make the Celery Stalk:

- Puree the cauliflower, cream and horseradish. Season with salt and chill. Just before serving, fill celery stalks with the puree.

To Finish and Serve:

- Heat the oven to 350°F. Split the vanilla beans in half, place on a sheet pan, and bake until slightly dried, about 3 minutes.
- Divide the sweetbread stew between serving bowls and top each with a stuffed celery stalk and an unmolded lobster brûlée. Garnish with the toasted vanilla bean halves and the lobster claw meat.

Lobster Hot Dog, Shaved Cucumber, Onion Jam and Vegetable Chips

Chef Daniel J. Scannell, CMC
Serves 4

Lobster Hot Dogs:

1 pound lobster meat
1 large egg
1 large egg yolk
1 cup heavy cream
1 tablespoon minced piquillo pepper
1 tablespoon minced chives
2 teaspoons kosher salt
1/2 teaspoon freshly ground pepper
2 feet washed lamb casings

Pâte à Choux Rolls:

2 cups milk
1/2 pound unsalted butter
1/2 teaspoon kosher salt
1 teaspoon sugar
10 1/2 ounces all-purpose flour
2 cups eggs
1 egg beaten with 2 teaspoons water

Onion Jam:

1 tablespoon unsalted butter
1 tablespoon olive oil
1 cup minced onions
1 tablespoon Pernod
2 teaspoons lemon juice
1 teaspoon sea salt
1 tablespoon whole-grain mustard
2 teaspoons Dijon mustard
1 tablespoon chopped fresh tarragon

Shaved Cucumber:

1/2 English cucumber,
   cut into fine julienne
2 tablespoons extra-virgin olive oil
2 teaspoons lemon juice
1/4 teaspoon sea salt
Pinch freshly ground pepper

Finish and Serve:

Unsalted butter
Dehydrated vegetable chips
Soufflé potatoes or fries

To Make the Lobster Hot Dogs:

- In a high-speed food processor, process the lobster meat for 15 seconds, until pureed. Add the egg and yolk and pulse until fully incorporated. Slowly add the cream and puree, being sure not to overwork the mixture. Transfer the puree to a stainless-steel bowl set over a larger bowl of ice. Fold in the piquillo pepper, chives, salt and pepper.
- Fit a disposable pastry bag with a medium piping tip. Have ready some fine butcher's string. Add the lobster mixture to the bag, find the opening to the lamb casings, and gently pull the casing up over the tip. Gently squeeze the pastry bag to fill the casing with the lobster mixture. Tie off the filled casing so you have hot-dog sized sausages.
- Bring a large pot of water to a simmer. Add the lobster hot dogs and simmer for 5 minutes. Immediately place in an ice-water bath to stop the cooking.

To Make the Pâte à Choux Rolls:

- In a medium saucepan, combine milk, butter, salt and sugar and bring to a gentle boil. Quickly whisk in the flour and continue to whisk for 2 minutes on low heat. Transfer the mixture to the bowl of an electric mixer fitted with a paddle attachment and mix on low speed for 5 minutes to cool.
- Preheat the oven to 375°F. Add the eggs one at a time to the batter, beating until fully incorporated. Using a piping bag fitted with a medium round tip, pipe 3-inch-long logs out onto a sheet pan lined with parchment. Make the logs as consistent as possible in size and shape. Brush the tops of the logs with the beaten egg and bake until golden brown, 10 to 15 minutes.

To Make the Onion Jam:

- Heat the butter and oil in a medium sauté pan and add the onion. Cook until light brown, then remove from the heat. Stir in the remaining ingredients, mix well and serve warm or at room temperature.

To Make the Shaved Cucumber:

- Toss the cucumber with the remaining ingredients; chill for 30 minutes

To Finish and Serve:

- Sauté the lobster hot dogs very gently in butter until golden brown; be careful not to let the pan get too hot or the dogs will burst. Split the pâte á choux buns, place a dog in each bun and serve hot with onion jam, cucumbers, vegetable chips, and soufflé potatoes or fries.

Mini Club Sandwiches with Mozzarella, Dried Tomatoes, Quail Eggs and Vegetable Purees

Chef Edward G. Leonard, CMC
Serves 4

Mushroom Puree:

1 teaspoon olive oil

1 shallot, minced

12 ounces assorted wild mushrooms, finely chopped

1 tablespoon brandy

1 tablespoon heavy cream

1/2 teaspoon finely chopped fresh tarragon

Kosher salt and freshly cracked black pepper

Golden Beet Puree:

6 ounces golden beets, peeled and diced

2 cups white grape juice

Kosher salt

Red Beet Puree:

6 ounces red beets, peeled and diced

2 cups apple juice

Kosher salt

Club Sandwiches:

6 slices brioche

8 slices fresh mozzarella

8 dried olive oil tomato petals

1 tablespoon unsalted butter

1 tablespoon extra-virgin olive oil

Finish and Serve:

4 tablespoons sweet garlic dressing

Extra-virgin olive oil

1 tablespoon unsalted butter

4 quail eggs

Sea salt

To Make the Mushroom Puree:

- Heat a medium sauté pan over medium heat for 2 minutes. Add the olive oil and heat 1 minute more. Add the shallot and cook, stirring often, until the shallot is translucent. Add the mushrooms and continue to cook, stirring often, until the mushrooms are cooked through. Add the brandy and cook for 2 minutes. Add the cream and tarragon and cook until all the liquid has evaporated but the mixture is still moist. Remove from the heat and season with salt and pepper.

To Make the Golden Beet Puree:

- Place the golden beets and grape juice in a small stainless-steel saucepan and simmer over medium heat until the beets are very tender. Drain the beets, reserving the cooking liquid. Place the beets in the container of a high-speed blender and puree until smooth, adding cooking liquid as necessary to form a smooth, thick puree. Season the mixture with salt.

To Make the Red Beet Puree:

- Place the red beets and apple juice in a small stainless-steel saucepan and simmer over medium heat until the beets are very tender. Drain the beets, reserving the cooking liquid. Place the beets in the container of a high-speed blender and puree until smooth, adding cooking liquid as necessary to form a smooth, thick puree. Season the mixture with salt.

To Make the Club Sandwiches:

- Using a 1 1/2-inch round cutter, cut out 12 brioche disks. Reserve the trim for another use. Place a medium skillet over medium heat and add the butter and oil. Once the butter has melted, add the brioche disks and cook until golden brown on both sides. Drain the disks on paper towels. Reserve at room temperature.
- Using the same round cutter, cut 8 disks from the mozzarella slices. Reserve excess mozzarella for another use. Place 4 of the browned brioche disks on a work surface. Top each with a mozzarella disk. Place a tomato petal on top of each and then top the pedals with a second brioche disk. Repeat the stacking, ending with a brioche disk.

To Finish and Serve:

- Place 4 room-temperature serving plates on a work surface. Place a sandwich in the center of a plate. Using 2 spoons, place a quenelle of each puree around the sandwich. Using a small spoon, place a dot of the sweet garlic dressing between vegetable purees. Place a small amount of extra-virgin olive oil on top of dot of sweet garlic dressing. Repeat with the remaining 3 plates.
- Place a non-stick sauté pan over medium heat and melt the butter. Fry the quail eggs in the pan, being careful not to break the yolks, until the whites are set. Transfer the eggs to a cutting board and use a 1-inch round cutter to cut the eggs into perfect circles around the yolks. Gently place an egg on top of each sandwich. Sprinkle the eggs with sea salt and serve immediately.

CHEF'S NOTES

- Chef Leonard serves this dish with Carrot Puree (see page 227) and Celery Root Puree (see page 228) .

Open-Face Supreme of King Crab with Creamed Fennel, Saffron Pasta, Truffled Pea Flan and Red Pepper Reduction

Chef Daniel J. Scannell, CMC
Serves 4

Crab:

4 king crab supremes

4 ounces basic lobster mousse

1 tablespoon shaved truffles

2 teaspoons snipped chives

2 teaspoons chopped parsley

1/4 teaspoon crushed red pepper flakes

Saffron Pasta:

4 ounces King Arthur flour

1 ounce semolina flour

1 lightly beaten egg

2 tablespoons saffron tea

2 tablespoons extra-virgin olive oil

1/2 teaspoon kosher salt

Warm water as needed to form dough

Creamed Fennel:

1 cup shaved fennel

1 cup heavy cream

1/2 ounce Pernod

1 teaspoon toasted fennel seeds

Unsalted butter

2 teaspoons snipped fresh fennel tops

Salt and freshly ground pepper

Truffled Pea Flan:

2 cups green pea puree

2 cups heavy cream

6 large eggs, lightly beaten

1/8 teaspoon ground mace

1 ounce minced truffle

1 tablespoon truffle oil

Finish and Serve:

4 crackers for garnish

4 Parmesan-dusted gougères

1/4 cup red pepper reduction

Fennel sprigs

To Make the Crab:

- Pat the crab supremes dry with paper towels. Pipe the mousse evenly along the underside of each supreme to form a cylinder. Sprinkle with the truffle, chives, parsley and red pepper flakes. Wrap each tightly in plastic wrap and tie the ends to seal. Cook the crab in gently simmering water until the flesh is firm to the touch and reaches an internal temperature of 130°F.

To Make the Saffron Pasta:

- Combine all the pasta ingredients and mix well, adding warm water as needed. Gently knead the dough until very smooth. Wrap the dough in plastic and allow it to rest for 20 minutes. Roll the dough through a pasta machine; cover the sheets and allow them to rest for 5 minutes before cutting them into the desire shape.
- Just before serving, cook the pasta in 2 quarts of salted boiling water until cooked through, about 2 minutes.

To Make the Creamed Fennel:

- Blanch the fennel in lightly salted water and drain. Place the cream, Pernod and fennel seeds in a small saucepan and reduce until thickened and silky. Stir in the blanched fennel, a touch of butter, and the snipped fennel. Season with salt and pepper.

To Make the Pea and Truffle Flan:

- Preheat oven to 275°F. Combine all the flan ingredients in a blender and blend until very smooth. Strain through a fine-mesh sieve into 4 buttered 4-ounce molds. Bake until the flan has set.

To Finish and Serve:

- Unmold the flans and place one on each serving plate. Garnish the flans with the crackers and Parmesan gougères. Place a portion of saffron pasta and creamed fennel on each plate. Slice the crab while still wrapped; remove and discard the wrap from the slices and arrange 5 segments on top of the fennel on each plate. Garnish the plates with red pepper reduction and fennel sprigs.

Pan-Seared Sea Scallops with Roasted Sweet Corn, Creamed Mushrooms and Lemon-Thyme Oil

Chef Daryl Shular
Serves 4

Lemon-Thyme Oil:

1 cup olive oil

2 ounces lemon zest

4 ounces thyme leaves

4 ounces parsley leaves

Creamed Wild Mushrooms:

2 tablespoons olive oil

4 ounces wild mushrooms

2 ounces roasted pearl onions

2 tablespoons sherry

1 Idaho potato, julienned

1 ounce chopped garlic

1/2 cup heavy cream

1 ear fresh sweet corn, roasted and kernels removed

12 asparagus spears (white or green)

2 ounces fresh shelled English peas

1 tablespoon truffle oil

Pan-Seared Scallops:

2 tablespoons olive oil

4 giant (U-10) dry-pack sea scallops

Sea salt and ground white pepper

To Make the Lemon-Thyme Oil:

- In a food processor, combine all the ingredients and pulse until the herbs are very finely chopped. Strain through a fine-mesh sieve; discard the solids. Refrigerate the oil in a clean glass container until ready to use.

To Make the Creamed Wild Mushrooms:

- In a medium sauté pan, heat the oil over medium-high heat. When very hot, add the mushrooms and sauté until lightly browned. Add the roasted onions and continue to sauté until the liquid from the mushrooms has almost evaporated. Add the sherry and cook until it is reduced by half. Add the potato and garlic and cook until the potato is tender.
- Add the cream and cook over low heat until it is reduced by half. Add the corn and asparagus and cook until just heated through. Season the mixture with salt and pepper. Stir in the peas and truffle oil.

To Make the Pan-Seared Scallops:

- Heat the oil in a sauté pan until very hot. Pat the scallops dry with paper towels and season them on both sides with salt and pepper. Place them in the pan and sear on both sides until golden brown.

To Finish and Serve:

- Place a scoop of the creamed mushroom mixture on each plate and top with a scallop. Drizzle the plates with the lemon-thyme oil.

Poached Oysters with Salmon Caviar and Israeli Couscous

Chef Joachim Buchner, CMC
Serves 4

Poached Oysters:

12 shucked oysters, juices reserved
1 shallot, finely chopped
1 cup white wine
Juice of 1 lemon
3 tablespoons heavy cream
1/4 teaspoon dry mustard
10 tablespoons unsalted butter, diced
Splash Tabasco sauce
Worcestershire sauce
Salt and freshly ground white pepper
Chopped flat-leaf parsley

Israeli Couscous:

1 teaspoon olive oil
1 cup Israeli couscous
1 shallot, diced
1 1/2 cups hot chicken stock
Salt and freshly ground black pepper

Finish and Serve:

1 ounce salmon roe caviar
Cracker bread (optional)
Fennel fronds (optional)
Fresh herbs (optional)

To Make the Poached Oysters:

- In a saucepan, combine the oyster juices, shallot, white wine and lemon juice. Simmer until reduced to 1/4 cup. Whisk in the cream and mustard. Add the butter, one cube at a time, whisking first on the heat and then removing the pan from the heat. Continue whisking in butter until the mixture is fully emulsified. Whisk in the Tabasco and Worcestershire sauce to taste.
- Heat the sauce to 150°F. Add the oysters and gently poach until the edges of the oysters start to curl. Season with salt and white pepper and add the chopped parsley.

To Make the Israeli Couscous:

- In a sauté pan, heat the oil over medium-high heat. Add the couscous and toast, tossing occasionally, until the couscous starts to brown. Add the shallot and half of the hot stock and bring to a simmer. If the stock evaporates before the couscous is tender, add the remaining stock and continue to simmer until the couscous done. Season with salt and pepper and keep hot.

To Finish and Serve:

- Place a little couscous on the bottom of serving plates or bowls. Spoon oysters and sauce on top, garnish with caviar, fennel fronds and herbs and serve with cracker bread.

While fans look on, Chef Buchner prepares braised petit shank & palm heart for National team hot food service.

Poached Salmon and Halibut with Cauliflower-Potato Terrine, Celery Salad and Pumpernickel Crisp

Chef Daniel J. Scannell, CMC
Serves 4

Fish:

8 ounces skinless salmon fillet

8 ounces skinless halibut fillet

8 ounces kosher salt

4 ounces sugar

1 teaspoon powdered gelatin

Pickled radish wrap

Cauliflower-Potato Terrine:

1 pound peeled, blanched Yukon gold potatoes

4 ounces cream cheese

1 ounce veal aspic

1 tablespoon saffron tea

2 teaspoons kosher salt

1 teaspoon freshly ground pepper

5 blanched, sliced fingerling potatoes

8 ounces cauliflower florets, poached in milk

1 tablespoon chopped herbs

2 tablespoons pickled red onions

Pumpernickel Crisps:

2 slices pumpernickel bread, crusts removed

2 tablespoons melted butter

2 pieces tempered glass

Finish and Serve:

Thinly sliced celery

Celery leaves

Diced carrot

Vinaigrette

For the Fish:

- Cut both the salmon and halibut into matching shapes, each about 2 ounces. Sprinkle the fish with the salt and sugar and let sit for 15 minutes. Rinse the fish and pat dry with paper towels. Sprinkle one side of each piece of fish with gelatin, then press the gelatin sides of the salmon firmly against the gelatin sides of the halibut and wrap each piece tightly in plastic.
- Poach the fish in simmering water until the internal temperature of the fish reaches 134°F. Immediately shock the fish in an ice-water bath. After the fish has chilled, unwrap each piece, discard the plastic wrap, and rewrap each piece in pickled radish wrap. Refrigerate 24 hours before serving.

To Make the Cauliflower-Potato Terrine:

- Run the Yukon gold potatoes through a ricer or food mill and fold in the cream cheese, aspic, saffron tea, salt and pepper and mix well. Adjust seasoning as needed. Fold in the sliced fingerling potatoes, cauliflower florets, herbs and pickled red onions.
- Line a small square terrine mold with plastic wrap. Spread the potato mixture evenly into the terrine; compact it by pressing down firmly; refrigerate overnight.

To Make the Pumpernickel Crisps:

- Preheat the oven to 350°F. Put the bread slices through a pasta machine until they are very thin. Cut the bread into the desired shape.
- Butter one side of each of the pieces of glass and lay the bread out onto one piece. Place the other piece on top, buttered side down. Transfer the glass to a half sheet pan and bake until the crackers are crisp, about 15 minutes. Carefully remove the glass from the oven, lift up the top piece of glass, and transfer the crackers to a wire rack to cool.

To Finish and Serve:

- Turn the cauliflower terrine out onto a cutting board and unwrap it. Cut into slices and place one on each plate. Slice the salmon-halibut pieces and lay one next to the terrine, along with a pumpernickel crisp. Toss together the celery, celery leaves, carrot and vinaigrette and place on the plates.

Salmon and Lobster Terrine with Asparagus and Golden Beets

Chef Joachim Buchner, CMC
Serves 4

Terrine:

1 pound skinless salmon fillet

Kosher salt and freshly ground pepper

4 ounces skinless halibut or sole fillet

1 1/2-pound lobster, tail meat removed raw, claw meat and knuckle meat cooked and chopped

1 large egg white

2 tablespoons brandy

1/4 cup heavy cream

2 tablespoons fennel fronds

Butter Sauce:

1 shallot, finely chopped

1 cup white wine

Juice of 1 lemon

1 tablespoon heavy cream

15 tablespoons unsalted butter, cubed

Salt and ground white pepper

1 tablespoon sliced dill or chives

Golden Beets:

12 baby golden beets

1/4 cup vegetable stock

2 tablespoons unsalted butter

Salt and ground white pepper

Asparagus:

12 stalks asparagus, trimmed and peeled

1 tablespoon unsalted butter

1/2 teaspoon grated lemon zest

1 teaspoon chopped chives

Salt and ground white pepper

Finish and Serve (optional):

Micro greens

Crackers

To Make the Terrine:

- Remove all blood lines from the salmon, then slice it into long strips and season it with salt and pepper. Place on a tray and refrigerate until needed.
- Place the halibut and the raw lobster tail meat in a food processor and puree. Add the egg white, brandy, and more salt and pepper. Continue to process until you have a smooth, light mousse. Transfer the mixture to a chilled mixing bowl and slowly fold in the heavy cream. Fold in the cooked lobster meat and the fennel fronds.
- Line a terrine mold with heat-resistant plastic wrap. Fill the terrine by alternating layers of salmon with the lobster mousse. Layer until the mold is filled. Wrap the terrine tightly with more heat-resistant plastic. Poach the terrine in a water bath at 180°F. until it reaches an internal temperature of 142°F. Remove from the water bath and place in ice water for 2 minutes. When cooled, unmold the terrine onto a platter and set aside for later.

To Make the Butter Sauce:

- In a stainless-steel saucepan, combine the shallot, white wine and lemon juice and cook over medium heat until the mixture is reduced to 2 tablespoons. Add the cream, bring to a boil, and reduce the heat to low. Add the butter, one cube at a time, whisking first on the heat and then off the heat. Continue whisking butter in until the mixture is fully emulsified. Season with salt and white pepper. Add the dill and keep the sauce warm until needed.

To Make the Golden Beets:

- Remove the greens from the beets and discard or save for another use. Simmer the beets in salted water until tender. Drain and, while still warm, rub the beets with a kitchen towel to remove the skins. Set aside.
- When ready to serve, to warm the beets, place the vegetable stock and butter in a saucepan. Add the beets, season with salt and pepper, and simmer until the stock has evaporated.

To Make the Asparagus:

- Cook asparagus in boiling salted water until tender. Drain and toss with the butter, lemon zest, chives, and salt and pepper. Keep warm until serving.

To Finish and Serve:

- Place a piece of the terrine on each serving plate. Top with butter sauce, micro greens, and serve with the asparagus, beets and crackers.

Shrimp Cone Cocktail

Chef Jamie P. Keating, CCC
Serves 4

Shrimp Cones:

8 U-10 (colossal) shrimp, split

1/4 cup scallops

1 tablespoon heavy cream

1 tablespoon egg, slightly whipped

Pinch kosher salt

Pinch white pepper

2 pieces thinly sliced prosciutto

Yellow Tomato Cocktail Sauce:

3 yellow tomatoes, peeled and seeded

Worcestershire sauce

Tabasco sauce

Juice of 1 lemon

3 tablespoons freshly grated
    horseradish

Kosher salt

Couscous Salad:

1 tablespoon canola oil

2 cups Lebanese couscous

1/4 cup diced fennel

1 shallot, chopped

2 teaspoons brunoise of celery

2 teaspoons brunoise of carrot

6 cups chicken stock

4 basil leaves, cut into chiffonade

Kosher salt and freshly ground pepper

Extra-virgin olive oil

Spring Lettuce Salad:

2 cups blend of oak, mâche,
    and frisée lettuces

16 slices garlic, fried

4 teaspoons extra-virgin olive oil

2 teaspoons tarragon vinegar

Sea salt

To Make the Shrimp Cones:

- Lay out 4 squares of plastic wrap and top each with 4 pieces of shrimp.
- Puree scallops, cream, egg, salt and pepper. Spread over the shrimp. Cut each prosciutto slice in half and lay it over the scallops. Using the plastic wrap, manipulate the shrimp into a cone shape by rolling and restricting one side more than the other. Tie the ends.
- Cook the shrimp in a water bath to 146°F. Drop the shrimp in an ice-water bath to stop the cooking. Refrigerate.

To Make the Yellow Tomato Cocktail Sauce:

- Purée the yellow tomatoes. Blend in Worcestershire, Tabasco, lemon juice, horseradish and salt to taste.

To Make the Couscous Salad:

- Heat the canola oil in a saucepan and sauté the couscous, fennel, shallot, celery and carrot briefly. Add the stock and simmer until the couscous is tender.
- Drain if necessary, and stir in the basil. Spread on a sheet pan to cool. Finish with salt, pepper and olive oil.

To Make the Spring Lettuce Salad:

- Toss the lettuces and garlic with the oil and vinegar. Season with salt.

To Finish and Serve:

- Unwrap the shrimp cones and place one on each plate. Place couscous salad and lettuce salad on plates and add a pool of tomato cocktail sauce.

Torte of Lump Crab Salad with Lime Snaps and Gazpacho Dressing

Chef Edward G. Leonard, CMC
Serves 4

Lime Snaps:

2 tablespoons brunoise of lime rind, blanched

5 ounces sugar

2 1/2 ounces all-purpose flour

Pinch vanilla powder

2 tablespoons cold water

Gazpacho Dressing:

1 tablespoon extra-virgin olive oil

1 tablespoon minced shallot

1 tablespoon minced garlic

1 1/2 cups tomato concassé

6 tablespoons crab jus

2 tablespoons diced roasted red pepper

2 tablespoons finely diced cucumber

1/4 cup cucumber water

Juice of 1 lime

Chipotle Tabasco sauce

Salt and freshly ground pepper

Lump Crab Salad:

1/2 cup mayonnaise

1/2 cup crème fraîche

1 teaspoon fines herbes

Juice of 1 lime

20 ounces lump crabmeat

Sea salt

To Make the Lime Snaps:

- Combine all the lime snap ingredients in medium bowl and blend until smooth. Place the mixture in cheesecloth; tie tightly with butcher's string, and hang overnight to drain.
- Preheat the oven to 325°F. Line a baking sheet with a Silpat. Roll 1 teaspoon at a time of the lime snap mixture into a ball and place on the baking sheet. Repeat until you have 12 balls, leaving at least 2 inches between each. Bake until crisp, about 10 minutes. Remove the pan from the oven and cool the snaps on the pan.

To Make the Gazpacho Dressing:

- In a small saucepan, combine the oil, shallot and garlic and cook over medium-low heat until the shallot is translucent. Add the tomato concassé, crab jus, roasted pepper, cucumber and cucumber water. Simmer for 1 minute. Remove from the heat and allow to cool. Stir in the lime juice and season with Chipotle Tabasco, salt and pepper. Set aside at room temperature until serving.

To Make the Lump Crab Salad:

- In a medium bowl, combine the mayonnaise, crème fraîche, fines herbes and lime juice. Gently fold in the crabmeat. Season with salt and refrigerate until serving.

To Finish and Serve:

- Divide the dressing evenly between 4 room-temperature serving bowls. Place a lime snap in the center of each bowl. Place 1/4 cup of the crab salad on each lime snap. Repeat with remaining ingredients, making 2 more layers of snaps and salad and ending with just a small dollop of the salad.

Tuna Carpaccio with Tomato Granita and Niçoise Salad

Chef Scott A. Fetty
Serves 4

Tomato Granita:

1 cup sugar

1 cup water

1 teaspoon lemon juice

2 pounds ripe beefsteak tomatoes, blanched, peeled and chopped

2 tablespoons tomato puree

1 teaspoon curry powder

2 teaspoons kosher salt, plus more as needed

1/2 teaspoon ground white pepper

Fennel Melba Toast:

1 small baguette, cut lengthwise into 1/8-inch-thick slices

Olive oil

Sea salt

Fennel pollen

Grated Parmesan cheese

Tuna:

8 ounces ahi tuna

Lemon-flavored olive oil

Sea salt and cracked white pepper

Niçoise Salad:

4 baby red potatoes, blanched, chilled and cut into small dice

20 haricot verts, blanched and chilled

4 quail eggs, hard cooked, chilled, peeled and halved

4 baby yellow tomatoes, halved

4 baby red tomatoes, halved

4 ounces red onion, cut into small dice

4 teaspoons pitted, sliced Niçoise or other small black cured olives

1 small bunch frisée lettuce, rinsed and separated into leaves

2 tablespoons rice vinegar

6 tablespoons extra-virgin olive oil

Sea salt and cracked black pepper

BEVERAGE RECOMMENDATION

Washington State Riesling, Portuguese vino verde, or a rosé

To Make the Tomato Granita:

- In a small saucepan, combine the sugar and water and place over medium heat. Stir just until the sugar melts and the mixture comes to a boil. Remove from the heat and stir in the lemon juice. Set aside.
- Heat a medium saucepan over medium heat and add the chopped tomatoes, tomato puree, curry powder, salt and pepper. Simmer the mixture for 5 minutes, then puree it in a food processor, strain through a fine-mesh sieve and chill.
- Whisk together the tomato mixture and 1 cup of the sugar syrup (save the remaining syrup for another use). Taste and season with more salt if necessary. Pour the mixture into a shallow pan and freeze for approximately 3 hours. Break the frozen mixture into chunks and pulse it in a food processor until smooth. Scrape back into the pan and freeze until ready to serve.

To Make the Fennel Melba Toast:

- Preheat the oven to 250°F. Drizzle the baguette slices with olive oil and sprinkle with salt, fennel pollen and Parmesan. Bake the toasts until dried and crisp.

To Make the Tuna:

- Season the fish with the lemon-flavored olive oil, salt and pepper. In a very hot pan, sear the tuna on all sides, leaving the middle raw. Cool the tuna, wrap it in plastic, and place in the freezer until lightly frozen. Remove from the freezer, unwrap, and shave the tuna into very thin slices. Roll each slice into a cylinder and transfer them to chilled appetizer plates. Refrigerate until serving.

To Make the Niçoise Salad:

- Combine the potatoes, haricot verts, quail eggs, tomatoes, onion, olives and lettuce in a large bowl. Drizzle with the vinegar and oil, season with salt and pepper and toss. Allow to marinate for 15 minutes before serving.

To Finish and Serve:

- Spoon a portion of the salad around each chilled plate with the tuna. Place a scoop of the granita on top of each portion of tuna, place toasts on the granita and serve.

CHEF'S NOTES

- The granita base in this recipe can be served melted as a cold soup.
- Fennel pollen can be found online and at stores specializing in spices.

Baked Sole with Corn and Roma Tomato Tart, Truffle Popcorn and Lobster Ravioli

Chef Edward G. Leonard, CMC
Serves 4

Baked Sole:

2 teaspoons extra-virgin olive oil

Kosher salt

4 (6-ounce) sole fillets, cleaned

4 teaspoons unsalted butter

1 lemon, quartered

Lobster Gastrique:

1 tablespoon unsalted butter

2 shallots, minced

2 garlic cloves, sliced

1 tablespoon tomato paste

1/3 cup vermouth

3 cups lobster stock

1 bay leaf

2 sprigs fresh thyme

1 cup merlot

6 tablespoons champagne vinegar

Kosher salt

Vanilla Butter Sauce:

3/4 cup lobster gastric (see above)

1 tablespoon heavy cream

1/2 vanilla bean, seeds scraped out

1 cup very cold unsalted butter, diced

Juice of 1/4 lime

2 tablespoons chopped fresh
    lobster meat

2 tarragon leaves, minced

Kosher salt

Finish and Serve:

8 baby carrots, peeled, blanched and
    halved lengthwise

Lobster ravioli

Truffle popcorn

4 fried sage leaves

4 tempura-fried thyme sprigs

To Make the Baked Sole:

- Lay four 7-inch squares of aluminum foil on a work surface. Gently rub each with the olive oil and sprinkle with salt. Place one fillet in the center or each square skin-side up. Lightly season the fish with kosher salt and place 1 teaspoon of butter on each piece of fish. Roll the aluminum around the sole and twist the ends closed to form a tube. Place the wrapped fillets on an ovenproof pan and reserve for service.

To Make the Lobster Gastrique

- Place a stainless-steel saucepan over medium heat and melt the butter. Add the shallots and garlic and cook until the shallots are translucent. Add the tomato paste and continue to cook, stirring constantly, for 3 minutes. Deglaze the pan with the vermouth. Add the lobster stock, bay leaf, thyme, merlot and vinegar. Bring to a simmer and continue to simmer until the mixture is reduced to 2 cups. Strain through a fine sieve and season with salt.

To Make the Vanilla Butter Sauce:

- Place the gastrique and cream in a small stainless-steel saucepan and place over medium heat. Simmer until reduced by half. Reduce the heat to low and add the vanilla bean seeds. Slowly whisk in the cold butter a chunk at a time, forming an emulsified sauce. Stir in the lime juice, lobster meat and tarragon. Season to taste with kosher salt and reserve in a warm spot until serving.

To Finish and Serve:

- Preheat the oven to 350°F. Bring 1 gallon of salted water to a boil over high heat.
- Place the wrapped sole in the oven and bake until cook through, about 10 minutes. Reheat both sauces. Warm 4 serving plates.
- Place the blanched baby carrots and lobster ravioli in the boiling water and cook for 2 minutes. Drain well. Place 4 pieces of carrot on each serving plate just to the right of center. Place 1 ravioli on top of the carrots on each plate. Remove the cooked sole from the foil and place a fillet in the center of each plate. Place a portion of the tart to the left of each fillet. Drizzle the vanilla butter sauce over each ravioli. Spoon small pools of the lobster gastric at the tip of the fillets. Garnish each plate with the truffle popcorn, fried sage and tempura thyme. Serve immediately.

CHEF'S NOTES

- Chef Leonard serves this dish with Corn and Tomato Tart (see page 230).

Braised Beef Short Ribs, Kimchee Slaw and Pineapple Ketchup

Chef Drew Garms
Serves 4

Pineapple Ketchup:

1/2 cup pineapple juice

1/4 cup rice-wine vinegar

2 tablespoons soy sauce

1 1/2 teaspoons minced ginger

1/4 cup ketchup

2 tablespoons dark-brown sugar

1 tablespoon chopped cilantro

1 tablespoon lime juice

Braised Short Ribs:

1/4 cup clarified butter

2 pounds boneless beef short ribs, silver skin and excess fat removed

Salt and freshly ground pepper

1/2 cup diced onion

1/4 cup diced celery

1/4 cup diced carrot

1 shallot, minced

1 garlic clove, minced

1 cup sake

1/2 cup hoisin sauce

2 quarts brown veal stock

1 sprig cilantro

1 kaffir lime leaf

Kimchee Slaw:

2 cups julienned kimchee

1/4 cup julienned radish

1/4 cup julienned carrot

1 tablespoon toasted sesame seeds

2 tablespoons lime juice

1 tablespoon olive oil

Salt and freshly ground pepper

Cilantro leaves

Potato Sticks:

1 pound cooked, warm riced potato

7 tablespoons cornstarch

2 large eggs

2 large egg yolks

6 tablespoons clarified butter

6 tablespoons heavy cream

4 large egg whites

1 tablespoon egg white powder

Oil for deep frying

1 sheet nori

1 teaspoon sea salt

To Make the Pineapple Ketchup:

- In heavy, non-reactive pot, combine the pineapple juice, vinegar and soy sauce and simmer until reduced by half. Add the ginger, ketchup and brown sugar and simmer for 5 minutes more. Remove from the heat, add the cilantro, cover the pan, and let steep for 10 minutes.
- Strain the sauce, discard the solids, and stir in the lime juice.

To Make the Braised Short Ribs:

- Preheat the oven to 375°F. In a large pot, heat the clarified butter over high heat. Season the ribs with salt and pepper and sear until golden brown. Remove the ribs from the pan and set aside. Add the onion, celery and carrot to the pan and cook until the vegetables are caramelized. Stir in the shallot and garlic and cook for a minute.
- Deglaze the pot with the sake and cook until evaporated. Stir in the hoisin and veal stock. Tie the cilantro and lime leaf together and add them to the pan along with the ribs. Bring to a simmer, cover the top of the pot with buttered parchment paper, then wrap in foil to form a lid. Place in the oven and braise until the ribs are very tender.
- Remove the ribs from the braising liquid. Strain the liquid, place it in a small saucepan, and simmer until reduced to a sauce consistency.

To Make the Kimchee Slaw:

- Just prior to serving, mix the kimchee, radish, carrot, sesame seeds, lime juice, olive oil, and salt and pepper. Garnish with cilantro.

To Make the Potato Sticks:

- Preheat the oven to 250°F. Butter a half sheet pan and line it with buttered parchment paper.
- Place the warm riced potatoes in a large bowl and sift the cornstarch over them. Stir in the eggs and yolks. Stir in the butter and cream. In separate bowl, whip the egg whites and egg white powder until it forms soft peaks; gently fold them into the potato mixture.
- Spread the mixture in the prepared pan and bake for 12 minutes. Cool and cut into sticks.
- When ready to serve, heat oil to 375°F. and fry the potato sticks until golden brown. Toast the nori over a flame and grind it in a spice grinder with the sea salt. Season the potato sticks with the nori salt.

To Finish and Serve:

- Portion the rib meat into 5-ounce pieces. Glaze the ribs with a mixture of half reduced sauce, half pineapple ketchup. Serve the ribs with the slaw and the potato sticks.

Braised Chicken Thighs "Coq au Vin" with Parsnip-Turnip Puree, Caramelized Shallots and Baby Green Beans

Chef Scott A. Fetty
Serves 4

Chicken:

2 slices smoked bacon, diced

12 cremini mushrooms, halved

8 pearl onions, peeled

8 chicken thighs, skin removed

Kosher salt and cracked white pepper

Flour as needed

Olive oil as needed

1 1/2 cups red wine

4 cups chicken stock or broth

1 garlic clove, minced

1 bay leaf

1 teaspoon chopped thyme

1 sprig fresh rosemary

Puree:

1 tablespoon unsalted butter

1 shallot, chopped

2 small turnips, peeled and chopped

3 parsnips, peeled and chopped

1 1/2 cups heavy cream

1 sprig fresh thyme

4 sundried tomato halves, rehydrated in
water and thinly sliced

Kosher salt and cracked white pepper

Shallots:

Olive oil

8 small whole shallots, peeled

2 sprigs fresh thyme

Sugar

Kosher salt and ground black pepper

Baby Green Beans:

4 tablespoons unsalted butter

32 baby green beans, trimmed,
blanched and shocked

2 tablespoons water

Kosher salt and cracked black pepper

BEVERAGE RECOMMENDATION

Red Burgundy or Oregon Pinot Noir

To Make the Chicken:

- Place a Dutch oven over medium heat and cook the bacon until crisp. Remove the bacon with a slotted spoon and reserve. Add the mushrooms and pearl onions to the bacon fat in the pan and cook until the vegetables are caramelized. Remove with a slotted spoon and reserve.

- Preheat the oven to 350°F. Season the chicken with salt and white pepper and dredge lightly in flour.

- Brown the chicken thighs in the remaining fat, adding a little olive oil to the pan if there is not enough bacon fat. Remove the chicken from the pan and pour out any remaining fat. Place the pan back on the flame and add the red wine. Simmer until the wine is reduced by about two-thirds. Return the chicken to the pan and add the stock, garlic and herbs. Bring back to a simmer, cover the pan, and place in the oven. Cook until the chicken is very tender.

- Remove the chicken from the liquid in the pan, strain the liquid, discard the solids, and place the liquid in a small saucepan. Simmer the liquid until it is concentrated and has a nice flavor and texture. Season to taste with salt and pepper. When ready to serve, combine the sauce, chicken, reserved mushrooms and onions and reheat.

To Make the Puree:

- Place a small saucepan over medium heat and melt the butter. Add the shallot and cook until softened. Add the turnips and parsnips and cook for 2 minutes. Add the cream and thyme, reduce the heat, cover the pan, and simmer until the vegetables are very soft.

- Remove and discard the thyme. Puree the vegetable mixture in a food processor, adding cream from the pan as needed, until they are very smooth. Fold in the tomatoes and season to taste with salt and pepper.

To Make the Shallots:

- Preheat the oven to 350°F. Heat a small sauté pan over medium heat and add some olive oil. Add the shallots to the pan and cook until they begin to caramelize. Add the thyme and season the shallots with sugar, salt and pepper. Place the pan in the oven and roast until the shallots are golden and soft. Remove the shallots from the oil and set them aside for serving.

To Make the Baby Green Beans:

- Heat a medium sauté pan over medium heat and melt the butter. Add the beans and sauté them until they are just warm. Add the water and season with salt and pepper. Set aside.

To Finish and Serve:

- Place some of the puree in the middle of each warmed serving bowl. Place 2 thighs over the puree and spoon some of the sauce, onions, and mushrooms over the chicken and sprinkle with the reserved bacon. Arrange a few green beans and shallots around the chicken and serve.

CHEF'S NOTES

- This classic French dish was designed to make the most of tough, older poultry. Using the dark meat of American poultry will simulate the flavor of the traditional preparation.

Braised Pig Cheek, Confit of Pig Feet Croquette, Yukon Puree and Serrano Ham Crisp

Chef Edward G. Leonard, CMC
Serves 4

Pigs' Feet Confit:

1 cup kosher salt

1 cup sugar

1 bunch fresh sage, chopped

1 teaspoon coriander seeds,
    toasted and crushed

6 black peppercorns, crushed

6 garlic cloves, crushed

6 pigs' feet, split lengthwise

6 shallots, peeled and quartered

1 sprig fresh rosemary

Manteca, melted

1 cup veal demi-glace

Fine sea salt and freshly ground pepper

1 cup seasoned flour

3 large eggs, whipped lightly

2 cups panko bread crumbs

Oil for deep frying

Pigs' Cheeks:

1/4 cup canola oil

4 pigs' cheeks

Kosher salt and freshly cracked black
    pepper

1/4 cup all-purpose flour

1 tablespoon finely diced onion

1 garlic clove, sliced

2 teaspoons finely diced carrot

2 teaspoons finely diced celery

1 teaspoon tomato paste

1/4 cup red wine

2 cups veal stock

1 bay leaf

1 sprig fresh thyme

To Make the Pigs' Feet Confit:

- In a medium bowl, combine the kosher salt, sugar, sage, coriander, peppercorns, and 3 of the crushed garlic cloves and mix well. Add the pigs' feet and toss to coat. Place the feet in a baking dish and sprinkle with the remaining salt mixture. Cover with plastic wrap and refrigerate overnight.

- The next day, preheat the oven to 275°F. Brush the salt mixture off the feet and rinse them well under cold water. Discard the curing mixture. Pat the feet dry with paper towels and place them in a 4-quart ovenproof baking dish. Add the remaining 3 cloves garlic, the shallots and rosemary. Pour in melted manteca until the pig's feet are covered. Cover the baking dish tightly with aluminum foil and bake until the meat easily pulls from the bones of the pig's feet, 6 to 8 hours. Remove from the oven and allow the feet to cool in the manteca.

- Once cool, gently remove the meat from the feet being sure to remove and discard all small bones. Place this meat in a bowl and add the demi-glace and season with salt and pepper. Divide the meat into 4 equal portions and use your hands to form each portion into a cylinder. Place the 4 cylinders in the refrigerator for 30 minutes.

- Place the seasoned flour, eggs and panko separately in shallow bowls. Remove the cylinders from the refrigerator and dust each in the seasoned flour, dip in the eggs, and then roll each in the panko. Place the breaded cylinders on a plate and cover lightly with plastic wrap.

- Just before serving, heat the oil to 350°F. and fry the cylinders until golden brown. Drain on paper towels and keep warm until serving.

To Make the Pigs' Cheeks:

- Place a small rondeau over medium heat. Add the canola oil and heat for 2 minutes. Season the pigs' cheeks with salt and pepper and dust with the flour. Place the floured cheeks in the pan and cook, turning them once, until golden brown on both sides. Remove the cheeks from the pan and set aside.

- Preheat the oven to 300°F. Add the onion, garlic, carrot and celery to the pan and cook, stirring occasionally, until the vegetables are lightly browned. Add the tomato paste and cook, stirring constantly, for 2 minutes. Deglaze the pan with the wine and cook until the wine is reduced. Add the stock, bay leaf and thyme and bring to a bare simmer over medium heat. Add the seared cheeks and cover the pan with aluminum foil. Place in the oven and bake until the cheeks are tender, 1 to 2 hours.

- Remove the cheeks from the pan and place on a tray. Cover loosely with plastic wrap and keep in a warm place until serving. Strain the liquid through a fine-mesh sieve and simmer over medium heat until thickened and reduced. Season with salt and pepper.

To Finish and Serve:

- Warm 4 serving plates. Using 2 spoons, make a medium quenelle of potato puree and place one left center on each warmed plate. Spoon portions of cabbage next to the potato puree. Place the warm pigs' cheeks next to the cabbage and place a fried pigs' feet croquette behind each cabbage portion. Spoon the heated braising liquid over the cheeks, allowing some extra to pour into the plates. Place a Serrano ham crisp on top of each serving of potato puree, leaning onto the croquette, and serve immediately.

CHEF'S NOTES

- Chef Leonard serves this dish with Cabbage and Chanterelles (see page 227), Serrano Ham Crisp (see page 236) and Yukon Potato Puree (see page 238).

Braised Pork Cheeks with Cauliflower and Black Truffle

Chef Joseph M. Leonardi
Serves 4

Braised Pork Cheeks:

4 pork cheeks

Salt and freshly ground pepper

1 tablespoon canola oil

1/3 cup chopped celery

1/3 cup chopped carrot

1/3 cup chopped leek

1/3 cup chopped onion

1 teaspoon tomato puree

3 1/2 ounces Madeira

1 cup beef stock

1 juniper berry

2 whole cloves

Cold unsalted butter, diced

Cauliflower Puree:

2 teaspoons canola oil

Florets from 3/4 head cauliflower

3 ounces diced Vidalia or other sweet
   onion

3 ounces chicken stock

1/4 cup heavy cream

2 tablespoons unsalted butter

Salt and freshly ground pepper

Ground nutmeg

Finish and Serve:

1/2 ounce sliced or finely diced truffle

To Make the Braised Pork Cheeks:

- Season the pork cheeks with salt and pepper. Heat the oil in a large skillet and sear the cheeks. Set the cheeks aside. Add the celery, carrot, leek and onion to the pan and sauté until browned. Stir in the tomato puree and cook a few minutes more. Deglaze with all but about 1 tablespoon of the Madeira and cook until all the wine has evaporated.

- Preheat the oven to 350° F. Add the stock, juniper and cloves and bring to a simmer. Place the beef cheeks in the hot liquid, cover the pan and place in the oven. Cook until very tender.

- Remove the cheeks from the liquid and set them aside. Strain the cooking liquid into a saucepan; discard the solids. Season the liquid with salt and pepper and whisk in butter until the sauce is thick and glossy.

- In a small sauté pan, heat a little butter and warm the truffle. Deglaze with the remaining Madeira.

To Make the Cauliflower Puree:

- Place the oil in a skillet and add the cauliflower and onion and cook slowly until the onion is soft. Add the stock and simmer until the cauliflower is very tender. Transfer the vegetables to a blender and add the cream. Blend until smooth, adding as much of the stock in the skillet as needed. Blend in the butter. Season with salt, pepper and nutmeg.

To Finish and Serve:

- Top the pork with the sauce and the truffle. Serve with the cauliflower puree and seasonal vegetables.

CHEF'S NOTES

- This dish can also be garnished with fried shallots and herbs.

Bronzini Rossini with Seared Foie Gras and Split Pea Puree

Chef Richard Rosendale, CEC
Serves 4

Split Pea Puree:
1/2 cup split peas
1/2 cup diced carrot
1/2 cup sliced onion
1 ham hock
1 sprig fresh thyme
4 cups chicken stock
1 cup baby spinach leaves
Salt and freshly ground pepper

Bronzini:
Olive oil
4 bronzini fillets
Salt and freshly ground white pepper
1/2 lemon

Foie Gras:
1/2 pound duck foie gras
Salt and freshly ground pepper

Finish and Serve:
4 small slices bread, toasted and
    brushed with olive oil
Braised savoy cabbage or other vegetable
4 slices black truffle
Chervil sprigs for garnish

To Make the Split Pea Puree:
- In a medium saucepan, combine the split peas, carrot, onion, ham hock, thyme and chicken stock and simmer until the peas are tender. Add the spinach. Remove the ham hock and thyme, and puree the mixture until silky smooth. Season with salt and pepper.

To Make the Bronzini:
- In a sauté pan, heat the oil until very hot. Season the fillets with salt and pepper. Sear the fish skin-side down until browned. Flip the fillets and sear the other side. Finish with a squeeze of fresh lemon juice.

To Make the Foie Gras:
- Cut the foie gras into 2-ounce slices and season with salt and pepper. In a very hot skillet, cook the slices for about 1 minute on each side. Season again with salt and pepper.

To Finish and Serve:
- Place a little of the pea puree on each plate and top with a bread crouton. Place a piece of the fish and a slice of the foie gras over the bread. Garnish with some braised cabbage and top with truffle slices and chervil.

The finsih line is in sight as chefs Leonard and Barnes take a final look at Chef Rosendale's platter display.

Cedar-Planked Atlantic Salmon with Orange and Coriander Glaze, Cauliflower Panna Cotta, Toasted Almonds and Caviar

Chef Timothy R. Prefontaine, CSC
Serves 4

Panna Cotta:

2 teaspoons olive oil

1 onion, diced

1 tablespoon chopped garlic

2 cups cauliflower florets

2 cups heavy cream

1 teaspoon kosher salt,
plus more to taste

Pinch ground white pepper, plus more
to taste

Gelatin sheets as needed,
bloomed in water

Salmon:

3/4 cup freshly squeezed orange juice

1/4 cup honey

1 tablespoon ground coriander

1 teaspoon sea salt

Pinch freshly ground pepper

3 tablespoons unsalted butter, diced

1 cedar cooking plank, soaked in water
for 1 hour

12-ounce piece salmon fillet

1 tablespoon sliced chives

1 tablespoon chopped dill

1 tablespoon chopped parsley

Finish and Serve:

1 tablespoon toasted almonds

1 tablespoon edible flower petals

2 strips celery, sliced and blanched in
salted water

4 chives, chopped

1/2 ounce caviar

1/4 cup micro arugula or chervil

For the Panna Cotta:

- Heat the oil in a large saucepan and add the onion and garlic. Cook until softened. Add the cauliflower, cream and salt and pepper and cook at a bare simmer (do not boil) until the cauliflower is tender.
- Use a slotted spoon to transfer the cauliflower and onion to the container of a blender. Add in as much cream as necessary and blend until smooth and pourable. Season with more salt and pepper and add bloomed gelatin as needed; reheat if necessary to melt the gelatin.
- Line a 1/4 sheet pan with plastic wrap and pour the gelatin mixture over it. Chill until set, at least 4 hours.

For the Salmon:

- Combine the orange juice, honey, coriander, salt and pepper in a saucepan and simmer until syrupy. Remove from heat and whisk in butter a little at a time. Set aside.
- Preheat the oven to 400°F. Spray the cedar plank with cooking spray and lay the salmon on top. Brush with some of the orange glaze, place the plank in the oven and cook until salmon reaches the desired doneness, about 12 minutes. Remove from the oven and brush again with the glaze and sprinkle with the chives, dill and parsley.

To Finish and Serve:

- Cut the panna cotta into rectangles and place one on each plate. Top with almonds, flower petals, celery strips, chives, caviar and micro greens. Cut the salmon into 4 serving pieces and place one on each plate.

Chicken Breast with Julienne Vegetables and Smoked Bacon and Potato Ravioli

Chef Richard Rosendale, CEC
Serves 4

Vegetables:

1 zucchini
1 yellow squash
1 carrot
1 bunch scallions
1 tablespoon unsalted butter
Chicken stock
1 sprig fresh dill
1 sprig fresh parsley
1 sprig fresh tarragon
Salt and freshly ground pepper

Ravioli:

1/2 pound diced smoked bacon
1 small onion, diced
1/4 cup plus 1 tablespoon truffle juice
4 cups baked, riced potatoes
1 teaspoon chopped fresh thyme
1 tablespoon white truffle oil
1/4 cup unsalted butter
2 tablespoons grated Parmesan
1 pound semolina flour
3 large eggs
2 large egg yolks
1 tablespoon olive oil
Few drops milk

Chicken:

1 tablespoon unsalted butter
1 tablespoon olive oil
Four 6-ounce skinless boneless chicken
    breast halves
Salt and freshly ground pepper
4 sprigs fresh thyme
3 garlic cloves, skin on, crushed

Finish and Serve:

Herb oil
Tomato concassé
Basil leaves

To Make the Vegetables:

- Trim the zucchini, yellow squash and carrot and use a mandoline to cut them into long, fine julienne strips; they should resemble spaghetti or linguine noodles. Use a knife to make julienne from the scallions. Keep the vegetables separate.
- Heat the carrots in a medium sauté pan with the butter and a little stock. Cook the carrots just until they begin to wilt, then add the zucchini and yellow squash and cook for another 2 minutes; add the scallion and herb sprigs. Season with salt and pepper.

To Make the Ravioli:

- For the ravioli filling, in a large skillet, cook the bacon until it renders its fat. Add the onion and cook until caramelized. Deglaze with the truffle juice and cook until the liquid has evaporated. Stir in the potatoes. Stir in the thyme, truffle oil, butter, and Parmesan. Set aside.
- To make the ravioli dough, place the semolina, eggs, yolks, olive oil and milk in a food processor and pulse until the dough comes together. Remove from the food processor and knead for 8 minutes. Let the dough rest for half an hour, then roll it out on the #1 setting of a pasta machine. Place one sheet of dough on a lightly floured surface. Drop potato filling by tablespoons in a grid across the dough. Cover with another sheet of dough, press down around the mounds of filling, and cut out ravioli with a ravioli cutter. Seal the edges with some egg wash. To cook, place the ravioli in boiling water for 3 minutes. Remove, and place on top of the cooked vegetables.

To Make the Chicken:

- Heat the butter and olive oil in a large skillet. Season the chicken with salt and pepper, add it to the pan and sear it on both sides. Add the thyme and crushed garlic to the pan and continue cooking the chicken, basting it with the fat in the pan, until it is golden brown. Finish the chicken in a hot oven until it is cooked through.

To Finish and Serve:

- Place a piece of chicken on each plate, followed by some of the vegetables and ravioli. Garnish with herb oil, tomato and basil.

Crispy Long Island Duck Breast, Grand Marnier Orange Sauce, Mustard Späetzle and Red Cabbage

Chef Daniel J. Scannell, CMC
Serves 4

Crispy Duck:

1 whole duck
1/2 orange
1 sprig thyme
1 garlic clove
3 teaspoons kosher salt
2 teaspoons freshly ground pepper

Red Cabbage:

8 slices bacon, diced
1 cup shaved onions
2 Granny Smith apples, peeled, cored
   and shaved
1 large head red cabbage
1 tablespoon peeled, grated fresh ginger
2 cups Cabernet Sauvignon
2 cups red-wine vinegar
1 cup sugar
1 cup red currant jelly
1 sachet made with 6 whole cloves, 1
   bay leaf, 6 peppercorns, 1 cinnamon
   stick and 10 juniper berries
2 teaspoons kosher salt
1 teaspoon freshly ground pepper

Mustard Späetzle:

6 ounces all-purpose flour
2 large eggs, lightly beaten
3 ounces milk
1 teaspoon kosher salt
1/2 teaspoon ground black pepper
1/2 teaspoon freshly grated nutmeg
1 teaspoon Dijon mustard
1 teaspoon whole-grain mustard
1 tablespoon fresh minced chives
2 tablespoons unsalted butter
Juice of 1 lemon
1 tablespoon chopped flat-leaf parsley

Orange Sauce:

1 quart fresh orange juice
1/4 cup Grand Marnier
2 teaspoons unsalted butter
Salt and freshly ground pepper

Finish and Serve:

Orange segments

To Make the Crispy Duck:

- Preheat the oven to 425°F. Cut off the neck and/or neck fat from the duck and set it aside. Stuff the cavity of the duck with the orange half, the thyme and garlic and sprinkle the inside with a 1 teaspoon of the salt and 1 teaspoon of the pepper. Tie the legs of the duck together with butcher's string. Use a meat fork to poke the duck all over to help the fat render off from the skin. Sprinkle the duck with the remaining salt and pepper. Remove the skin from the neck and place it on a rack set into a roasting pan. Place the duck on top of the skin; this will help keep the duck from sticking to the rack. Roast the duck for 30 minutes.
- Lower the oven temperature to 325°F. and continue roasting the duck for about 2 more hours. Remove from the oven and let the duck rest for 1 hour, then debone the duck and reheat in a 375°F. oven for 15 minutes to crisp the skin.

To Make the Red Cabbage:

- Heat a large, deep sauté pan over medium heat and cook the bacon until lightly browned. Add the onions and apples and cook for 2 minutes. Mix in the cabbage and ginger. Stir in the remaining ingredients and bring to a boil. Reduce the heat, cover the pan, and cook until the cabbage is tender and the liquid has been reduced to light syrup; boil uncovered to reduce the liquid if necessary.
- Remove the cabbage from the heat. Discard the sachet. Serve immediately, or cool rapidly, refrigerate, and reheat as needed.

To Make the Mustard Späetzle:

- In a large mixing bowl, stir together the flour, eggs, milk, salt, pepper, nutmeg, mustards and chives until well mixed. Set aside to rest for 15 minutes.
- Fill a 4-quart pot half full of salted water and bring to a rolling boil. Have ready a bowl of ice water. Working in batches, place some späetzle dough on a marble tile and use a 10-inch pallet knife to scrape off bits of it into the boiling water (or run the dough through a späetzle machine). Stir the water frequently and gently; if using a pallet knife, stir with the knife to keep the dough from sticking to it. Cook the späetzle until it floats, then remove it from the boiling water with slotted spoon and transfer it to the ice water to cool. Transfer to paper towels to dry.
- When ready to serve, sauté the späetzle in the butter and until just browned; add lemon juice and parsley and serve hot.

To Make the Orange Sauce:

- In a stainless-steel saucepan, heat the orange juice over medium heat until it is the consistency of maple syrup. Add the Grand Marnier. Remove from the heat and whisk in the butter. Season with salt and pepper and keep warm.

To Finish and Serve:

- Place a portion of duck and späetzle on each plate. Pool some of the orange sauce around the duck and garnish with orange segments. Serve with the cabbage on the side,

Kielbasa-Stuffed Pork Loin with Braised Sauerkraut, Brussel Sprout and Chestnut Sauté and Crispy Potatoes

Chef Michael Matarazzo
Serves 4

Pork:

1 (1 1/2-pound) piece boneless pork
   loin
1 Polish kielbasa sausage
1/4 cup clarified butter
1 tablespoon unsalted butter
Kosher salt and freshly ground pepper
2 shallots, peeled and halved
4 garlic cloves, crushed
4 sprigs fresh thyme
3 fresh sage leaves

Crispy Potatoes:

2 Yukon gold potatoes, peeled
1 quart clarified butter
2 sprigs fresh rosemary
Kosher salt and freshly ground pepper

Brussel Sprout and Chestnut Sauté:

16 Brussel sprouts, quartered
1 tablespoon olive oil
2 slices apple wood-smoked bacon,
   finely diced
1 tablespoon paper-thin slices shallot
1/4 cup chicken stock
2 roasted chestnuts, roughly chopped
1 tablespoon unsalted butter
Kosher salt and freshly ground pepper

Pork Jus:

1/4 cup clarified butter
Meat from 1 smoked ham hock, diced
3 slices apple wood-smoked bacon
1/2 cup diced onion
1/4 cup finely diced celery
1/4 cup finely diced leeks
1/2 cup apple brandy
3 sprigs fresh thyme
2 fresh sage leaves
20 black peppercorns
1 quart pork or veal stock

To Make the Pork:

- Preheat the oven to 350°F. Butterfly the pork loin by cutting deeply but not all the way through it lengthwise. Open the pork up and lay it flat. Using a meat mallet, pound the pork until it is about ½ inch thick. Lay the kielbasa down the length of the loin, trim any that hangs over, and then roll the pork up tightly to enclose the sausage. Tie the pork every few inches with butcher's string to hold it together.
- Heat the clarified butter and whole butter together in a cast-iron skillet until just smoking. Generously season the loin with salt and pepper. Place the loin in the hot pan along with the shallots, garlic, thyme and sage. Roll the loin back and forth in the pan to promote even browning and baste it with the butter in the pan. Once the loin is nicely browned, transfer it to a roasting pan fitted with a rack and roast in the oven until it reaches an internal temperature of 135°F. Remove the loin from the oven and allow to rest for at least 10 minutes before slicing.

To Make the Crispy Potatoes:

- Using a melon baller, scoop out balls of potato flesh. Cook the potato balls in salted boiling water until just tender. Drain and pat dry.
- In a medium saucepan, combine the clarified butter and rosemary. Bring the butter to 350°F., making sure to remove the rosemary once it begins to sizzle. Carefully drop the potato balls into the hot butter and fry until golden brown. Remove from the pan with a slotted spoon and drain on a paper towel-lined pan. Season with salt and pepper.

To Make the Brussel Sprout and Chestnut Sauté:

- Blanch the Brussel sprouts in salted boiling water until tender. Immediately shock in ice water. When cool, drain and pat dry.
- Heat the olive oil in a sauté pan. Add the diced bacon and cook slowly until it has rendered its fat and is crispy. Add the shallot and cook until softened. Add the blanched Brussel sprouts and chicken stock and heat through. Finish with the chestnuts and butter and season with salt and pepper.

To Make the Pork Jus:

- In a small rondeau, heat the clarified butter until it just smokes. Add the ham hock meat and cook until lightly browned. Add the bacon and cook until it renders its fat. Drain excess fat from the pan and add the onion, celery and leeks and sauté briefly. Deglaze the pan with the brandy and cook until evaporated. Add the thyme, sage and peppercorns. Add the stock 1 cup at a time, reducing until only a third of the liquid is left each time.
- Strain the jus through a fine chinois and return it to a clean heavy saucepan. Simmer until reduced to the desired consistency.

To Finish and Serve:

- Spoon Brussel sprout sauté down the middle of each serving plate. Spoon sauerkraut along one side of the sprouts. Slice the stuffed loin in slices about 1/4-inch thick and shingle 4 slices on top of the sauerkraut on each plate. Garnish the plates with crispy potatoes and spoon jus around the sliced pork.

CHEF'S NOTES
- Chef Matarazzo serves this dish with Braised Sauerkraut (see page 226).

Lamb Tenderloin with Potato Cake, Parmesan Crisp and Tomato Preserves

Chef Joachim Buchner, CMC
Serves 4

Lamb Tenderloin:

4 lamb tenderloins, trimmed

1 scallion, sliced

1 garlic clove, crushed

1 teaspoon chopped fresh herbs
   (preferably a mix of thyme,
   rosemary and sage)

Pinch cracked black pepper

2 tablespoons olive oil

Kosher salt

Potato Cakes:

2 small russet potatoes, baked and riced

1/4 cup clarified butter

5 tablespoons cornstarch

1 large egg

2 large egg yolks

1/4 cup heavy cream

1 teaspoon salt

Pinch white pepper

Pinch nutmeg

3 large egg whites

Oil for frying

Parmesan Crisp:

1/4 cup grated Parmesan cheese

Tomato Preserves:

2 tablespoons olive oil

1/2 small red onion, finely diced

1 garlic clove, finely chopped

5 Roma tomatoes, peeled,
   seeded and diced

1 tablespoon champagne vinegar

Pinch Italian seasoning

Smidgen cayenne pepper

Pinch paprika

Salt and freshly ground pepper

3 tablespoons tomato ketchup

1 cup white wine or champagne

Finish and Serve:

Lamb sauce

Basil and rosemary

Herb oil

Olive halves

Crumbled feta cheese

To Make the Lamb Tenderloin:

- In a zip-close plastic bag, combine the tenderloins and all the remaining ingredients except the salt. Shake the bag until all the items are mixed and the lamb is well coated. Refrigerate for 2 hours.
- Remove the tenderloins from the bag, season with salt, and grill over hot coals until medium rare. Let rest at room temperature for 5 minutes before carving.

To Make the Potato Cakes:

- Preheat the oven to 300°F. Line a baking sheet with parchment paper. In a mixing bowl, stir together the cooked and riced potatoes, clarified butter and cornstarch. Slowly stir in the egg, egg yolks and cream. Stir in the salt, pepper, and nutmeg, stirring until everything is well incorporated.
- In a separate bowl, whip the egg whites until they hold soft peaks. Fold the egg whites into the potato mixture in two additions. Spread the mixture onto the prepared baking sheet and bake until cooked through, about 40 minutes. Let cool, then cut into desired shapes. Just before serving, fry the potato cakes in oil until golden.

To Make the Parmesan Crisp:

- Heat a small nonstick skillet over medium heat. When hot, sprinkle 1 tablespoon of the cheese into the pan. Let the cheese melt; as soon as it starts to brown, flip it over and cook until the other side is lightly browned as well. Remove the chip from the pan and cool on a wire rack. Repeat with the remaining cheese, making 4 chips.

To Make the Tomato Preserves:

- Heat the oil in a medium saucepan and sauté the onion and garlic until soft but not browned. Add the tomatoes, vinegar, Italian seasoning, cayenne, paprika and salt and pepper. Cook over low heat until the tomato liquid evaporates and the mixture becomes almost dry. Stir in the ketchup and continue to cook until most of the liquid has evaporated.
- Add 1/4 cup of the wine to the pan and continue to cook until it has evaporated. Repeat with the remaining wine, adding it a 1/4 cup at a time. Set aside.

To Finish and Serve:

- Slice the lamb, place the slices on and around a hot potato cake and top with a Parmesan crisp and tomato preserves. Garnish with lamb sauce, herbs, herb oil, olives and feta.

Madeleine's Fried Turkey

Chef Chris Desens, CEC
Serves 4

Turkey:

8 (2-ounce) portions turkey tenderloin,
  slightly pounded

4 thin slices prosciutto,
  halved lengthwise

1 cup all-purpose flour

1 teaspoon garlic powder

1 teaspoon smoked paprika

1 teaspoon curry powder

1 teaspoon salt

1 cup buttermilk

2 large eggs

Root Vegetable Hash:

1/4 cup peeled, diced Yukon gold potato

1/4 cup peeled, diced parsnip

1/4 cup peeled, diced turnip

1/4 cup peeled, diced celery root

1/4 cup peeled, diced rutabaga

1/4 cup diced yellow onion

1/4 cup diced red bell pepper

1/4 cup diced celery

Olive oil

Unsalted butter

Fresh herbs of choice

Salt and freshly ground pepper

Sweet Potato Sauce:

1/4 cup diced yellow onion

1/4 cup diced celery

1/4 cup diced carrot

Olive oil

1/2 cup peeled, mashed roasted
  sweet potato

2 teaspoons minced peeled fresh ginger

1/2 teaspoon red curry paste

2/3 cup coconut milk

2 tablespoons lime juice

2/3 cup chicken stock

Unsalted butter

Salt and ground white pepper

Finish and Seve:

Yukon gold potato chips

BEVERAGE RECOMMENDATION

White Burgundy or Spätlese Riesling

To Make the Turkey:

- Wrap each piece of turkey in a half a slice of prosciutto. On a plate, combine the flour, garlic powder, paprika, curry powder and salt. In a bowl, whisk together the buttermilk and eggs. Measure out 2/3 cup of the flour mixed with spices and whisk it into the buttermilk mixture just until smooth. Dredge each piece of turkey in some of the remaining 1/3 cup seasoned flour, dip each in the batter, then dredge again in the flour.

- Deep-fry the turkey pieces in 350°F. oil until golden brown and cooked through. Drain well.

To Make the Root Vegetable Hash:

- Sauté the vegetables in olive oil until cooked through and the flavors combine. Stir in the butter, herbs, and salt and pepper to taste.

To Make the Sweet Potato Sauce:

- Sweat the onion, celery and carrot in olive oil until soft. Add the sweet potato, ginger, curry paste, coconut milk, lime juice and stock and cook until the flavors meld. Puree the sauce and finish with butter and season to taste with salt and pepper.

To Finish and Serve:

- Place 2 pieces of turkey on each plate, serve with the vegetable hash and parsnip-potato puree, and garnish each plate with some cranberry compote and a potato chip. Place a line of the sauce on the side.

CHEF'S NOTES

- Chef Desens serves this dish with Parsnip-Potato Puree (see page 233) and Cranberry Compote (see page 230).

- Turkey is great any time of year, and this dish can be enjoyed with family and friends year-round. The sweet potato and curry add a different twist to the traditional flavors that we all remember from our childhoods.

Mint Pesto Rack of Lamb and Braised Denver Rib

Chef Jamie P. Keating, CCC
Serves 4

Denver Rib:

4 ounces lamb trimmings

1 1/2 ounces fat back, diced

1 teaspoon chopped fresh rosemary

1 egg white

2 teaspoons heavy cream

1 garlic clove, roasted and mashed

Kosher salt and freshly ground pepper

Cayenne

4 pieces lamb Denver ribs
(3 bones only from short end)

1 tablespoon canola oil

1/2 cup seasoned flour

1/4 cup diced carrot

1 garlic clove, mashed

1/4 cup red wine

5 cups lamb stock

1 sachet made with bay leaf,
peppercorns and rosemary
tied in cheesecloth

Rack of Lamb and Pesto:

Loin meat from 4 pounds
domestic lamb racks

Crushed fennel seed

Kosher salt and cracked black pepper

Canola oil

1/2 pound mint fresh, stems discarded

1 tablespoon chopped garlic

1/3 cup extra-virgin olive oil

1/4 cup shredded Asiago cheese

1/4 cup panko bread crumbs

1 tablespoon toasted pine nuts

Smoked Tomato Coulis:

10 Roma tomatoes, peeled and seeded

3 garlic cloves, peeled

2 shallots, peeled

1 tablespoon tomato paste

Salt and freshly ground pepper

**BEVERAGE
RECOMMENDATION**

Atlas Peak Sangiovese

To Make the Denver Rib:

- In a meat grinder, grind together the lamb and fat back. Transfer the mixture to a food processor and add the rosemary, egg white, cream and garlic. Pulse until smooth. Season the mixture with salt, pepper and cayenne and pass the mixture through a fine sieve.
- Cut out 2 of the three bones from each piece of Denver rib, leaving the meat attached (like a flap) to the third bone. Sprinkle the meat with salt and pepper and fill it with the ground lamb mixture. Roll the flap over the filling and tie the pieces with butcher's twine.
- Heat the oil in a pressure cooker. Dredge the lamb pieces in the seasoned flour and sear them on all sides. Remove from the pan and add the carrot and garlic and cook until browned. Add the wine, stock and sachet, cover the pressure cooker and cook the lamb for 90 minutes.
- Remove the lamb from the pan and cut the strings. Strain the sauce in the pan, discard the solids, and season the sauce with salt and pepper.

To Make the Rack of Lamb and Pesto:

- Sprinkle the lamb with the fennel, salt and pepper and rub with canola oil. Heat a large skillet over high heat and sear the lamb until browned. Set aside.
- In a food processor, combine the mint, garlic, oil, Asiago, bread crumbs and pine nuts and pulse until smooth. Transfer the mixture to a pastry bag fitted with a medium plain tip. Make an incision through the lamb that runs the length of the loins. Pipe the pesto into the incision. Place the lamb in roasting pans and roast until it reaches the desired doneness.

To Make the Smoked Tomato Coulis:

- Place the tomatoes, garlic and shallots in a stovetop or outdoor smoker and smoke until they take on good flavor. Puree the vegetables in a food processor with the tomato paste. Season the mixture with salt and pepper.

To Finish and Serve:

- Place some of the tomato coulis on each plate. Slice the lamb and top the coulis with a few slices. Place a pool of the sauce from the Denver rib on each plate, top with an unmolded ring of polenta, and place a rib piece on top of each. Divide the fava beans between the plates.

CHEF'S NOTES

- Chef Keating serves this dish with Polenta (see page 235) and Fava Beans (see page 231) .

Monkfish Osso Buco over Eggplant Risotto

Chef Jamie P. Keating, CCC
Serves 4

Monkfish:

4 monkfish tails

1 cup seasoned flour

Blended oil for searing
(olive and canola oil)

2 ounces dry white wine

2 cups fish stock

1 leek, diced

1 small sachet of peppercorns, parsley
stems and a bay leaf

Eggplant Risotto:

2 tablespoons blended oil
(olive and canola oil)

1 eggplant, peeled and diced

2 shallots, diced

1 garlic clove, finely chopped

1 cup Arborio rice

2 cups lobster stock, or as needed

1/2 cup shredded Pecorino-Romano

1 cup heavy cream, or as needed

12 basil leaves, sliced into chiffonade

10 sun-dried tomatoes, rehydrated in
Marsala wine and julienned

2 tablespoons unsalted butter

Kosher salt and crushed black pepper

Broccoli Rabe:

1 tablespoons unsalted butter

1 garlic clove, sliced

2 bunches broccoli rabe, blanched

Kosher salt and crushed black pepper

Tomato Coulis:

3 vine tomatoes, peeled and seeded

1/4 cup chicken stock, heated

Pinch kosher salt

Pinch fennel powder

To Make the Monkfish:

- Preheat the oven to 325°F. Dredge the monkfish in the seasoned flour. Heat the oil in a skillet and sear the fish. Remove the fish from the pan and set aside. Add the wine, stock, leek and sachet to the pan and bring to a boil. Add the fish, cover the pan and bake 8 to 10 minutes.

To Make the Eggplant Risotto:

- Heat the oil in a large skillet. Add the eggplant and sauté until tender. Add the shallots and garlic cook until softened.
- Place the rice in a saucepan and toast lightly. Add half of the stock and cook until most of the liquid has been absorbed. Add the remainder of the stock and cook until it has been absorbed, adding more stock if needed until rice is tender. Stir in cheese and cream. Stir in basil, tomatoes, eggplant and butter. Season with salt and pepper.

To Make the Broccoli Rabe:

- Heat the butter in a large sauté pan. Add the garlic slices and sauté briefly. Add the broccoli rabe and cook until heated through. Season with salt and pepper.

To Make the Tomato Coulis:

- Combine all the ingredients in a blender and blend until smooth. Season to taste.

To Finish and Serve:

- Place a serving of risotto on each plate. Top with monkfish. Surround plates with broccoli rabe and dollops of the coulis. Garnish monkfish as desired.

Moussaka of Veal with Tomato Gravy and Braised Sweetbread and Cipollini Tarting

Chef Edward G. Leonard, CMC
Serves 4

Moussaka:

5 tablespoons extra-virgin olive oil

1 veal shank

Kosher salt and fresh cracked pepper

1/2 cup diced onion

1/2 cup diced carrot

1/2 cup diced celery

3 cloves garlic, sliced

1 tablespoon tomato paste

1 cup red wine

5 cups veal stock

1 sprig fresh rosemary

1 sprig fresh sage

1 bay leaf

1 large eggplant, sliced lengthwise into 1/4-inch-thick slices

2 Idaho potatoes, peeled and cut into 1/4-inch-thick slices

8 tomato petals

2 beefsteak tomatoes, peeled, seeded and diced

Finish and Serve:

4 dried eggplant strips

Sea salt

To Make the Moussaka:

- Place a small rondeau over medium heat and add 1 tablespoon of the olive oil. Once the oil begins to smoke, season the veal shank with salt and pepper and brown it on all sides. Remove the shank from the pan and add the onion, carrot, celery and garlic. Cook, stirring often, until the vegetables are lightly caramelized. Add the tomato paste and cook, stirring constantly, for 2 minutes. Deglaze the pan with the wine and simmer until the liquid is reduced by half. Add the stock, rosemary, sage and bay leaf. Add the veal shank and bring to a simmer.

- Preheat the oven to 325°F. Cover the pan with aluminum foil and bake until the veal is so tender that the meat falls off the bone, about 1 hour. Remove the pan from the oven and allow to cool to room temperature.

- Remove the veal shank; strain the liquid through a fine-mesh sieve and set aside. Gently pull the meat from the bone and remove and discard any connective tissue (try to keep the meat in medium-size pieces). Set the meat and cooking liquid aside.

- Place a large sauté pan over medium heat and add 3 tablespoons of the oil. Sauté the eggplant slices on each side for about 2 minutes. Drain the slices on paper towels and set aside.

- Preheat the oven to 325°F. Grease a small loaf pan that measures approximately 3 x 3 x 12 inches and line the mold with the eggplant slices; leave some eggplant hanging over the sides (this will be folded over to cover the top of the pan later). Place a layer of sliced potatoes into the pan and season them lightly with salt and pepper. Combine the cooked meat with 2 cups of the cooking liquid and mix well; season with salt and pepper and place a thin layer of the mixture over the potatoes. Place the tomato petals on top of the meat and season lightly with salt and pepper. Top with a second layer of the meat and another layer of potatoes; season with salt and pepper. Fold the excess eggplant over the top of the pan, cover the pan with aluminum foil, and bake until the potatoes are tender, about 20 minutes. Remove from the oven and allow to rest for 10 minutes.

- Place a medium saucepan over medium heat and add the remaining 1 tablespoon oil. Add the diced beefsteak tomatoes and cook, stirring occasionally, for 2 minutes. Add the remaining cooking liquid from the veal, bring to a simmer, and cook 10 minutes. Using a hand blender, puree the sauce. Season to taste with salt and pepper.

To Finish and Serve:

- Heat 4 serving plates. Remove the moussaka from the pan, use a sharp knife to cut it into 8 equal portions and place 2 portions on each plate. Spoon tomato gravy onto the plates and garnish each with a tartin, dried eggplant chip and a sprinkle of sea salt.

CHEF'S NOTES

- Chef Leonard serves this dish with Braised Sweetbread and Cipollini Tartin (see page 226).

Olive-Brined Lamb Loin with Sun-Dried Red Pepper and Herb Crust, Potato Sponge, Braised Lamb Neck and Shallot Marmalade

Chef Timothy R. Prefontaine, CSC
Serves 4

Braised Lamb Neck:

1 pound lamb neck

Salt and freshly ground pepper

1 tablespoon olive oil

2 cups diced mirepoix

4 white anchovies

2 shallots, minced

2 garlic cloves, chopped

1 tablespoon sugar

1 teaspoon cornstarch

2 tablespoons tomato paste

1/4 cup white wine

3 cups lamb stock

8 whole peppercorns

3 bay leaves

6 fresh thyme sprigs

1 fresh rosemary sprig

Lamb:

1 cup pureed kalamata olives

3 tablespoons plus 1/4 cup olive oil

1 tablespoon chopped garlic

2 lamb loins, trimmed of silver skin

1 cup fresh bread crumbs

2 tablespoons minced
   sun-dried peppers

1/2 teaspoon chopped fresh
   rosemary leaves

1/2 teaspoon chopped fresh
   thyme leaves

2 teaspoons chopped parsley

2 tablespoons minced kalamata olives

Salt and freshly ground pepper

Vegetables:

2 tablespoons olive oil

1/2 cup cremini mushrooms,
   sliced if large

1/2 cup peeled, sliced salsify,
   blanched and shocked

1/2 cup fresh peas,
   blanched and shocked

1 tablespoon minced shallot

1/4 cup julienned roasted
   red bell pepper

1/4 cup julienned red onion

3 tablespoons chicken stock

Salt and freshly ground pepper

2 tablespoons unsalted butter

To Make the Braised Lamb Neck:

- Season the neck with salt and pepper. Heat the oil in a heavy saucepan and brown the meat. Remove it from the pan and set aside.
- Add the mirepoix to the pan and cook until lightly caramelized. Add the anchovies, shallots, garlic, sugar, cornstarch and tomato paste and sauté for 1 more minute. Add wine and cook for 2 more minutes. Add lamb neck and enough stock so the lamb is half submerged. Add the peppercorns, bay leaves, thyme and rosemary. Cover the pan and simmer gently on low heat until the meat is very tender and the stock has reduced.
- Remove the neck meat and cool it slightly. Pull it into medium-size pieces. Strain the braising liquid and add about 3/4 of it to the meat and set this aside. Reserve the remaining liquid for plating.

To Make the Lamb:

- Whisk together pureed olives, 3 tablespoons of the oil, and the garlic. Coat the loins with this mixture and wrap them in plastic. Refrigerate for 4 to 6 hours.
- Remove from the plastic, brush off any excess marinade, and sear the loins on all sides in a very hot pan. Transfer to a rack set over a sheet pan.
- Preheat the oven to 350°F. Mix together the bread crumbs, sun-dried peppers, rosemary, thyme, parsley, minced olives and remaining 1/4 cup oil. Season the mixture with salt and pepper and use it to coat the top of the seared loins. Bake until the lamb reaches the desired doneness, about 9 minutes. Let rest about 5 minutes, then slice.

To Make the Vegetables:

- Heat the oil in a sauté pan over medium-high heat. Add the mushrooms and sauté for 2 minutes. Add the salsify and cook for 1 minute. Add the peas, shallot, roasted pepper and onion and sauté for an additional 1 minute. Add stock and season with salt and pepper. When stock is almost reduced, finish with the butter.

To Finish and Serve:

- Spoon the vegetables onto 4 warm plates. Arrange the lamb on top of the vegetables and spoon a little of the braised lamb neck next to lamb. Place a spoon of the shallot marmalade on each plate and top with a piece of potato sponge. Drizzle a little of the reserved braising liquid around each plate.

CHEF'S NOTES

- Chef Prefontaine serves this dish with Potato Sponge (see page 236) and Shallot Marmalade (see page 237).

Pan-Roasted Pork Lion with Twice-Cooked Pork Shank

Chef Drew Garms
Serves 4

Pork Loin:

4 pieces boneless center-cut pork loin,
about 7 ounces each

Salt and freshly ground pepper

3 tablespoons clarified butter

1 shallot, quartered

1 clove garlic

1 sprig fresh thyme

2 tablespoons unsalted butter

Pork Shanks:

2 bone-in pork shanks

Salt and freshly ground pepper

1/4 cup clarified butter

1/2 cup diced onion

1/4 cup diced carrot

1/4 cup diced celery

1 shallot, minced

1 garlic clove, minced

2 cups white wine

2 quarts pork stock
(or rich chicken stock)

1 sprig fresh thyme

1 sprig parsley

1 bay leaf

1/4 cup brunoise of bacon

1/2 cup brunoise of onion

1/4 cup brunoise of carrot

1/4 cup brunoise of celery

2 tablespoons chopped parsley

1 tablespoon whole-grain mustard

Breading mixture

Oil for deep frying

Sweet Potato Silk:

2 large sweet potatoes, peeled and diced

2 cups chicken stock

2 cups heavy cream

1 sprig fresh thyme wrapped in
cheesecloth

Salt and freshly ground pepper

To Make the Pork Loin:

- Preheat the oven to 350°F. Season the pork with salt and pepper. In heavy skillet, heat the clarified butter and until very hot and sear the pork on all sides. Once the pork is browned, add the shallot, garlic, thyme and butter to the skillet. Continue to cook until the shallot browns, basting the pork frequently. Transfer the skillet to the oven and cook until the pork is medium rare.

To Make the Pork Shanks:

- Preheat the oven to 375°F. Season the shanks with salt and pepper. In a large heavy pot, heat the clarified butter until very hot and sear the shanks on all sides. Remove from the pot and set aside.
- In the same pot, add the onion, carrot and celery and cook until the vegetables are golden brown. Stir in the shallot and garlic and quickly sauté. Pour in the white wine, deglaze the skillet, and simmer until the wine is reduced by half.
- Place shanks, stock, thyme, parsley and bay leaf into the pot and bring to a boil. Cover the top of the pot with buttered parchment and them with foil to make a lid. Place in the oven and braise until the pork is tender, 3 to 3 1/2 hours.
- Remove the shanks from the braising liquid and pull the meat from the bones. Cover and keep warm. Strain the liquid into a saucepan and simmer until reduced to a sauce-like consistency.
- Meanwhile, place the bacon in a skillet and cook until it renders its fat. Add the brunoise of onion, carrot and celery and cook until the vegetables are just tender. Scrape the vegetables into a bowl and add the pulled pork, parsley, mustard and half of the reduced braising liquid (reserve the other half for plating). Shape the mixture into a cylinder using plastic wrap and tying both ends with butcher's string. Chill in an ice bath.
- When ready to serve, cut the cylinder into 1-inch-thick medallions and double bread them for frying. Fry in oil at 350°F. until golden brown and liquid in the center.

To Make the Sweet Potato Silk:

- In a saucepan, combine the sweet potatoes, stock, cream and thyme. Simmer until the potatoes are tender. Strain, reserving the cooking liquid and potatoes separately. Puree the potatoes at high speed in a blender, adding enough cooking liquid to yield a silky smooth puree. Season with salt and pepper.

To Finish and Serve:

- Place some sweet potato silk on each plate and top with some greens. Place a serving of the pork loin and fried pork shank on each plate and surround with some of the reserved liquid from the pork shanks.

CHEF'S NOTES:

- Chef Garms serves this dish with Braised Collard Greens (see page 225).

Pan-Roasted Veal Porterhouse with Asparagus and Morels

Chef Jonathan P. Moosmiller, CEC
Serves 4

Porterhouse:
Juice of 1 lemon
2 sprigs fresh rosemary, leaves finely chopped
1/4 cup extra-virgin olive oil
4 veal Porterhouse steaks, each about 12 ounces
Kosher salt and freshly cracked pepper
1/4 cup canola oil

Red Wine Sauce:
2 tablespoons unsalted butter
1 tablespoon finely diced onion
1 teaspoon finely diced carrot
1 teaspoon finely diced celery
1 sprig fresh thyme
2 tablespoons all-purpose flour
1 cup red wine
1 cup veal stock

Asparagus and Morels:
10 jumbo asparagus stalks
1 tablespoon unsalted butter
1 shallot, thinly sliced
8 ounces fresh morels, cleaned
1/2 cup chicken stock
Kosher salt and freshly cracked pepper

Finish and Serve:
Sea salt

To Make the Porterhouse:

- In a small bowl, combine the lemon juice, rosemary and olive oil. Spread half of the mixture into a shallow pan just large enough to hold the veal steaks in a single layer. Add the veal and pour the remaining oil mixture evenly over the top. Cover with plastic wrap and refrigerate overnight.

- Preheat the oven to 400°F. Remove the steaks from the marinade and season both sides with salt and cracked pepper. Place a large cast-iron skillet over medium-high heat and heat for 5 minutes. Add the canola oil and allow the oil to heat until it just begins to smoke, about 2 minutes. Add the steaks (work in batches if necessary) and cook until golden brown on both sides. Remove the steaks from the pan and place them on a roasting rack set over a baking sheet. Repeat until all steaks are seared on both sides. Transfer to the oven and bake until the steaks reach the desired doneness. Allow to rest for 10 minutes in a warm place before serving.

To Make the Red Wine Sauce:

- Place a medium saucepan over medium heat and melt the butter. Add the onion, carrot, celery and thyme. Cook, stirring often, until the onion is translucent. Add the flour and stir until all the flour is incorporated, forming a roux. Continue to cook, stirring, for 5 minutes.

- Stir in the wine, stirring until the mixture is smooth. Simmer 3 minutes. Stir in the veal stock and bring back to a simmer; simmer gently for 10 minutes. Strain the sauce through a fine-mesh sieve, season to taste with salt and pepper and keep warm until serving.

To Make the Asparagus and Morels:

- Using a sharp knife, trim the bottom inch off the asparagus stalks. Using a vegetable peeler, carefully peel the skin off the bottom 2 inches of 8 of the stalks and set them aside.

- Using the vegetable peeler, make long, thin strips of the remaining asparagus stalks. Place the strips in a food dehydrator and dehydrate until crisp. Set aside until serving. (This can be done the day before and the strips placed in an airtight container until serving.)

- Place 1 gallon of heavily salted water into a large pot and bring to a boil over high heat. Add the reserved 8 stalks of asparagus and cook 2 minutes. Drain the asparagus and cool in an ice-water bath. Drain again and pat dry.

- Place a large sauté pan over medium heat and melt the butter. Add the shallot and cook 2 minutes. Add the morels and cook 2 minutes more. Add the asparagus and stock and cook until the stock has reduced and glazes the vegetables. Season with salt and cracked pepper.

To Finish and Serve:

- Warm 4 large serving plates. Using a sharp knife, cut out the sirloin side of the Porterhouses and slice each into 5 slices. Place the tenderloin side of the Porterhouses onto the right side of the plate. Shingle the slices of sirloin back into place next to the tenderloin. Place two asparagus spears in alternating direction on the left side of each plate. Divide the morels equally between the plates. Garnish the asparagus with 2 pieces of the dried asparagus. Lightly nap the steak with the red wine sauce. Sprinkle the meat with sea salt and serve immediately.

Pepper-Crusted Strip Steak with Chocolate Salt, Beet Risotto and Beet Foam

Chef Richard Rosendale, CEC
Serves 4

Beet Risotto:

2 cups chicken stock

1 cup beet juice

1 tablespoon olive oil

1 tablespoon minced white onion

1 cup Carnaroli rice

3 tablespoons grated Parmesan

2 tablespoons unsalted butter

Salt and freshly ground pepper

Steaks and Chocolate Salt:

1/4 cup chopped bittersweet chocolate, frozen

1 tablespoon kosher salt

Four 8-ounce strip steaks

Fine sea salt

2 tablespoons freshly ground pepper

1/4 cup olive oil

Beet Foam:

2 cups beet juice

Zest and juice of 1 orange

1 star anise pod

1 vanilla pod (not scraped)

Salt and freshly ground pepper

1 tablespoon soy lecithin

Finish and Serve:

Steamed seasonal vegetables

To Make the Beet Risotto:

- Heat the stock and beet juice together in saucepan until hot. In another medium saucepan, heat the olive oil and cook the onion until translucent. Add the rice and stir until all the grains are coated in the oil. Start adding the hot beet stock a ladle at a time, stirring occasionally and adding more stock only after the rice is almost dry again. Cook until the rice grains are tender but still have some bite to them. Remove from the heat and stir in the cheese and butter. Season with salt and black pepper.

To Make the Steaks and Chocolate Salt:

- Put the frozen chocolate and the kosher salt in a coffee grinder. Process just until the mixture is finely ground, about 20 seconds. Refrigerate until serving. (If the chocolate gets too warm, it will begin to melt.)
- Rub the steaks with the sea salt, black pepper and oil. Heat a grill until very hot and sear the steaks on both sides until cooked to desired doneness. Let the steaks rest for 10 minutes. Before serving the steaks, sprinkle with a little chocolate salt.

To Make the Beet Foam:

- Place the beet juice in a medium saucepan. Reduce for 5 minutes. Add the orange zest and juice, star anise, and vanilla pod and simmer for 8 minutes more. Season with salt and pepper, strain the mixture, and stir in the lecithin. The sauce can be frothed with a hand-held blender.

To Finish and Serve:

- Place some of the risotto on each plate, followed by a steak and some frothed beet foam. Garnish with some steamed seasonal vegetables and sprinkle the plates with some chocolate salt.

Persillade and Mustard-Crusted Corned Rack of Lamb

Daniel J. Scannell, CMC
Serves 4

Lamb:

2 quarts water

3 ounces kosher salt

4 ounces sugar

1/4 cup honey

10 juniper berries

2 star anise pods

1 cinnamon stick

1 tablespoon pickling spice

2 racks of lamb

1 ounce TCM (tinted cure mix)

Lamb stock as needed for poaching

Persillade Crust:

1 cup chopped fresh parsley

2 slices white bread, crusts removed,
 bread diced

1 cup light toasted fine panko crumbs

1/4 teaspoon kosher salt

1 tablespoon finely grated Parmesan

1 tablespoon melted butter

Mustard as needed

Soufflé Potatoes:

2 Idaho potatoes

Oil for frying

Kosher salt

To Make the Lamb:

- In a large pot, combine the water, salt, sugar, honey, juniper, star anise, cinnamon and pickling spice. Bring to a boil, skimming off any foam that rises to the surface. Remove from the heat and chill.
- Inject the lamb with the cure mix. Submerge the lamb in the brine and refrigerate overnight.
- Remove the lamb from the brine; discard the brine. Gently poach the lamb in the stock until fully cooked and tender, about 1 hour. Slice and serve hot.

To Make the Persillade Crust:

- Combine the parsley, bread, panko and salt in a food processor and process until very finely chopped. Stir in the cheese and butter. Brush the lamb with mustard and press the persillade mixture over it to coat.

To Make the Soufflé Potatoes:

- Slice potatoes to the thickness of a dime. Trim and shape as desired. Heat oil to 299°F. Add potatoes and cook until they begin to blister. Quickly remove. Drain, then fry again in 375°F. oil until golden brown. Season with salt and serve warm.

To Finish and Serve:

- Warm the lamb in the oven, slice and serve with the potatoes. Garnish the plates as desired.

Pork and Clam Duo

Chef Jonathan P. Moosmiller, CEC
Serves 4

Pork Loin:

3 pounds bone-in pork loin

1/4 cup blended oil

1/4 cup unsalted butter

3 unpeeled shallots, quartered

2 unpeeled garlic cloves, crushed

1 sprig fresh sage

1 sprig fresh rosemary

Kosher salt and fresh cracked pepper

Pork Jowl:

1/4 cup blended oil

2 pork jowls

Kosher salt and freshly cracked pepper

2 ounces diced carrot

3 ounces diced onion

2 ounces diced celery

1 garlic clove, sliced

1 tablespoon tomato paste

1/2 cup red wine

1 quart veal stock

2 sprigs fresh thyme

1 bay leaf

Finish and Serve:

1/4 cup extra-virgin olive oil

4 roasted cipollini onions

To Make the Pork Loin:

- Using a sharp knife, remove the bones from the pork loin and reserve them for the Pork Jowl recipe below. Trim off all excess fat and silver skin from the loin. Truss the loin with butcher's string and season the loin with salt and cracked pepper.
- Preheat the oven to 400°F. Place a heavy bottomed sauté pan over medium heat and allow to heat for 2 minutes. Add the blended oil and heat 2 minutes more. Place the pork loin in the pan and brown for 2 to 3 minutes on one side. Turn the loin ¼ of a turn; add the butter, shallots, garlic, sage and rosemary. Continue to cook the pork loin on all sides, continuously basting with a spoon, until all sides are gold brown. Remove the loin from the pan and place in a baking dish fitted with a wire rack. Place in the oven and roast until the loin reaches an internal temperature of 120°F. Remove from the oven and allow to rest 20 minutes before slicing.

To Make the Pork Jowl:

- Place a pressure cooker over medium heat and allow to preheat for 2 minutes. Add the blended oil and heat for another 2 minutes. Season the pork jowls with salt and pepper, add them to the pressure cooker and cook on both sides until golden brown. Remove from the pressure cooker and reserve.
- Add the reserved bones from the pork loin to the pressure cooker and brown evenly on all sides. Once browned remove from the pan and reserve. Add the carrot, onion, celery and garlic and cook, stirring often, until the vegetables are lightly caramelized. Add the tomato paste and continue to cook for 3 minutes, stirring constantly. Deglaze the pan with the wine and allow the wine to reduce by half. Add the stock, thyme and bay leaf. Return the pork jowls and pork bones to the pressure cooker. Bring the mixture to a simmer over medium heat. Cover the pressure cooker according to the manufacturer's directions. Once the cooker begins to release pressure, lower the heat slightly and continue to cook for 25 minutes.
- Remove the cooker form the heat and remove the cover according to the manufacturer's directions. Remove the pork jowls and place them on a cutting board. Cut them into serving pieces and keep warm until serving.
- Strain the liquid the jowls cooked in into a stainless-steel saucepan and place over medium heat. Discard the bones and solids. Simmer the liquid until reduced to the desired consistency. Season with salt and pepper and set aside until serving.

To Finish and Serve:

- In a nonstick sauté pan, heat the oil over medium heat. Add 4 chorizo potato bars and brown lightly on one side. Add the roasted onions to the pan and heat through.
- Divide warm spinach evenly between 4 warmed serving plates. Using a sharp knife, slice the warm pork loin into 12 slices and shingle 3 slices on each plate on top of the spinach. Place 1 potato bar on each plate. Place 5 clams from the poached clams on each potato bar. Spoon the clam froth over the poached clams. Place 1 piece of pork jowl onto each plate and top with a roasted onion. Gently spoon the reduced sauce over the pork jowl and sliced pork loin and serve immediately.

CHEF'S NOTES

- Chef Moosmiller serves this dish with Chorizo Potato Bar (see page 229), Spinach (see page 237), Clam Foam (see page 229) and Poached Clams (see page 234).

Potato-Crusted Scallops with Cheese and Basil Mousse, Pumpkin Confit, Frisée and Tomatoes

Chef Edward G. Leonard, CMC
Serves 4

Cheese and Basil Mousse:

2 sheets gelatin, soaked in ice water

4 ounces goat cheese

2 ounces ricotta cheese

1/4 cup heavy cream

1 teaspoon honey

1 large egg white, whipped to
    medium peaks

1 tablespoon basil chlorophyll

Pumpkin Confit:

1 cup sugar

1 cup water

1/2 vanilla bean, split lengthwise

1/4 cup brunoise of pumpkin

Potato-Crusted Scallops:

1 Idaho potato, peeled

Kosher salt and fresh cracked
    black pepper

1/4 cup clarified butter

12 sea scallops

1/4 cup olive oil

Finish and Serve:

1 cup frisée, trimmed,
    washed and dried

12 grape tomatoes, peeled (optional)

1/2 teaspoon red-wine vinegar

1 tablespoon extra-virgin olive oil

Kosher salt and fresh cracked pepper

To Make the Cheese and Basil Mousse:

- Place the softened gelatin sheets in a small stainless-steel bowl and place over simmering water. Stir gently with a rubber spatula until the gelatin is completely melted. Add the goat cheese, ricotta, cream and honey and mix until smooth. Place the bottom of the bowl over and ice water and stir continuously until the mixture begins to firm slightly. Remove from the ice bath and fold in the whipped egg white. Add the chlorophyll and mix slightly to create a marbled effect.
- Place the mixture in a piping bag fitted with a medium tip. Line a pan with parchment paper. Pipe the mousse onto the paper, making 4 tubes about 2 inches in length. Refrigerate until serving.

To Make the Pumpkin Confit:

- Place the sugar, water and vanilla bean in a small stainless-steel saucepan. Cook over medium heat until the sugar is completely dissolved. Add the pumpkin and simmer until tender. Drain, reserving the pumpkin and liquid separately.
- Preheat the oven to 200°F. Place the pumpkin on a baking sheet lined with a Silpat and bake until it is dried, about 1 hour. Remove from the oven and store in an airtight container until serving.

To Make the Potato-Crusted Scallops:

- Place the potato in a spiral vegetable slicer and slice the entire potato into thin strands. Place the potato in a bowl and season with kosher salt and pepper.
- Place a nonstick sauté pan over medium heat; add the clarified butter and heat for 2 minutes. Place a metal ring mold that is slightly larger than the scallops into the pan. Place enough of the potato strands into the ring mold to cover the bottom. Remove the cutter and cook the potato until golden brown. Using a small spatula, turn the potato disk over and cook until golden brown. Remove the disk from the pan and drain on paper towel. Repeat until you have 12 potato crusts.
- Place a cast-iron sauté pan over medium-high heat and heat it for 5 minutes. Season the scallops with salt and pepper. Add the olive oil to the pan; once the oil has just begun to smoke, add the scallops and cook until golden brown, about 2 minutes on each side. Remove the scallops from the pan and drain on paper towels. Place the scallops in an ovenproof dish and top each with one of the potato crusts.

To Finish and Serve:

- Warm 4 serving plates. Place the potato-crusted scallops in a preheated 400°F. oven for 5 minutes.
- While the scallops are cooking, toss together the frisée, tomatoes, vinegar and oil. Season with salt and pepper. Remove the scallops from the oven and place 3 on each plate. Place one of the basil mousse tubes on each plate and garnish the top with the pumpkin. Finish each plate with the frisée salad and serve immediately.

Potato-Wrapped Grouper in Tomato-Shellfish Stew with Roasted Artichokes

Chef Daryl Shular
Serves 4

Potato-Wrapped Grouper:

1 large Idaho potato, peeled and sliced paper thin

1 ounce lemon zest, finely chopped

Salt and freshly ground pepper

2 pounds grouper fillet

Olive oil

Tomato-Shellfish Stew:

1/4 cup olive oil

2 ounces peeled and deveined shrimp

2 ounces shelled mussels

2 ounces canned clams (reserve juice)

6 ounces roast artichoke hearts

1 ounce chopped garlic

1/2 ounce chopped shallot

2 ounces cleaned sliced calamari

1/2 cup clam juice

1/4 cup lemon juice

1/2 cup chopped tomatoes

1 ounce drained capers

1 ounce chopped black olives

1/2 ounce chopped basil

Salt and freshly ground pepper

Finish and Serve:

Herbs and greens of choice

To Make the Potato-Wrapped Grouper:

- On a large sheet of parchment paper, lay the potato slices out to form a sheet, overlapping each slightly so you have a solid layer of potatoes with no holes. Sprinkle with zest, salt and pepper.
- Place the grouper fillet 3/4 inch from the edge of the potato sheet. While holding the parchment, begin to roll the potato around the fish, completely enclosing it. Make sure to apply gentle pressure to the roll to assure a tight, even wrapping around the fish. Once fish is wrapped, cut it into 4 portions.
- In a medium nonstick skillet, heat the oil over medium-high heat. Place fish pieces seam-side down and cook until browned and the potatoes are firmly sealed. Using a fish spatula, turn fish over and cook until potato is golden brown and crisp and fish is cooked through.

To Make the Tomato-Shellfish Stew:

- In a medium saucepan, heat the oil over medium-high heat. Add the shrimp, mussels and clams and cook until browned on all sides. Add the artichokes, garlic and shallot and continue to cook for an additional 2 to 3 minutes. Add all the remaining ingredients and simmer 2 to 4 minutes more. Season with salt and pepper.

To Finish and Serve:

- Ladle stew into serving bowls and top with a wrapped fish fillet. Garnish with herbs and greens.

Pumpkin Seed Crusted Elk Loin

Chef Jamie P. Keating, CCC

Serves 4

Elk Loin:

1/2 cup toasted pumpkin seeds

1 teaspoon cumin seeds

2 teaspoons kosher salt

1 1/2 teaspoons chili powder

1/2 teaspoon ground fennel

2 teaspoons paprika

1 1/2 pounds elk loin

3 tablespoons canola oil

Butternut Squash:

1 butternut squash, top only, peeled

2 cups chicken stock

1/2 cinnamon stick

Kosher salt

1 tablespoon melted unsalted butter

2 teaspoons brown sugar

Sauce:

2 cups veal demi-glace

1 cup elk stock

12 peeled, roasted cippolini onions

2 ounces diced foie gras

Salad:

40 fresh currants

4 ounces chanterelle mushrooms, sautéed

1 teaspoon chopped fresh thyme

Finish and Serve:

Micro greens or herbs for garnish

BEVERAGE RECOMMENDATION

Coppola Claret 2006

To Make the Elk Loin:

- Combine the pumpkin seeds, cumin seeds, salt, chili powder, fennel and paprika in a coffee grinder and pulse until the pumpkin seeds are finely ground. Press the mixture onto the elk loin.
- Preheat a convection oven to 375°F. In a skillet, heat the oil over medium-high heat and sear the elk. Transfer the elk to a pan fitted with a roasting rack and roast for about 12 minutes. Allow to rest before slicing.

To Make the Butternut Squash:

- Trim the squash into 1-inch-thick rectangles that measure 3 x 2 inches. Place the stock, cinnamon stick and salt to taste in a large saucepan and poach the squash. Allow to cool to room temperature.
- Preheat the oven to 325°F. Cut each piece of squash into 8 slices. Sprinkle with butter and brown sugar, shingle the pieces on a baking sheet, and bake for about 4 minutes.

To Make the Sauce:

- Combine the demi-glace and stock and simmer for 20 minutes. Add the onions and simmer for 5 minutes. Just before serving, fold in the diced foie gras.

To Make the Salad:

- Gently toss the currants and mushrooms together. Toss again with the thyme.

To Finish and Serve:

- Place some of the squash on each plate and top with a serving of the elk. Spoon sauce and salad around plates. Garnish with micro greens or herbs.

CHEF'S NOTES

- Venison, pork or lamb can be substituted for the elk.

Pressed Honey-Cured Long Island Duck Breast with Pressed Cheesy Potatoes

Chef Daniel J. Scannell, CMC
Serves 4

Duck Breast:

1 gallon water

6 ounces kosher salt

8 ounces sugar

2 ounces TCM (tinted curing mixture)

2 cinnamon sticks

1/2 cup honey

2 tablespoons pickling spice

1 tablespoon juniper berries

4 cleaned and trimmed duck breasts

1 cup foie gras mousse

1/4 cup fine wood chips for smoking

Potatoes:

2 large Yukon gold potatoes, sliced very thinly lengthwise

1/2 cup grated Parmesan

4 ounces thinly sliced aged sharp Cheddar cheese

1 teaspoon kosher salt

1/2 teaspoon ground white pepper

Pinch nutmeg

1 tablespoon snipped chives

4 ounces Mornay sauce

20 chervil leaves

Finish and Serve:

Pickled duck leg ham

8 slices toasted brioche

4 sliced roasted fresh chestnuts

8 pickled gooseberries

To Make the Duck Breast:

- In a large stainless-steel pot, combine the water, salt, sugar, TCM, cinnamon, honey, pickling spice and juniper. Bring to a boil and boil for 1 minute; skim off and discard any foam that forms on the surface of the liquid. Allow the mixture to cool to room temperature, then place the duck breasts in the liquid and refrigerate for 24 hours.

- Remove the duck from brine; discard the brine and pat the duck dry with paper towels. Place the mousse in a piping bag fitted with a 1/2-inch round tip and pipe it evenly onto the breasts. Wrap the duck in plastic, secure both ends tightly and tie with butcher's string. Place the wrapped duck between two 1/4-inch-thick boards and wrap again.

- Place the wrapped duck breasts in simmering water until they are cooked through and reach an internal temperature of 145°F. Remove from the simmering water and shock in an ice bath for 5 minutes. Unwrap the breasts and smoke them over wood chips at medium-low heat until they take on a nice golden color.

To Make the Potatoes:

- Cut the potatoes to fit in a small terrine or other mold. Grease the mold, then make layers of potatoes, topping each layer with some of the Parmesan, Cheddar, salt, pepper, nutmeg, chives and Mornay sauce. Finish the terrine with the chervil leaves and top them with a very thin (almost translucent) layer of potato slices so that the leaves will show through once the potatoes are cooked.

- Preheat the oven to 275°F. Place the terrine in a bain-marie and bake until the potatoes are just tender and the terrine is fully set, about 30 minutes (do not overcook). Remove from the water and allow the terrine to rest for 5 minutes. Slice the potatoes into the desired shape.

To Finish and Serve:

- Slice the duck breasts and place the slices on serving plates. Place the potatoes on the plates and serve with the duck leg ham, brioche, chestnuts and gooseberries.

Quail Two Ways with Foie Gras, Cranberry Wild Rice, Haricot Verts and Mushrooms

Chef Jonathan P. Moosmiller, CEC
Serves 4

Quail:

4 semi-boneless quail
1/2 cup prepared cranberry relish
Kosher salt and freshly ground pepper
1 cup all-purpose flour
2 large eggs, cracked and beaten
2 cups panko bread crumbs
Oil for deep frying
1/2 pound Grade A foie gras
2 tablespoons cognac
2 tablespoons heavy cream
4 (7-inch) squares caul fat
2 tablespoons extra-virgin olive oil

Red Wine Reduction:

1 tablespoon extra-virgin olive oil
Reserved bones and scraps from quail
2 garlic cloves, sliced
3 cups fruity red wine
2 cups roasted chicken stock
1 tablespoon cold unsalted butter,
   diced
Kosher salt and freshly ground pepper

To Make the Quail:

- Using a sharp knife, remove the leg section from each quail. Remove the wing tips and French the remaining wing section on each quail; reserve all bones and trim. Divide each leg section into two. Remove the thigh bone and French the leg bone. Lay the legs skin-side down and season lightly with salt and pepper. Place 1 tablespoon of cranberry relish into each thigh section. Fold the thigh over onto the leg and pull excess skin over to seal in the relish. Wrap each snugly with plastic and refrigerate for 1 hour.
- Remove the stuffed legs from the refrigerator and discard the plastic. Gently dust each leg in the flour, shaking off any excess flour. Dip the legs into the eggs and then thoroughly coat with panko. Place the breaded legs in a small dish and set aside until serving. When ready to serve, heat oil to 350°F.; fry the legs until golden brown. Drain on paper towels and season lightly with salt.
- Place the foie gras in a food processor and puree. With the motor running, add the cognac and heavy cream. Remove from the food processor and season the mixture with salt and pepper. Divide the mixture into 4 equal portions. Place one portion into each of the quail breasts. Lay out the squares of caul fat and season them lightly with salt and pepper. Place each stuffed quail breast skin-side down on a square. Gently warp the breasts in the fat and trim off any excess with scissors. Refrigerate the wrapped breasts for 1 hour.
- When ready to serve, preheat the oven to 350°F. Place a large sauté pan over medium heat. Add the olive oil and heat for 2 minutes. Place the breasts in the pan skin-side down and cook until golden brown, about 2 minutes. Flip the breasts, then place the pan in the oven and bake until the quail is just cooked through, about 7 minutes.

To Make the Red Wine Reduction:

- Place a 1-quart saucepan over medium-high heat for 2 minutes. Add the olive oil and heat until the oil just begins to smoke. Add the reserved quail bones and trim and cook, stirring occasionally, until the bones are golden brown. Add the garlic and cook 2 more minutes. Deglaze the pan with the wine. Simmer until the wine is reduced and thick enough to coat the back of a spoon. Add the roasted chicken stock and continue to simmer until the mixture is again thick enough to coat the back of a spoon.
- Strain the sauce through a fine-mesh sieve into a small saucepan. Reheat the sauce just before serving, remove from the heat, and whisk in the cold butter, whisking until it is melted. Season with salt and pepper.

To Finish and Serve:

- Warm 4 dinner plates. Place a ring mold in the center of each and fill with wild rice. Place 1 quail breast on top of each mound of rice and place 2 quail legs on each plate. Divide haricot verts and mushrooms between the plates and arrange them around the rice and quail. Gently spoon the red wine reduction over the quail breasts and serve immediately.

CHEF'S NOTES

- Chef Moosmiller serves this dish with Cranberry Wild Rice (see page 231) and Haricot Verts and Mushrooms (see page 232)

Roasted Pork Loin with Chorizo Crisps, Clam Butter Sauce and Pork Rillettes

Chef Edward G. Leonard, CMC
Serves 4

Pork Rillettes:

2 garlic cloves

1 teaspoon five-spice powder

1 tablespoon kosher salt,
plus more to taste

1/2 teaspoon fresh cracked pepper,
plus more to taste

1 pound boneless pork shoulder,
cut into 1 1/2-inch pieces

1/2 pound skinless pork fatback,
cut into 1/2-inch pieces

1/2 large carrot, peeled and
roughly chopped

1/2 sweet onion, peeled and
roughly chopped

5 sprigs flat-leaf parsley

1 bay leaf

1/3 cup dry sherry

2 cups pork or chicken stock

Pork Loin:

4 1/2 pounds boneless pork loin,
trimmed

Kosher salt and fresh cracked pepper

2 tablespoons olive oil

2 tablespoons unsalted butter

2 garlic cloves, unpeeled, smashed

2 shallots, unpeeled, quartered

1 sprig fresh rosemary

2 sprigs fresh thyme

Clam Butter Sauce:

1 tablespoon melted butter

1 tablespoon brunoise of chorizo

1 tablespoon minced shallot

1 tablespoon brunoise of carrot

1 tablespoon brunoise of peeled celery

16 manila clams

2 tablespoons dry sherry

1 cup clam broth

Leaves from 1 sprig fresh thyme

1/4 cup heavy cream

1 pound very cold diced unsalted butter

Kosher salt

Finish and Serve:

8 chorizo crisps

1/4 cup fried garlic chips

To Make the Pork Rillettes:

- Using a knife, mince and mash the garlic with the five-spice powder, 1 tablespoon of the kosher salt, and 1/2 teaspoon of the pepper.
- Preheat the oven to 325°F. Combine the diced pork and fatback in a cast-iron Dutch oven. Add the garlic and spice mixture and mix well. Add the carrot, onion, parsley, bay leaf, sherry and stock. Place over medium heat and bring to a simmer. Cover the pan, place in the oven, and cook until the meat is very tender, about 3 hours.
- Remove from the oven and drain the meat, reserving all of the liquid separately. Shred the meat and fat back finely and place it in a mixing bowl. Skim and reserve the fat from the cooking liquid. Add 1/2 cup of the cooking liquid to the shredded pork and season to taste with salt and pepper. When cooled, press the mixture lightly into a terrine. Cover with a 1/4-inch layer of the skimmed fat. Refrigerate for 8 hours.
- Remove the rillettes from the refrigerator at least an hour before service so they will come to room temperature.

To Make the Pork Loin:

- Preheat the oven to 325°F. Using butcher's string, tie the pork loin and season it on all sides with salt and pepper. Place a cast-iron skillet over medium heat and allow it to heat for 5 minutes. Add the olive oil and butter. Place the loin in the pan and cook until golden brown on all sides. Add the garlic, shallots, rosemary and thyme to the pan; baste the pork loin.
- Place in the oven and roast until the loin reaches the desired doneness, basting every 5 minutes.
- Once cooked, remove the loin from the oven and place on a wire rack. Allow to rest for 15 minutes.

To Make the Clam Butter Sauce:

- Place a stainless-steel saucepan over medium heat and add the melted butter and chorizo. Cook, stirring frequently, for 2 minutes. Add the shallot, carrot and celery and continue to cook, stirring often, until all the vegetables are cooked through. Add the clams and sherry. Cover the pan and cook gently until the clams have opened.
- Remove the clams from the pan. Remove the clam meats from the shells and reserve for service.
- Add the clam broth and thyme to the pan and simmer until the mixture has been reduced to 1/4 cup of liquid. Add the cream and reduce again until the mixture measures 1/4 cup.
- Reduce the heat to low and slowly whisk in the cold butter, forming an emulsified sauce. Season with salt and keep warm until serving. Before serving, add the clam meats back to the sauce and heat through.

To Finish and Serve:

- Warm 4 dinner plates. Place 3 or 4 pieces of potato on the right side of each plate in a straight line. Top each piece with 1/2 teaspoon of the pork rillettes. Spoon 4 clam meats and some sauce in the center of each plate. Slice the pork loin and shingle 4 slices to the left of the clams on each plate. Garnish each plate with 2 chorizo crisps and some of the fried garlic chips. Serve immediately.

CHEF'S NOTES

- Chef Leonard serves this dish with Potato Disks (see page 235).

Roast Pork Tenderloin with Cider Cream Sauce and Fall Flavors

Chef Mike Bush
Serves 4

Rice Medley:

2 teaspoons canola oil

2 tablespoons minced white onion

1 cup white rice

1 cup wild rice

4 3/4 cups warm chicken stock

1/4 cup dried cherries

1/4 cup toasted pine nuts

3 tablespoons unsalted butter

Brussel Sprouts:

10 Brussel sprouts

1/2 white onion, sliced

Oil as needed

Splash of dry sherry

1 tablespoon unsalted butter

Salt and freshly ground pepper

Sweet Potatoes:

2 sweet potatoes, peeled and
    turned or cut into medium dice

1 tablespoon olive oil

1 tablespoon maple syrup

1 tablespoon chopped parsley

Salt and freshly ground pepper

Cider Cream Sauce:

2 cups hard cider

1 shallot, sliced

1 cup heavy cream

1 1/2 tablespoons cider vinegar

1 tablespoon unsalted butter

Salt and freshly ground pepper

Crackers:

2 pieces white sandwich bread,
    crusts removed

1 tablespoon flax seeds

Pork:

2 teaspoons cracked pepper

2 teaspoons dried thyme

2 teaspoons granulated garlic

2 teaspoons kosher salt

1 pork tenderloin, about 1 1/2 pounds,
    sinew removed

3 tablespoons oil

Hawaiian sea salt

To Make the Rice Medley:

- Preheat a convection oven to 350°F. Place two small oven-proof saucepans on the stove over medium heat and add a teaspoon of the oil in each. Add a tablespoon of the onion to each and cook until softened. Add the white rice to one pan and the wild rice to the other and cook, stirring, 1 more minute. Add 2 cups of the warm chicken stock to the white rice and 2 3/4 cups of the stock to the wild rice. Season with salt. When the stock comes to a simmer, cover the pans and place them in the oven. Bake until the rice is tender, about 25 minutes for the white rice, 45 minutes for the wild rice.
- Combine the rices and stir in the cherries, pine nuts and butter. Keep warm.

To Make the Brussel Sprouts:

- Bring a 2-quart saucepan 2/3 filled with salted water to a boil. With a paring knife, remove and discard the tough outer leaves of each sprout. Trim the bottom of each and cut an X into the stem. Drop the sprouts into the boiling water and cook until bright green and just tender, about 5 1/2 minutes. Drain the sprouts and cool them in ice water. Drain again and cut each spout in half.
- Place a sauté pan over high heat and caramelize the onion in a little oil, stirring constantly. Deglaze the pan with sherry; set aside until serving. When ready to serve, add the Brussel sprouts, butter, and salt and pepper to taste to the pan and reheat.

To Make the Sweet Potatoes:

- Preheat a convection oven to 350°F. and place a small oven-proof sauté pan inside to heat up. When hot, add the potatoes and oil to the pan and return it to the oven. After 8 minutes, shake the pan to toss the potatoes. Continue to roast until the potatoes are tender when poked with a toothpick.
- Toss the potatoes with the maple syrup, parsley and salt and pepper and keep warm.

To Make the Cider Cream Sauce:

- In a small saucepan, combine the cider and shallot and simmer until the liquid is reduced to 1/2 cup. Add the cream and reduce until you have about 3/4 cup of liquid. Strain the sauce and stir in the vinegar, butter and salt and pepper.

To Make the Crackers:

- Preheat a convection oven to 250°F. Sprinkle the bread with the flax seeds and use a rolling pin or pasta roller to flatten the slices until they are very thin. Cut each slice into 2 long triangles. Place a rolling pin on a sheet pan and lay the triangles over the rolling pin to get a curve. Bake until crisp, about 5 minutes.

To Make the Pork:

- Combine the pepper, thyme, garlic and salt and rub the mixture over the pork. Let sit for at least 30 minutes.
- Preheat a convection oven to 350°F. Place a medium sauté pan over medium-high heat and add the oil. When hot, sear the pork on all sides. Transfer the pork to a sheet pan and bake until cooked to medium (145 to 150°F. on an instant-read thermometer), 12 to 15 minutes. Allow to rest 5 minutes before slicing.

To Finish and Serve:

- Place a scoop of rice medley on each plate and top with slices of pork. Sprinkle with a little sea salt. Tuck a cracker behind the last piece of pork. Place some of the cream sauce next to the pork and serve with the Brussel sprouts and potatoes.

Roasted Cobia Shank with Smoked Bacon Savoy Cabbage

Chef Joachim Buchner, CMC
Serves 4

Cobia Shanks:

4 cobia shanks (cut from the tail section
of the fish)

Salt and freshly ground pepper

Seafood seasoning (either Old Bay or
Spice de Cosette)

1/4 cup olive oil

1 shallot, sliced

2 garlic cloves, sliced

1 sprig fresh thyme

2 tablespoons unsalted butter

4 tablespoons white wine

Juice of 1 lemon

Cabbage:

1/2 cup diced smoked bacon

1/4 cup thinly sliced sweet onion, such
as Vidalia or Maui Sweets

Caraway seeds

2 cups julienned and blanched savoy
cabbage

1 spice sachet made with bay leaves,
whole cloves, lemon zest and juniper
berries wrapped in cheesecloth

Salt and freshly ground pepper

1 cup heavy cream

Cornstarch or potato starch if needed

Finish and Serve:

Crisp bacon (optional)

Herbed potatoes (optional)

To Make the Cobia Shanks:

- Preheat the oven to 350° F. Season the cobia with salt, pepper and seafood seasoning. Heat the oil in a large skillet over high heat and sear the cobia on all sides until lightly browned. Reduce the heat to medium; add the shallot, garlic, thyme and butter and sauté until the shallot and garlic are tender, occasionally basting the cobia with the fat in the pan.
- Deglaze the pan with the wine and lemon juice, transfer the pan to the oven and continue roasting until the fish is cooked through. Remove from the oven and let rest in a warm place.

To Make the Cabbage:

- Put the bacon in a large cold pot, place over medium-low heat, and cook, stirring frequently, until it begins to render its fat. Turn the heat up to medium and continue cooking until it becomes crispy. Remove the bacon from the pot with a slotted spoon and set aside.
- Add the onion to the hot bacon fat in the pot and sauté until softened. Add the caraway seeds and cook for a minute or two. Add the cabbage, spice sachet, and salt and pepper. Continue to cook for 2 minutes. Reduce the heat and add the heavy cream. Simmer gently, uncovered, until the cream is thickened and the cabbage is soft. Return the crispy bacon to the pot and season again with salt and pepper. If the cabbage is too watery, stir in a slurry of cornstarch or potato starch to thicken it slightly.

To Finish and Serve:

- Place some cabbage on each plate, top with a cobia shank, and garnish the plate with crisp bacon and herbed potatoes.

Roasted Lamb Loin with Lavender Honey Glaze and Truffled Spring Vegetables

Chef Scott A. Fetty
Serves 4

Lavender Honey Glaze:

2 tablespoons mashed roasted garlic

1 cup lavender honey

2 tablespoons sherry vinegar

2 tablespoons tomato paste

1 tablespoon Dijon mustard

1/2 teaspoon herbes de Provence

Salt

Lamb Loin:

1 lamb loin (approximately 3 pounds), trimmed

2 tablespoons roasted garlic oil

1 tablespoon herbes de Provence

Sea salt and cracked pepper

Lavender honey glaze (see recipe above)

Vegetables:

4 tablespoons truffle butter

Water as needed

8 baby carrots or turned carrots, blanched and shocked

16 baby green beans, trimmed

1/4 cup fresh green peas, blanched and shocked

8 fingerling potatoes, diced and blanched

8 yellow pattypan squash (optional), trimmed and blanched

Sea salt and freshly ground pepper

Finish and Serve:

Black Hawaiian sea salt (optional)

BEVERAGE RECOMMENDATION

Côtes du Rhône or Spanish Rioja

To Make the Lavender Honey Glaze:

- Combine all the ingredients in a small saucepan and cook over low heat for 10 minutes. Set aside.

To Make the Lamb Loin:

- Rub the lamb with the garlic oil and sprinkle with the herbes de Provence and salt and pepper. Marinate for 1 hour.
- Preheat the oven to 375°F. Place a large skillet over medium heat and sear the lamb until caramelized. Transfer the meat to a roasting pan fitted with a rack and roast until the lamb reaches an internal temperature of 110°F, then begin basting the lamb with the glaze. Continue to roast, basting frequently, until the lamb reaches 130°F.
- Transfer the meat to a cutting board, allow it to rest for 10 minutes, and baste again with the glaze. Thinly slice the meat.

To Make the Vegetables:

- Melt the truffle butter in a large skillet and add a little water to create an emulsion. Add the carrots, green beans, peas, potatoes and squash and heat until the vegetables are warmed. Season with salt and pepper.

To Finish and Serve:

- Divide the lamb and vegetables between 4 plates and sprinkle with black sea salt. Spoon some of the leftover glaze around the lamb and serve.

CHEF'S NOTES

- Lavender honey and truffle butter can be found in most specialty markets.
- Most butchers and meat purveyors will be happy to trim the lamb loin for you if you ask.

Roasted Organic Chicken Breast, Confit of Leg, Roasted Salsify and Carrots with Balsamic Sauce

Chef Edward G. Leonard, CMC
Serves 4

Chicken Leg Confit:

4 chicken legs, thigh attached

1 tablespoon kosher salt

1/2 teaspoon freshly cracked
black pepper

10 cloves garlic, peeled

4 bay leaves

4 sprigs fresh thyme

1 1/2 teaspoons black peppercorns

4 cups rendered chicken fat or olive oil

Chicken Breast:

4 organic half chicken breasts,
wing section attached

1/4 cup olive oil

1/4 cup unsalted butter

Kosher salt and freshly
cracked black pepper

1 sprig fresh thyme

Potato Puree:

1 pound Yukon gold potatoes, peeled

1 1/2 teaspoons kosher salt,
plus more to taste

1/2 cup heavy cream

6 tablespoons unsalted butter, softened

Finish and Serve:

12 slices fried salsify

4 roasted cipollini onions

To Make the Chicken Leg Confit:

- Place the chicken legs on a platter skin-side down. Sprinkle with the salt and pepper. Place the garlic, bay leaves and thyme on top of two of the chicken legs. Place one of the remaining legs on top of each, flesh side to flesh side. Wrap the leg pairs in plastic and refrigerate for 12 hours.
- Preheat the oven to 200°F. Unwrap the chicken. Remove the garlic, bay leaves and thyme and place them in a cast-iron Dutch oven. Rinse the chicken legs under cold running water to remove the salt. Pat them dry with paper towels. Place the legs skin-side down in the Dutch oven and sprinkle evenly with the peppercorns. Add the chicken fat or olive oil, cover, and bake until the meat pulls away from the bones, 12 to 14 hours.
- Remove the chicken from the fat. Strain the fat and refrigerate for later use. Gently pick the meat from the chicken legs, being sure to remove and discard all skin, bones and sinew. Place the pulled chicken in an ovenproof dish along with 1/4 cup of the strained fat; cover and reserve. When ready to serve, place the dish in a preheated 350°F. oven and bake until the chicken is warmed through.

To Make the Chicken Breast:

- Preheat the oven to 350°F. Using a sharp knife, french the chicken breasts by removing all meat and skin from the wing sections. Heat a large, heavy skillet over medium-high heat for 3 minutes. Add the oil and butter. Once the butter is melted and begins to bubble, add the chicken breasts skin-side down to the pan. Season the breasts with salt and pepper. Continue to cook the chicken until the skin is crispy and golden brown, about 5 minutes. Turn the chicken over and season again with salt and pepper. Add the thyme and baste the chicken breasts. Place the skillet in the oven and roast the chicken until it is cooked through.
- Transfer the chicken to a rack and allow to rest 5 minutes. Reserve in a warm place until serving.

To Make the Potato Puree:

- Cut the potatoes into large pieces and place them in a stock pot. Add the 1 1/2 teaspoons kosher salt and pour in cold water to cover the potatoes by 2 inches. Place the pot over medium-high heat and simmer until the potatoes are tender, about 20 minutes.
- Heat the cream in a small saucepan until it boils and then remove it from the heat. Drain the potatoes and immediately transfer them to a food mill placed over a mixing bowl. Add the softened butter to the potatoes and pass them through the mill. Stir in the heated cream. Season with salt and keep warm until serving.

To Finish and Serve:

- Warm 4 dinner plates. Place about 4 ounces of the hot potato puree just to the left of center on one of the plates. Gently place a chicken breast on the potato puree. Place 3 pieces salsify next to the chicken breast and top with 3 roasted carrots, making a triangular stack. Place 1 ounce of the reheated chicken confit just in front of the vegetables. Place one roasted onion next to the chicken confit. Gently spoon balsamic sauce over the chicken breast and over the roasted onion and garnish the plate with fried salsify. Repeat with the remaining 3 plates.

CHEF'S NOTES

- Chef Leonard serves this dish with Balsamic Sauce (see page 225) and Roasted Salsify and Carrots (see page 236).

Roasted Veal Loin, Marrow and Parmesan Sauce, Eggplant and Veal Rib Quenelles and Soufflé of Carrot and Truffle

Chef Edward G. Leonard, CMC
Serves 4

Veal Rib and Eggplant:

1 rack veal ribs, trimmed

Kosher salt and freshly cracked pepper

2 tablespoons olive oil

3 tablespoons diced onion

1 tablespoon diced carrot

1 tablespoon diced celery

1 garlic clove, sliced

1 tablespoon tomato paste

1 cup red wine

2 cups veal stock

2 sprigs fresh thyme

1 bay leaf

2 peppercorns

1 small eggplant, diced, salted and drained

Marrow and Parmesan Sauce:

1 teaspoon olive oil

2 tablespoons bone marrow

2 shallots, minced

1/3 cup white wine

1 cup veal stock

1 tablespoon heavy cream

1 bay leaf

1/3 cup grated Parmigiano-Reggiano

Salt and freshly ground pepper

Veal Loin:

1/4 cup olive oil

1 pound veal loin, cleaned

Salt and freshly ground pepper

1/4 cup unsalted butter

2 shallots, unpeeled, quartered

2 garlic cloves, unpeeled, crushed

1 sprig fresh rosemary

1 sprig fresh sage

Finish and Serve:

8 truffle slices

Coarse sea salt

4 dried carrot slices

To Make the Veal Rib and Eggplant:

- Cut the rack into single ribs and season them with salt and pepper. Place a heavy rondeau over medium heat and heat 1 tablespoon of the oil for 2 minutes. Add the ribs and brown evenly on both sides. Remove from the pan and set aside.

- Add the onion, carrot, celery and garlic to the pan and cook, stirring occasionally, until the vegetables are lightly caramelized. Add the tomato paste and continue to cook, stirring constantly, for 5 minutes. Deglaze the pan with the red wine and simmer until the liquid is reduced by half. Add the stock, thyme, bay leaf and peppercorns and bring to a simmer over medium heat. Add the ribs back to the pan and cover the top of the pan tightly with aluminum foil.

- Preheat the oven to 300°F. Bake the ribs until the meat pulls away easily from the bones, 1 to 2 hours. Remove the ribs from the sauce, cool slightly, and pull all meat from the bones. Set aside. Strain the cooking liquid through a fine-mesh sieve and set aside separately.

- Heat the remaining tablespoon of oil in a sauté pan for 2 minutes. Add the eggplant and sauté until lightly browned. Add the rib meat and enough of the strained cooking liquid to moisten the mixture. Season with salt and pepper. Cover and set aside until serving.

To Make the Marrow and Parmesan Sauce:

- Place a 1-quart saucepan over medium heat. Add the oil and heat for 2 minutes. Add the marrow and brown lightly. Add the shallots and cook for 2 minutes, stirring often. Add the wine and reduce by half. Add the stock, cream and bay leaf and reduce by half. Add the cheese and whisk until incorporated. Season with salt and pepper, strain through a fine-mesh sieve and set aside until serving.

To Make the Veal Loin:

- Preheat the oven to 350°F. Place a heavy skillet over medium heat and allow to heat for 5 minutes. Add the oil and heat 2 minutes more. Season the veal with salt and pepper and place in the heated skillet. Add the butter, shallots, garlic, rosemary and sage and continue to cook, basting, until the veal is golden brown on the bottom, about 3 minutes. Flip the veal and continue to cook, basting, until it is browned on the other side, about 2 minutes. Transfer the skillet to the oven and roast until the veal reaches the desired doneness. Place the veal on a cutting board and let rest for 10 minutes before slicing.

To Finish and Serve:

- Heat 4 serving plates. Place a soufflé to left of center on each plate and garnish with sliced truffle. Using 2 spoons, form the eggplant and rib meat mixture into 4 quenelles and place one on each plate at 6 o'clock. Gently spoon about 1/4 cup of the marrow sauce onto the center of each plate. Slice the veal loin into 12 slices and place 3 slices in the center of each serving plate. Sprinkle the veal with sea salt and garnish the plates with dried carrots.

CHEF'S NOTES

- Chef Leonard serves this dish with Carrot and Truffle Soufflé (see page 227).

Roulade of Duck with Foie Gras and Pistachio, Ragout of White Beans and Duck Confit, Broccolini and Natural Jus

Chef Timothy R. Prefontaine, CSC
Serves 4

Broccolini:

1 bunch Broccolini, trimmed

1 tablespoon very finely diced bacon

1 teaspoon minced shallot

3 tablespoons chicken stock

1 tablespoon unsalted butter

Salt and freshly ground pepper

Jus:

1 duck carcass, quartered, skin removed

2 teaspoons canola oil

1 cup diced mirepoix

6 fresh thyme sprigs

1 star anise pod

2 bay leaves

8 peppercorns

1/2 cup Madeira

2 tablespoons tomato paste

1 quart duck stock or double-strength
   chicken stock

Cold unsalted butter, diced

Salt and freshly ground pepper

Roulade:

Four 2-ounce slices foie gras

Salt and freshly ground pepper

Meat from one duck leg and thigh

1/2 cup heavy cream

Zest of 1 orange, chopped

Dried black trumpet mushrooms,
   rehydrated, drained, patted dry
   and coarsely chopped

1 teaspoon chopped fresh thyme leaves

1 teaspoon chopped parsley leaves

1/4 cup pistachios, coarsely chopped

Toasted pâté spice as needed

4 slices prosciutto

2 duck breasts

To Make the Broccolini:

- Blanch the Broccolini in salted water for about 1 minute, then immediately cool in ice water. Drain.
- Sauté bacon over medium heat until rendered and almost crispy. Add Broccolini and shallot and sauté 1 minute. Add stock and simmer until almost dry. Stir in butter and season with salt and pepper to taste.

To Make the Jus:

- Preheat oven to 425° F. Place the carcass on a small sheet pan and roast until browned, about 30 minutes.
- In a medium saucepan, heat the oil and caramelize the mirepoix. Add the thyme, star anise, bay leaves and peppercorns and cook 1 more minute. Deglaze the pan with the Madeira and cook until reduced by half. Stir in the tomato paste and cook for 1 more minute. Add the duck bones and stock. Simmer for 1 hour, skimming any foam that forms on the surface of the liquid. Strain, return the liquid to a clean saucepan, and continue simmering, skimming if needed, until the liquid is reduced by 2/3. Strain again, return to the pan, and whisk in cold butter until the jus reaches the desired consistency. Season with salt and pepper.

To Make the Roulade:

- Soak the foie gras, then cut it in pieces about as long as a duck breast. Season it with salt and pepper and cook in a very hot pan just until seared. Place on paper towels to soak up any excess fat. Set aside.
- Place the duck leg meat in a food processor and process until smooth. Add the cream and pulse. Pass the mixture through a tamis into a bowl set over ice. Fold in the zest, mushrooms, thyme, parsley and pistachios and season with pâté spice, salt and pepper; poach a small amount of the mixture and taste for seasoning. Transfer to a piping bag fitted with a plain tip.
- Moisten a work surface with a clean wet towel and lay out a piece of plastic wrap, smoothing out as many wrinkles as possible. Place two slices of prosciutto on the plastic and cover with a duck breast. Place a piece of foie gras on top of the breast, then pipe mousse on top and spread until it is about 1/4-inch thick. Roll the breast and prosciutto up, enclosing the filling and wrapping securely in the plastic. Refrigerate until ready to cook.
- Preheat the oven to 350° F. Place the roulade on a rack in the oven and roast until it reaches an internal temperature of 155° F., about 9 minutes. Allow to rest.

To Finish and Serve:

- Spoon about 1/3 cup of ragout onto each of 4 plates. Slice the roulade and arrange around the ragout. Place the broccolini on each plate and drizzle about 3 tablespoons jus onto each plate.

CHEF'S NOTES

- Chef Prefontaine serves this dish with Ragout (see page 235).

Saffron Cod with Shrimp Toast, Ribbon Vegetables and Red Pepper-Shellfish Broth

Chef Richard Rosendale, CEC
Serves 4

Broth:

1/4 cup olive oil

1 shallot, thinly sliced

1 white onion, thinly sliced

1 carrot, thinly sliced

2 cloves unpeeled garlic, crushed

2 tablespoons tomato paste

1/2 cup seafood trimmings (lobster shells, shrimp shells, and fish bones)

1/4 cup white wine

1 cup red bell pepper juice

1 1/2 cups fish fumet or water

1 spice sachet made of a bay leaf, tarragon, basil, peppercorns, parsley, and fennel seeds

Salt and freshly ground pepper

Shrimp Toast:

2 teaspoons unsalted butter

1 tablespoon chopped shallot

6 medium shrimp, peeled and deveined

1 egg yolk

1/4 cup heavy cream

Salt and freshly ground pepper

4 slices high-quality crusty white bread

Oil for deep frying

Ribbon Vegetables:

1 zucchini

1 yellow squash

1 carrot

Olive oil

Salt and freshly ground pepper

Cod:

Four 5-ounce pieces cod fillet

1 tablespoon saffron tea (see Chef's Notes)

Salt and freshly ground white pepper

1 tablespoon olive oil

1 lemon

1 tablespoon chopped parsley

To Make the Broth:

- Heat the olive oil in a pan and add the shallot, onion, carrot and garlic. Add the tomato paste and cook 5 minutes. Stir in the seafood trimmings. Deglaze the pan with the white wine. Stir in the pepper juice. Stir in the fumet and sachet and cook over low heat for 20 minutes. Strain, discard the solids, and season the broth with salt and pepper.

To Make the Shrimp Toast:

- Heat the butter in a small skillet and add the shallot. Cook until the shallot is just translucent. Cool.
- Mince the shrimp until you have a fine paste, then place in a bowl set over a larger bowl of ice. Emulsify the egg yolk into the shrimp. Stir in the cream, shallots and salt and pepper. Spread the paste over the bread. Fry in 350°F. oil until golden brown, then drain on paper towels.

To Make the Ribbon Vegetables:

- Slice the vegetables into long thin ribbons on a European mandoline. Dip the ribbons into boiling salted water just until softened. Drain and toss with olive oil, salt and pepper.

To Make the Cod:

- Preheat the oven to 350°F. Brush the cod fillets with the saffron tea and sprinkle with salt and white pepper. Drizzle a little olive oil over the fish and bake until just cooked through. Remove from the oven, drizzle with lemon juice and sprinkle with parsley.

To Finish and Serve:

- Ladle the broth into shallow bowls. Place a shrimp toast and piece of cod in each. Twirl the ribbon vegetables together and place them around the cod.

CHEF'S NOTES

- Saffron tea is made by heating water and saffron threads together to extract the color and flavor from the threads. The amount of saffron you use is a personal choice. You can refrigerate leftover tea in an airtight container for future use.

Seared Pheasant Breast, Creamed Cabbage, Mustard Späetzle and Calvados Cider Sauce

Chef Wayne Sieve
Serves 4

Späetzle:

1 large egg

1 1/4 cups milk

1 cup all-purpose flour

1 tablespoon whole-grain mustard

1 tablespoon Dijon mustard

1 tablespoon chopped parsley

1 tablespoon unsalted butter

Salt and freshly ground pepper

Calvados Sauce:

1 cup Calvados

1 cup apple cider

2 cups chicken stock

Cabbage:

1 head Savoy cabbage

2 slices hickory smoked bacon, diced

1 shallot, minced

1 garlic clove, minced

2 carrots, peeled and sliced

1 1/2 cups heavy cream

1 tablespoon unsalted butter

Salt and freshly ground pepper

Pheasant:

4 half pheasant breasts, frenched

Salt and freshly ground pepper

1 tablespoon unsalted butter

Finish and Serve:

1 cup French green beans,
trimmed and blanched

To Make the Späetzle:

- Whisk the egg and milk together in a medium bowl. Gradually stir in the flour, stirring until incorporated. Stir in the whole-grain mustard, Dijon mustard and parsley.
- Bring a pot of salted water to a boil. Place a metal colander over the pot, place the dough in the colander, and use a rubber spatula to press the dough through the holes in the colander and into the boiling water. Cook the späetzle until most of it floats, 3 to 4 minutes. Strain out the späetzle and cool it in an ice-water bath.
- To serve, heat a nonstick skillet over medium-high heat. Melt the butter and add the späetzle. Cook, stirring frequently, until browned. Season with salt and pepper.

To Make the Calvados Sauce:

- Combine the Calvados and apple cider in a small saucepan and simmer until reduced to about 1/2 cup. Add the stock and continue to simmer until reduced to the desired consistency.

To Make the Cabbage:

- Cut the cabbage in half and slice out the core. Cut the halves into wedges and then chop them coarsely. Blanch the chopped cabbage briefly in boiling water, then cool in an ice-water bath.
- Heat the bacon in a sauté pan until it renders its fat. Add the shallot and garlic and cook, stirring, 1 minute. Add the carrots and the blanched cabbage and cook, stirring, for 4 minutes. Add the cream and cook until slightly thickened. Season with salt and pepper.

To Make the Pheasant:

- Pat the pheasant dry with paper towels and season with salt and pepper. Heat a skillet over medium-high heat. Add the breasts skin-side down and let cook for 1 minute. Add the butter and continue to cook until the skin is brown and crispy. Turn the breasts over, lower the heat to low, and cook until the breasts reach the desired doneness.

To Finish and Serve:

- Reheat the green beans. Spoon some sauce on each plate and top each with a pheasant breast. Place cabbage, späetzle and green beans on plates and serve.

Chef Sieve finalizes a plating arrangement on the junior team cold food display.

Seared Sea Bass, White Bean Ravioli and Roasted Tomato-Kalamata Olive Ragout

Chef Mike Palazzola, CC

Serves 4

Ravioli:

1/2 cup white beans, soaked overnight and simmered in chicken stock until tender

1 tablespoon finely diced ham

1 teaspoon chopped roasted garlic

1 tablespoon heavy cream

1/2 teaspoon truffle oil

Pasta dough of choice for making ravioli (see Chef's Notes)

Ragout:

2 Roma tomatoes, quartered and seeded

2 tablespoons balsamic vinegar

2 tablespoons olive oil

1 teaspoon chopped fresh thyme

2 tablespoons pitted, halved kalamata olives

1 tablespoon drained capers

2 tablespoons white wine

2 tablespoons unsalted butter

Salt and freshly ground pepper

Fennel-Lime Slaw:

2 jalapeño peppers, seeded and cut into fine julienne

1/2 cup finely julienned fennel

1 lime, segmented

1/4 cup cilantro leaves

1/4 cup lemon juice

Olive oil

Salt and freshly ground pepper

Sea Bass:

Four 4-ounce pieces skinless sea bass fillet

Extra-virgin olive oil

Lemon juice

Chopped fresh flat-leaf parsley

Salt and freshly ground pepper

To Make the Ravioli:

- In a food processor, combine the cooked beans, ham, roasted garlic and cream and blend until smooth. Stir in the truffle oil.
- Roll pasta dough out into 2 thin sheets in a pasta machine or by hand and place on a lightly floured surface. Drop bean filling by tablespoons in a grid across one sheet of the dough. Cover with the other half of the dough, press down around the mounds of filling, and cut out ravioli. Seal the edges. When ready to serve, cook in salted boiling water and keep warm.

To Make the Ragout:

- Preheat the oven to 350° F. In a small, ovenproof sauté pan, combine the tomatoes, balsamic, olive oil and thyme and roast in the oven for about 10 minutes. Add the olives, capers and wine and cook until the pan is deglazed. Remove from the heat and stir in butter. Season with salt and pepper to taste.

To Make the Fennel-Lime Slaw:

- In a small bowl toss together jalapeño, fennel, lime segments, cilantro leaves, lemon juice and olive oil. Season with salt and pepper.

To Make the Sea Bass:

- Marinate the sea bass in olive oil, lemon juice, and parsley. When ready to cook, season the fish with salt and pepper and cook until browned on the outside and just cooked through.

To Finish and Serve:

- Place a piece of sea bass on each plate and top with some of the slaw. Place a few ravioli on each plate and top with the ragout.

CHEF'S NOTES

- Chef Palazzola makes his pasta dough using 8 ounces flour, 1 teaspoon olive oil, 1 tablespoon milk, 1 egg and 6 egg yolks.

Smoked Salmon Belly and Crab Terrine

Chef Jamie P. Keating, CCC
Serves 4

Terrine:

3 cups spinach leaves

1/8 cup hot salted water

1 1/2 pounds salmon belly,
    skin removed

1 cup kosher salt

6 ounces scallops (U10-20 dry pack)

2 large egg whites

1 tablespoon heavy cream

Cayenne

Fine sea salt

6 ounces lump crabmeat

6 chives, finely chopped

Saffron Cream:

6 ounces sour cream

1 teaspoon saffron tea

1/2 teaspoon truffle oil

Kosher salt

Prosciutto Rings:

1 thin sliced prosciutto

Vegetable oil cooking spray

Navy Bean Ragout:

1 cup navy beans, soaked overnight

2 slices bacon

6 cups chicken stock

1 cup brunoise of mirepoix, blanched

2 teaspoons chili powder

2 cloves roasted garlic, mashed

1 roasted shallot, mashed

1 teaspoon chopped fresh dill

Kosher salt

Fried Quail Eggs:

4 quail eggs

1 cup seasoned flour

1 large egg, lightly beaten

1 cup cornflakes, finely ground

Oil for frying

Asparagus:

1 tablespoon unsalted butter

24 asparagus spears, blanched

1/2 teaspoon chopped garlic

Salt and freshly ground pepper

To Make the Terrine:

- Combine the spinach and hot salted water and blend until smooth. Chill over an ice bath. Trim the salmon belly to fit in a terrine. Season the belly heavily on both sides with the kosher salt and let sit for 5 minutes. Rinse under cold water. Line the terrine with plastic wrap, place salmon in the bottom of the terrine and refrigerate.

- Combine the scallops, egg whites and cream and puree. Season with cayenne and sea salt and divide between two bowls. Add the spinach to one bowl and the crabmeat and chives to the other. Layer the spinach mousse over the salmon, then layer the crab mixture on top. Top with a piece of blue Styrofoam and wrap tightly in plastic wrap, tying off each end. Poach in a 140°F. water bath until an instant-read thermometer inserted into the terrine registers 134°F. Immediately chill the terrine in an ice bath.

To Make the Saffron Cream:

- Whisk together all the ingredients. Pass the mixture through a fine-mesh sieve. Refrigerate.

To Make the Prosciutto Rings:

- Preheat the oven to 350°F. Cut thin strips of the prosciutto and wrap the strips around a metal cylinder that has been coated with vegetable oil spray. Wrap a small piece of parchment paper around the cylinder and secure it. Bake for 10 minutes.

To Make the Navy Bean Ragout:

- In large saucepan, combine the beans, bacon and stock. Simmer until the beans are tender. Strain the beans, discard any excess stock, and toss the beans with the mirepoix, chili powder, garlic, shallot and dill. Season with salt.

To Make the Fried Quail Eggs:

- Gently crack the quail eggs into the seasoned flour. Dredge in the flour and then coat in beaten egg. Dredge in cornflakes. Fry in 325°F. oil until golden brown. Drain on paper towels.

To Make the Asparagus:

- In sauté pan, melt the butter. Add the asparagus and garlic and cook until heated through. Season with salt and pepper.

To Finish and Serve:

- Unwrap the terrine and smoke it over hickory for 3 minutes. Slice the terrine.

- Create a template design for the plates; place the template on each plate and spread the saffron cream across it. Place terrine slices on each plate. Divide the quail eggs, prosciutto rings and ragout between the plates and serve with frisée salad.

CHEF'S NOTES

- Chef Keating serves this dish with Frisée Salad (see page 231).

Soy-Soaked Salmon with Steamed Vegetables

Chef Kevin Taylor
Serves 4

Salmon:

2 tablespoons soy sauce

1 teaspoon sugar

1 teaspoon salt

1 teaspoon ground black pepper

4 pieces salmon fillet, each about 6
ounces

1 tablespoon vegetable oil

Broth:

1 teaspoon sesame oil

1 teaspoon minced ginger

1 teaspoon minced garlic

3/4 cup chicken or fish stock

1/2 cup soy sauce

2 tablespoons rice-wine vinegar

1 tablespoon sugar

1 tablespoon miso paste

Vegetables:

1 large carrot, cut into 12 pieces

12 snow peas

1 celery stalk, cut into 12 pieces

1 leek, sliced

1/2 zucchini, halved and sliced

Rice:

3/4 cup sushi rice

1 1/2 cups water

Slaw:

1/4 cup julienned cucumber

2 tablespoons bean or radish sprouts

1 tablespoon canola oil

1 teaspoon rice-wine vinegar

1/2 teaspoon black sesame seeds

Pinch sugar

Pinch salt

Finish and Serve:

White sesame seeds

BEVERAGE RECOMMENDATION

Tsingtao Chinese beer

To Make the Salmon:

- Whisk together the soy sauce, sugar, salt and pepper. Add the salmon and marinate for about 1 hour.
- When ready to cook, heat a large, heavy skillet over medium-high heat. Add the oil. When hot, cook the salmon until seared and just warmed in the center, 3 to 4 minutes per side.

To Make the Broth:

- In a medium saucepan, heat the oil over medium heat. Add the ginger and garlic and cook, stirring, 2 minutes. Add the remaining ingredients and simmer 20 minutes.
- Strain the broth and discard the solids. Reheat before serving if necessary.

To Make the Vegetables:

- Steam each vegetable separately until just tender, about 6 minutes for the carrot, 4 minutes for the snow peas and celery, and 2 minutes for the leek and zucchini. Cool each vegetable in ice water after cooking. Drain and pat dry.

To Make the Rice:

- Combine the rice and water in a medium saucepan. Bring to a boil, lower heat, cover and cook at a bare simmer for 18 minutes. Remove from the heat and let sit, covered, for 10 minutes before serving.

To Make the Slaw:

- Combine all the ingredients in a small bowl.

To Finish and Serve:

- Place a scoop of rice in each serving bowl and surround each with vegetables. Place a piece of salmon on top and pour hot broth into the bowls. Top each portion with slaw, sprinkle with white sesame seeds, and serve.

CHEF'S NOTES

- Specialty ingredients like miso paste and black sesame seeds are available at Asian grocery stores.

Truffle Risotto with Pecorino, Sunny-Side Free-Range Eggs and White Asparagus

Chef Edward G. Leonard, CMC
Serves 4

Asparagus Sauce:

2 tablespoons olive oil

2 stalks asparagus, sliced

1 shallot, diced

1/3 cup dry sherry

1/3 cup white wine

1 bay leaf

1/2 cup chicken stock

1/4 cup veal jus

2/3 cup heavy cream

1/4 cup crème fraîche

1 tablespoon unsalted butter, diced

Sea salt

Truffle Risotto:

1 tablespoon unsalted butter

1 small shallot, minced

1/2 cup Vialone Nano rice

1/2 cup white wine

2 tablespoons truffle juice

1 cup chicken stock

1/4 cup heavy cream

3 tablespoons grated pecorino

1 tablespoon cold butter, diced

1 small fresh winter truffle, thinly sliced

Salt and freshly ground black pepper

Asparagus:

1 teaspoon unsalted butter

16 stalks white asparagus, peeled and
    blanched

Salt and freshly ground pepper

Sunny-Side Eggs:

4 large free-range eggs

1/4 cup olive oil

Salt and freshly ground pepper

Finish and Serve:

1 winter truffle, thinly sliced

Shaved pecorino

To Make the Asparagus Sauce:

- Place a 1-quart saucepan over medium heat. Add the oil, asparagus and shallot. Cook, stirring frequently, for 2 minutes. Add the sherry, white wine and bay leaf and simmer until the liquid is reduced by half. Add the stock and veal jus and reduce again by half. Stir in the cream and simmer for 2 minutes. Strain the sauce through a fine-mesh sieve. Whisk in the crème fraîche and butter. Season with salt and keep warm until serving.

To Make the Truffle Risotto:

- In a 2-quart saucepan, melt the butter. Add the shallot and cook, stirring, until translucent. Add the rice and cook, stirring constantly, for 2 minutes. Add the wine and continue to cook, stirring, until all the wine has evaporated. Add the truffle juice and half of the stock. Cook over medium heat, stirring constantly, until all the liquid has been absorbed by the rice. Add the remaining stock and cook, stirring, until all of the liquid has again been absorbed.
- Add the cream, pecorino, cold diced butter and truffle and continue to cook until the butter is incorporated. Season with salt and pepper.

To Make the Asparagus:

- Place a large skillet over medium heat and melt the butter. Add the blanched asparagus and sauté until heated through, about 2 minutes. Season with salt and pepper. Keep warm until serving.

To Make the Sunny-Side Eggs:

- Place a nonstick skillet over medium heat and allow to heat for 2 minutes. Pour the oil into the pan. Place four egg rings in the skillet and crack one egg into each ring. Cook until all of the whites of the eggs are almost set. Remove from the heat and season with salt and pepper.

To Finish and Serve:

- Warm 4 serving plates. Place a square mold in the center of one plate and fill with a quarter of the risotto. Remove the mold and repeat with the remaining risotto on the remaining plates. Place one egg on top of each pile of risotto. Using 4 asparagus stalks for each plate, form a square border around each egg. Drizzle the sauce lightly over and around the risotto. Garnish the top of each egg with sliced truffle and shaved pecorino and serve immediately.

Truffled Lobster Tail over Risotto Milanese with Buttered Baby Vegetables and Crispy Serrano Ham

Chef Michael Matarazzo
Serves 4

Truffled Lobster:

4 raw Maine lobster tails, shells removed

1 teaspoon Activa powder

8 very thin slices fresh black truffle

2 tablespoons extra-virgin olive oil

1 teaspoon white truffle oil

1 sprig fresh tarragon

1/2 teaspoon kosher salt

Pinch freshly ground pepper

Crispy Serrano Ham:

2 thin slices Serrano ham

Risotto Milanese:

1 tablespoon olive oil

1 teaspoon finely minced shallot

1/2 teaspoon finely minced garlic

3/4 cup Arborio rice

1/4 cup white wine

1 1/4 cups chicken stock, plus more if needed

20 saffron threads

1/3 cup fresh shelled peas

2 tablespoons Mascarpone cheese

2 tablespoons grated Parmesan

1 tablespoon unsalted butter

Salt and freshly ground pepper

Baby Vegetables:

1 tablespoon olive oil

6 baby carrots, sliced obliquely

1/4 cup chicken stock

4 baby zucchini, sliced on the bias

1 yellow squash, scooped into small balls with a melon baller

1/2 teaspoon fresh thyme leaves

1 tablespoon unsalted butter

Salt and freshly ground pepper

Finish and Serve:

Good-quality extra-virgin olive oil

To Make the Truffled Lobster:

- Place the lobster tails on a work surface. Wrap the Activa powder in cheesecloth and sprinkle it very lightly over the bottom side of the tails. Shingle the slices of the black truffle down 2 of the tails. Set the other tails on top of the first 2, lining up the smaller tapered ends over the thicker ends so that they are even in thickness. Roll both of the pairs of tails up firmly in plastic wrap so you have two perfect cylinders. Puncture any air holes with a needle. Refrigerate the lobster overnight so the Activa will set and hold them together securely.
- The next day, remove the tails from the plastic wrap and transfer to a vacuum bag. Add the olive oil, truffle oil, tarragon, salt and pepper; vacuum seal the bag, making sure the lobster tails are not touching. Place the sealed bag in a 140°F. water bath for about 30 minutes.

To Make the Crispy Serrano Ham:

- Square off the sides of the ham slices and cut each in half lengthwise. Place the slices in a food dehydrator until crisp, about 3 hours.

For the Risotto Milanese:

- Heat the olive oil in a small saucepan. Add the shallot and garlic and cook briefly. Add the rice and stir about 2 minutes. Deglaze the pan with the white wine and reduce by 2/3. Add about a third of the chicken stock along with the saffron threads. Cook, stirring, until almost dry. Repeat with another third of the stock. Add the remaining stock and peas and cook again, stirring almost constantly, until most of the stock has evaporated and the rice grains are tender; add more stock if necessary.
- When the rice is just tender, remove the pan from the heat and fold in the Mascarpone, Parmesan and butter. Season with salt and pepper and serve.

For the Baby Vegetables:

- Heat the olive oil in a medium sauté pan over medium heat. Add the carrots and sauté briefly. Add the stock and simmer gently until the carrots begin to soften. Add the zucchini and yellow squash, raise the heat, and continue to cook until the stock is reduced to a glaze. Remove from the heat and stir in the thyme and butter. Season with salt and pepper.

To Finish and Serve:

- Lay a line of the risotto across the center of each plate. Slice the lobster into 1/2-inch-thick medallions and place 3 slices on top of the risotto. Spoon the vegetables across the front of the risotto. Lay the crispy ham across the top of the lobster and finish the plates with a drizzle of some really good olive oil.

The Ultimate Short Ribs

Chef Joachim Buchner, CMC
Serves 4

Braised Short Ribs:

4 beef short ribs
Zest of 2 oranges
Zest of 2 lemons
Salt and freshly ground pepper
1/4 cup olive oil
1/2 cup unsalted butter
2 medium onions, chopped
1/2 cup diced carrot
1/2 cup diced leek
1/2 cup diced celery
4 garlic cloves, minced
1 cup diced tomato
3 tablespoons tomato paste
1 1/2 cups dry red wine
1 spice sachet made with peppercorns,
　　bay leaf, thyme sprig and parsley
　　sprig wrapped in cheesecloth
3 cups veal stock

Garnishes (optional):

Cipollini onions
Haricot verts
Potatoes
Artichoke hearts
Red bell pepper

To Make the Braised Short Ribs:

- Rub the short ribs with the orange and lemon zest, sprinkle with salt and pepper, and place in a large bowl. Cover and refrigerate for 2 hours.
- Place the oil in a large, heavy-bottomed saucepan and place over medium-high heat. When the oil is just at the smoking point, carefully add the short ribs and cook until browned on all sides. Remove the ribs from pan and set aside. Add the butter, onions and carrot to the pan and sauté until the vegetables are lightly caramelized. Add the leek, celery and garlic and continue to cook the vegetables until soft. Stir in the diced tomato and tomato paste and cook for a few minutes more.
- Preheat the oven to 325°F. Deglaze the pan with the wine and cook until the wine is reduced by about three-quarters. Add the spice sachet and the veal stock. Bring to a simmer, add the short ribs back into the pan and cover with a layer of parchment paper. Cover the pan with a lid and seal the top with aluminum foil. Place in the oven and braise for approximately 3 hours, or until tender.
- Remove the short ribs from the pan and keep warm. Strain the sauce, discard the solids, and reduce the sauce over medium heat until thickened.

To Finish and Serve:

- Serve the ribs and sauce with your choice of garnishes: cipollini onions, haricot verts, potatoes, artichokes or red bell pepper.

*Chefs Buchner, Leonard and Carroll discuss
last minute plating changes.*

Veal Steak and Lobster Sausage with Baked White and Green Asparagus and Baby Fennel

Chef Joachim Buchner, CMC
Serves 4

Lobster Sausage:

2 feet hog or sheep casing

1 cup raw lobster meat

1 large egg white

Salt and freshly ground white pepper

1/2 cup heavy cream

1/2 cup diced cooked lobster meat

1 teaspoon finely chopped parsley

1 teaspoon finely chopped fresh chervil

2 teaspoons finely sliced chives

1 teaspoon Dijon mustard

Court bouillon or fish stock for
     poaching the sausage

Veal Steak:

4 (6-ounce) veal New York strip steaks

Sea salt and cracked black pepper

3 tablespoons clarified butter

2 tablespoons cold unsalted butter

1 shallot, sliced

Herb sprigs of choice

Vegetable Gratin:

2 tablespoons unsalted butter, plus
     more for coating dishes

2 tablespoons all-purpose flour

1 cup milk or vegetable stock, heated

1/4 cup heavy cream

1 cup grated white Cheddar cheese

1 teaspoon fresh thyme leaves

Salt and freshly ground pepper to taste

12 white asparagus spears, bottoms
     peeled, spears blanched

12 green asparagus spears, bottoms
     peeled, spears blanched

4 heads baby fennel, blanched

8 yellow carrots, peeled and blanched

1/2 cup shelled edamame (green soy
     beans) or fava beans

1/2 cup coarse fresh bread crumbs

2 tablespoons Parmesan cheese

Garnishes (optional):

Demi-glace

White sauce

Fennel fronds

Fresh herbs

To Make the Lobster Sausage:

- Rinse the casings well, then soak in cold water, refrigerated, for 24 hours.
- Combine the raw lobster with the egg white in a food processor and pulse until the lobster is very finely puréed and pink in color. Season with salt and pepper, then slowly pour the cream in through the feed tube while the motor is running. Transfer the mixture to a chilled mixing bowl and fold in the cooked lobster meat, parsley, chervil, chives and mustard. Adjust the seasoning of the mixture if necessary. Scrape the mixture into a pastry bag fitted with a plain tip and pipe it into the casing. Chill the sausages a few hours before cooking.
- Poach the sausages in simmering court bouillon or fish stock for about 4 minutes. Finish them by grilling or pan frying just before serving.

To Make the Veal Steak:

- Preheat the oven to 350°F. Season the veal with salt and pepper. Heat the clarified butter in a large skillet over high heat, add the veal, and sear on all sides until lightly browned. Reduce the heat to medium; add the butter, shallot and herbs to the pan and cook, basting the veal with the butter, until the shallots are soft. Transfer to the oven and continue roasting until the veal is cooked to the desired doneness. Let rest in a warm place.

To Make the Vegetable Gratin:

- Preheat the oven to 350°F. In a medium skillet, melt the butter over medium-low heat. Stir in the flour and cook, stirring, for 2 minutes. Whisk in the hot milk or vegetable stock and whisk until the sauce is smooth and thickened. Whisk in the cream and continue to cook, uncovered, for 20 minutes.
- Stir in the Cheddar, thyme, salt and pepper, stirring just until the cheese melts. Remove the sauce from the heat.
- Butter the sides and bottom of individual baking dishes and place a layer of the white asparagus, green asparagus, fennel, carrots and edamame on the bottom of each. Spoon 3 to 4 tablespoons of the cheese sauce over each. Sprinkle the bread crumbs and Parmesan over the tops and bake until golden.

To Finish and Serve:

- Place the vegetable gratin on the bottom of serving plates or bowls. Top with sausage and sliced veal. Garnish each plate with demi-glace, white sauce, fennel fronds and fresh herbs if desired.

Veal Tenderloin Filled with Foie Gras and Mushrooms, Served with Root Vegetables and Soft Polenta

Chef Joachim Buchner, CMC
Serves 4

Veal:

3 slices foie gras

Kosher salt and freshly ground pepper

1 tablespoon olive oil

1 cup assorted forest mushrooms,
    cleaned and trimmed

2 shallots, chopped

6 tablespoons unsalted butter

1 tablespoon chopped fresh
    herbs of choice

4 slices Parma ham, plus more if needed

1 veal tenderloin,
    trimmed and butterflied

Steak seasoning blend,
    such as Chefnique

1 cup baby spinach

1/4 cup clarified butter

1 sprig fresh thyme

1 sprig fresh rosemary

2 shallots, quartered

3 whole garlic cloves

Root Vegetables:

1/4 cup vegetable stock

1 shallot, finely diced

2 tablespoons unsalted butter

2 tablespoons sugar

2 cups assorted root vegetables (such as
    baby carrots, celery root, rutabaga,
    turnips, baby onions), blanched

Salt and freshly ground pepper

1 teaspoon chopped fresh marjoram

Soft Polenta:

2 cups chicken stock

1 cup heavy cream

1/2 teaspoon freshly grated nutmeg

1 teaspoon salt

Pinch ground white pepper

1/3 cup polenta

2 tablespoons semolina

1/2 cup Taleggio cheese

2 tablespoons unsalted butter

Chopped fresh herbs

Finish and Serve:

1 cup veal demi-glace

To Make the Veal:

- Season the foie gras with salt and pepper. Heat a large, heavy-bottomed pan over high heat and quickly sear the foie gras on both sides until nicely browned. Set aside.
- In a medium skillet, heat the oil over medium-high heat and sauté the mushrooms until lightly browned. Add the chopped shallots and 2 tablespoons of the butter and continue to cook until the mushrooms are tender. Add the chopped herbs and set aside to cool.
- Lay a sheet of plastic wrap down on a work surface, and lay the ham over the wrap. Place the veal tenderloin on top of the ham and sprinkle it with steak seasoning. Place the spinach, foie gras and mushrooms on top of the veal. Use the plastic wrap to roll the veal into a log, covering the outside with the Parma ham (make sure all the veal is covered; use more ham if necessary). Wrap up tightly to form a cylindrical shape. Place in the freezer to chill.
- After the meat is fully chilled, preheat the oven to 350°F. Remove the plastic wrap and secure the veal roll with butcher's twine. When ready to cook, heat the clarified butter in a heavy skillet and brown the veal on all sides. Add the remaining 4 tablespoons butter, the thyme and rosemary sprigs, the quartered shallots, and garlic to the pan. Continue to cook, basting the veal with the butter in the pan, until the veal is nicely browned. Transfer the skillet to the oven and continue cooking until the veal reaches the desired doneness, about 8 minutes. Remove from the oven and let rest before carving.

To Make the Root Vegetables:

- Heat the stock in a large skillet and add the shallot, butter, sugar and vegetables. Simmer until most of the stock has evaporated. Season the vegetables with salt, pepper and marjoram. Keep warm.

To Make the Soft Polenta:

- In a heavy saucepan, combine the stock and cream and bring to a boil. Whisk in the nutmeg, salt and pepper. Slowly whisk in the polenta and semolina. Switch to a spoon, and cook over low heat for 20 to 30 minutes, stirring often, until the mixture is thick and the grains of polenta are tender. Fold in the cheese, butter and herbs. Serve immediately or reserve.

To Finish and Serve:

- Place some warm polenta on each plate. Slice the veal and place a few slices on top of the polenta along with some vegetables. Surround with a little demi-glace.

Wild Pheasant Ravioli

Chef Joseph M. Leonardi
Serves 4

Ravioli:

2 large eggs

1 1/3 cups all-purpose flour

Salt

1 tablespoon olive oil

2 shallots, finely diced

1 pound pheasant breast, diced

1/2 cup Madeira

1 cup heavy cream

1 cup grated Parmigiano-Reggiano

Red Onion Jam:

3 tablespoons sugar

1 tablespoon olive oil

1 red onion, finely sliced

2 tablespoons red-wine vinegar

1 cup Cabernet Sauvignon

Apple Cider:

1 cinnamon stick

3 black peppercorns

1 bay leaf

Pinch red pepper flakes

4 cups apple cider

2 shallots, finely diced

Finish and Serve:

2 tablespoons unsalted butter

Blanched ribbons of leek

1 tablespoon toasted pecans

4 fried sage leaves

To Make the Ravioli:

- Stir together the eggs and flour and season with salt. Knead the dough for 10 minutes, adding water or more flour as needed. Let the dough rest for 30 minutes.
- In a sauté pan, heat the oil and sweat the shallots for 5 minutes. Add the pheasant and cook, stirring frequently, just until cooked through. Deglaze the pan with the Madeira and cook until all the alcohol has evaporated. Add the heavy cream and bring the mixture to a simmer. Stir in the cheese. Chill the mixture completely and season with salt.
- Divide dough in half. Roll half the dough out thinly in a pasta machine or by hand and place on a lightly floured surface. Drop the pheasant filling by tablespoons in a grid across the dough. Roll out the remaining dough and place it on top. Press down around the mounds of filling and cut out ravioli with a round pastry cutter. Seal by using an egg wash and by pinching the edges together.

To Make the Red Onion Jam:

- In a medium sauté pan, cook the sugar and oil together until caramelized and golden brown. Add the onion and cook for 3 minutes. Stir in the vinegar and Cabernet. Cook the mixture until all liquid has evaporated. Keep warm.

To Make the Apple Cider:

- In a medium dry skillet set over medium heat, toast the cinnamon stick, peppercorns, bay leaf and pepper flakes until fragrant. Add the cider and shallots. Simmer the mixture until reduced by about half. Strain, discard the spices, and reserve the cider.

To Finish and Serve:

- Cook the ravioli in salted water for 4 minutes. Drain. Heat the apple cider in a pan and whisk in the butter to emulsify. Gently toss ravioli and leek ribbons in the apple cider. Divide between plates, place the warm onion jam on top of the ravioli and garnish with the pecans and fried sage.

Apple Layers

Chef Mariana Delgado Gambini, CPC
Serves 4

Chiffon Cake:

2 1/4 **cups** cake flour

1 1/2 **cups** sugar

1 **tablespoon** baking powder

1/2 **teaspoon** plus 1 pinch salt

1/2 **cup** vegetable oil

7 **large** egg yolks

3/4 **cup** fresh orange juice

2 **tablespoons** freshly grated orange zest

2 **teaspoons** vanilla extract

9 **large** egg whites

1 **teaspoon** cream of tartar

Poached Apples:

6 **medium** Gala apples, cored from the
    bottom and peeled

1/2 lemon

1/2 **gallon** apple cider

1 **cup** packed light-brown sugar

1 cinnamon stick

2 **whole** cloves

Vanilla Mousse:

900 **grams** milk

3 vanilla beans, split

270 **grams** sugar

342 **grams** egg yolks

24 sheets gelatin, bloomed

1,500 **grams** heavy cream

Finish and Serve:

Thin layers of crispy phyllo

Short dough cookies

Small apples filled with vanilla mousse

Caramel sauce

Chocolate sauce

Chocolate garnishes and other
    garnishes of choice

To Make the Chiffon Cake:

- Preheat the oven to 325°F. Sift the flour, 3/4 cup of the sugar, the baking powder, and the 1/2 teaspoon salt into a large bowl. In another bowl, whisk together the oil, yolks, orange juice, zest and vanilla, then whisk this mixture into the flour mixture, whisking until the batter is smooth.

- In the bowl of an electric mixer, beat the egg whites and the pinch of salt until foamy. Add the cream of tartar and continue beating until the whites hold stiff peaks. Gradually beat in the remaining 3/4 cup sugar, beating until the mixture makes stiff, glossy peaks. Stir a third of the whites into the batter to lighten it. Fold in the remaining whites gently but thoroughly. Spoon the batter into a 10-inch greased and floured cake pan. Bake in the middle of the oven until a cake tester inserted into the center of the cake comes out clean, about 1 hour. Invert the pan immediately onto a rack and let the cake cool completely in the pan upside down on the rack.

To Make the Poached Apples:

- Put the apples in a wide, heavy 5-quart pot and add the lemon, cider, brown sugar, cinnamon and cloves. Cover and bring to a boil over medium heat (this will take 25 to 30 minutes). Remove from the heat and cool the apples in the cider, covered. Finely dice the apples before serving.

To Make the Vanilla Mousse:

- In a medium saucepan, heat the milk, vanilla beans, and half the sugar until small bubbles form around the edges of the pan. In a large bowl, beat the yolks with the remaining sugar. Whisking constantly, very slowly whisk the hot milk into the yolks. Pour the mixture back into the saucepan and cook over medium-low heat, stirring constantly with a wooden spoon, until the mixture thickens enough to coat the back of the spoon. Immediately remove from the heat and strain into a large bowl. Add the bloomed gelatin and stir until dissolved. Place the bowl over an ice bath and stir until cooled but not set. Whip the cream to medium peaks and fold it into the cooled custard.

To Finish and Serve:

- Cut out rectangles of the chiffon cake and cover the top of the cake with the diced poached apples. Place a rectangle of crispy phyllo sheets on top of the apples and cover the top with dollops of the vanilla mousse. Place another layer of phyllo on top. Place a stack on each plate. Place a cookie on each plate and top with an apple filled with mousse. Pipe sauces on plates and garnish as desired.

Chocolate Custard with Coconut Sorbet and Chocolate-Banana Empanadas

Chef Jennifer Kopp, CEPC
Serves 4

Chocolate Custards:

1/2 cup milk

1 tablespoon cocoa powder

2 tablespoons plus 1 teaspoon sugar

1/3 cup plus 1 tablespoon heavy cream

1/3 cup chopped dark chocolate couverture

1 large egg

2 large egg yolks

1/2 teaspoon rum

1/2 teaspoon vanilla extract

Coconut Sorbet:

2 cups Coco Lopez cream of coconut

1 1/2 cups coconut milk

3/4 cup hot water

2 tablespoons rum extract

Chocolate-Banana Empanadas:

2 cups all-purpose flour

1/2 cup unsalted butter

1 large egg

1/4 cup water

1/4 cup sugar

1 1/2 teaspoons cinnamon

1/4 teaspoon ground ginger

1/4 teaspoon salt

1 banana

1/4 cup chocolate pieces

Canola oil for frying

Finish and Serve:

Raspberry powder (optional)

Chocolate garnish (optional)

To Make the Chocolate Custards:

- Preheat the oven to 300°F. Place the milk in a saucepan. Stir together the cocoa powder and half of the sugar and whisk it into the milk. Whisk in the cream and bring the mixture to a boil. Place the chocolate in a bowl and pour in a third of the hot milk mixture. Whisk to incorporate, then pour in another third. Whisk again and add the remaining milk.

- In a bowl, whisk together the egg, yolks, remaining sugar, rum and vanilla. Whisk in the chocolate mixture. Strain the mixture through a fine-mesh sieve. Grease small ovenproof ceramic or metal cups and place them in a glass or metal baking dish that is approximately twice the height of the cups. Pour custard mix into each cup. Pour water into the baking dish until water comes about halfway up the sides of the cups. Bake until the custard is set and a paring knife inserted into the center of each comes out clean. Remove the custards from the water bath and refrigerate until completely cold and set.

To Make the Coconut Sorbet:

- In a medium saucepan, bring the cream of coconut, coconut milk and water to a boil. Strain through a fine-mesh sieve, stir in the rum extract, and chill the mixture. Freeze the sorbet according to the manufacturer's directions for your ice-cream maker.

To Make the Chocolate-Banana Empanadas:

- Combine the flour and butter in the bowl of a food processor and pulse until the mixture resembles cornmeal. Add the egg and water and pulse just until combined. Form into a disk and refrigerate until chilled. Roll the chilled dough out on a floured surface. Cut the dough into circles 2 inches in diameter.

- In a bowl, combine the sugar, cinnamon, ginger and salt. Cut the banana into small pieces and toss in the spice mixture; save remaining spice mixture. Place a few chocolate pieces and banana pieces on the bottom half of each dough circle. Fold the top of each over to enclose the filling. Seal the edges and press down all around the edges of the dough with the tines of a fork. (If the edges don't seal firmly, paint the edges of the dough circles with water or egg white before folding in half.) Deep fry the empanadas until golden brown. Drain on paper towels. Coat the empanadas in the remaining spice mixture and serve warm.

To Finish and Serve:

- Dust the plates with raspberry powder. Place a cookie on each plate. Unmold the custards by running a paring knife around the inside of the custard cups and then inverting them over the cookies. Put fruit salsa and a warm empanada on each plate. Top the custards with quenelles or scoops of coconut sorbet. Garnish with chocolate decorations and serve.

CHEF'S NOTES

- Chef Kopp serves this dish with Cinnamon-Almond Cookies (see page 229) and Fruit Salsa (see page 232)

- Raspberry powder is available in some specialty stores. You can also substitute raspberry sauce or thinned raspberry jam for the powder to make your plate design.

Chocolate Meets Raspberries

Chef Mariana Delgado Gambini, CPC
Serves 4

Chocolate Mousse:

4 large eggs, separated

1/2 cup sugar

1/4 cup unsalted butter

1/4 cup water

1 teaspoon instant espresso powder

8 ounces bittersweet or semisweet chocolate, chopped

Raspberry Gelée:

8 ounces raspberry puree

2 gelatin sheets, bloomed

1/2 vanilla bean

8 ounces champagne

Finish and Serve:

Chocolate curls

Chocolate sticks

Chocolate ganache for brushing

Raspberry sauce

Fresh raspberries

To Make the Chocolate Mousse:

- In a large metal bowl, whisk together the yolks, 1/4 cup of the sugar, the butter, water and espresso powder. Set the bowl over a saucepan of simmering water (do not let bowl touch water) and whisk constantly until a thermometer inserted into mixture registers 160°F., about 3 minutes. Add the chocolate and whisk until melted and smooth. Turn off the heat; leave the bowl with the chocolate mixture over the hot water.

- In the bowl of an electric mixer, beat the egg whites until they hold soft peaks. Gradually beat in remaining 1/4 cup sugar, beating until the mixture is stiff and glossy. Remove the bowl of the chocolate mixture from the water. Fold a third of the egg whites into the warm chocolate mixture to lighten it. Fold in the remaining whites. Transfer the mixture to a pastry bag and pipe it into the desired molds. Freeze overnight.

To Make the Raspberry Gelée:

- Heat about a third of the puree up until just hot. Remove from the heat and stir in the bloomed gelatin, stirring until dissolved. Add the vanilla bean and remaining puree. Pour the mixture through a fine-mesh sieve into a large bowl; discard the solids. Pour into serving glasses and refrigerate until set. Top off glasses with cold champagne just before serving.

To Finish and Serve:

- Unmold a mousse on each plate and garnish with chocolate curls. Place a glass of raspberry gelée directly across from mousse. Balance a chocolate stick between glass and mousse. Using a paint brush, brush chocolate ganache on the plates. Pipe raspberry sauce where desired and garnish plates with raspberries.

Long hours and teamwork pay off with gold for the pastry team of chefs Root, Aoyama, Gambini and Camato.

Coconut Panna Cotta, Passion Fruit Curd with Macerated Mango and Strawberry, and Vanilla Pound Cake with Flambé Peaches

Chef Mellisa K. Root
Serves 8

Passion Fruit Curd:

412 grams egg yolks

488 grams sugar

266 grams passion fruit puree

6 grams gelatin, bloomed

453 grams unsalted butter

Coconut Panna Cotta:

960 milliliters heavy cream

300 grams desiccated
unsweetened coconut

96 grams sugar

3 grams gelatin, bloomed

Mango and Strawberry:

Corn syrup

Vanilla bean

Pineapple sage

Fresh ripe mango, peeled,
seeded and finely diced

Fresh strawberries,
hulled and finely diced

Vanilla Sauce:

480 milliliters milk

480 milliliters heavy cream

1 vanilla bean

160 grams egg yolks

180 grams sugar

Vanilla Pound Cake:

500 grams unsalted butter, at room
temperature

500 grams brown sugar

500 grams eggs, at room temperature

500 grams all-purpose flour

Flambé Peaches:

50 grams unsalted butter

500 grams dark-brown sugar

50 grams orange juice

2 vanilla beans

Dash cinnamon

3 peaches, peeled, flesh removed
with a melon baller

50 grams Maker's Mark
Kentucky bourbon

35 grams 151 proof rum

To Make the Passion Fruit Curd:

- Whisk together the yolks, sugar and puree in a microwavable bowl. Microwave in 1-minute intervals until the mixture starts to thicken. Continue heating in 30-second intervals until the mixture is very, very thick. Cool. Whisk in the bloomed gelatin and the butter, whisking until emulsified. Pour into individual molds and refrigerate until set.

To Make the Coconut Panna Cotta:

- Heat the cream until bubbles form around the edges of the saucepan. Add the coconut and allow to steep for at least 3 hours. Strain through a fine-mesh strainer and use a ladle to force all the liquid through the strainer. Discard the solids. Warm up the liquid and add the sugar and the bloomed gelatin. Stir until the sugar and gelatin are dissolved. Pour this mixture over the top of the passion fruit curd in the molds and refrigerate until this layer is set.

To Make the Mango and Strawberry:

- Infuse the corn syrup with vanilla and pineapple sage; strain out the solids. Combine the mango and strawberries, coat the mixture with a little of the corn syrup and macerate.

To Make the Vanilla Sauce:

- Heat the milk, cream and vanilla bean together until small bubbles form around the edges of the pan. In a medium bowl, whisk together the yolks and sugar until light and fluffy. Temper in the hot milk and return the mixture to the pan. Cook, stirring, until the mixture reaches 85°C. Strain through a fine-mesh sieve and cool. Transfer to a squeeze bottle.

To Make the Vanilla Pound Cake:

- Preheat the oven to 350°F. Beat the butter and brown sugar together until very light and fluffy. Slowly beat in the eggs. Stir in the flour. Pour the batter into greased ramekins. Bake until golden brown. Serve warm in the ramekins.

To Make the Flambé Peaches:

- Melt the butter in a large sauté pan and whisk in the brown sugar. Whisk in the orange juice, vanilla beans and cinnamon and bring to a boil. Add the peaches. Pour in the bourbon and rum and cook until the alcohol has burned off and the peaches are soft.

To Finish and Serve:

- Place some peaches on top of a piece of warm pound cake and drizzle with some of the juices in the pan the peaches cooked in. Place on a plate with a serving of the curd and panna cotta. Place mango and strawberry mixture to one side and dot the plate with the vanilla sauce. Garnish as desired.

Lemon Extravaganza

Chef Mellisa K. Root
Serves 8

Lemon Poppy Seed Cake:

448 grams almond paste

224 grams unsalted butter

196 grams sugar

3 lemons, zested

6 large eggs

56 grams Grand Marnier

63 grams cake flour

1 teaspoon baking powder

20 grams poppy seeds

Cream Cheese Mousse:

320 grams sugar

180 grams egg yolks

800 grams heavy cream

1,400 grams cream cheese

400 grams hot milk

27 grams gelatin, bloomed

White chocolate spray (optional)

Lemon Curd:

412 grams egg yolks

488 grams sugar

266 grams lemon puree

453 grams unsalted butter

Lemon-Vanilla Bean Pate Fruit:

15 grams pectin

230 grams sugar

200 grams lemon puree, warmed

100 grams glucose

Vanilla bean

12 grams citric acid solution 1:1

Fried red beet strips for garnish

Frozen Lemon Parfait:

750 grams milk

400 grams sugar

3 vanilla beans

500 grams egg yolks

200 grams trimoline

Zest from 4 lemons

2,000 grams heavy cream

To Make the Lemon Poppy Seed Cake:

- Preheat the oven to 350°F. Beat the almond paste, butter, sugar and zest together until smooth. Beat in the eggs one at a time. Beat in the Grand Marnier. When no lumps remain, beat in the flour, baking powder and poppy seeds. Pour onto a pan lined with a Silpat and bake at 350°F. until light golden brown. Remove from the oven and let cool completely before removing from the Silpat. Cut out the shape of the cake to fit into your chosen mold and reserve.

To Make the Cream Cheese Mousse:

- Cook the sugar in a saucepan until it reaches 121°C. Meanwhile, with an electric mixer, begin beating the egg yolks on high speed. Continue beating while slowly pouring the hot sugar into the yolks. Keep beating on high until cooled.
- In another bowl, whisk the cream and set aside. In a third bowl beat the cream cheese with the paddle attachment and slowly beat in the hot milk. Fold the cream cheese mixture into the egg yolk mixture and add the gelatin. Make sure everything is well mixed and fold in the whipped cream. Pour the mixture into molds. Place a piece of poppy seed cake on the surface of the mousse and press down gently so the edges are covered with mousse. Freeze all the way through before unmolding. Spray the frozen mousse with white chocolate if you desire.

To Make the Lemon Curd:

- Whisk together the yolks, sugar and lemon puree in a microwavable bowl. Microwave the curd until it starts to thicken, stopping and stirring at 1-minute intervals. Continue to microwave at 30-second intervals until the mixture becomes very, very thick. Allow to cool, then whisk in the butter. Cool fully, then pipe the mixture into empty spaces left in your mousse cake.

To Make the Lemon-Vanilla Bean Pate Fruit:

- In a saucepan, stir together the pectin and 30 grams of the sugar. Slowly stir in warm lemon puree. Bring to a boil, stir in the glucose, and bring back to a boil again. Add the vanilla bean and the remaining sugar and bring to a boil. Add the citric acid and cook until the mixture reaches 106°C. Pour into a thick mold and allow to set for one day before removing the paste and cutting it into squares of candy. Place one candy on the top of the mousse cake and garnish with fried beet strips.

To Make the Frozen Lemon Parfait:

- Combine the milk, sugar, vanilla beans, egg yolks, trimoline and lemon zest and steam the mixture over a bain marie until it reaches 85°C. Cool the mixture. Whip the cream and fold it into the cooled parfait base. Pour into molds and freeze.

To Finish and Serve:

- Place a cream cheese mousse cake, parfait topped with a meringue cookie, and marinated strawberries on each plate. Place 3 dots on the chocolate sauce on each plate and pull a brush through the dots to create a painted effect.

CHEF'S NOTES

- Chef Root serves this dish with Chocolate Sauce (see page 228), Marinated Strawberries (see page 233) and Meringue Cookies (see page 233).

Macadamia Nut Streusel Cake with Coconut Crème Brûlée, Pineapple Chips and Pina Colada Sorbet

Chef Jennifer Kopp, CEPC
Serves 4

Pineapple Chips:

1 pineapple, peeled
1 cup sugar
1 cup water
1/2 vanilla bean, seeded

Coconut Crème Brûlée:

1 cup heavy cream
3 large egg yolks
2 tablespoons sugar
1/2 teaspoon vanilla extract
1/2 teaspoon coconut compound

Pina Colada Sorbet:

1 cup fresh pineapple juice
1 cup coconut milk
3 tablespoons light rum
1/3 cup corn syrup
1/4 cup water

Crumb Topping:

1/4 cup brown sugar
2 tablespoons chopped
   macadamia nuts
1 teaspoon cinnamon
1 tablespoon unsalted butter, melted

Macadamia Nut Streusel Cake:

3 tablespoons sugar
3 tablespoons unsalted butter
1/4 teaspoon vanilla extract
1 large egg
1/2 cup all-purpose flour
1/4 teaspoon baking powder
1/4 teaspoon baking soda
Pinch salt
1/4 cup sour cream

Finish and Serve:

Cookie disks
Sugar for caramelizing the crème brûlées
Chocolate sticks (optional)
Diced pineapple, strawberries and mint
   (optional)

To Make the Pineapple Chips:

- Preheat the oven to 200°F. Slice the pineapple almost paper-thin using a mandoline. In a saucepan, bring sugar, water and vanilla bean to a boil. Add pineapple slices and cook until translucent, about 30 seconds. Drain well, place on a baking sheet covered with a Silpat and bake until dried and crisp, about 3 hours.

To Make the Coconut Crème Brûlée:

- Preheat the oven to 300°F. In a saucepan, scald the cream. In a mixing bowl, whisk together the egg yolks and sugar. Pouring in a thin, steady stream and whisking constantly, whisk the hot cream into the egg mixture. Whisk in the vanilla and coconut compound. Strain through a fine-mesh sieve.
- Set small ceramic cups in a glass or metal baking dish that is approximately twice the height of the cups. Pour custard into each cup. Pour water into the baking dish so that the water comes halfway up the sides of the cups. Bake until the custards are set and they don't ripple when the sides of the cups are tapped. Remove from the water bath and refrigerate until chilled and set.

To Make the Pina Colada Sorbet:

- Bring the pineapple juice to a boil in a stainless-steel saucepan. Whisk in the remaining ingredients. Strain through a fine-mesh sieve and refrigerate until chilled. Process the sorbet according to the manufacturer's instructions for your ice-cream maker.

To Make the Crumb Topping:

- Mix all ingredients until crumbly in texture.

To Make the Macadamia Nut Streusel Cake:

- Preheat the oven to 350°F. In the bowl of an electric mixer, cream together the sugar and butter. Beat in the vanilla. Beat in the egg. Combine the flour, baking powder, baking soda and salt. Add the dry ingredients to the bowl in 3 additions, alternating with additions of the sour cream.
- Scoop the batter into well-greased individual pans, filling them a quarter full. Sprinkle some of the crumb topping on top. Add more batter to pans to fill them three-quarters full, and top with another sprinkling of the crumb topping. Bake until cakes are firm and a toothpick inserted into the center comes out clean.

To Finish and Serve:

- On each plate, place a scoop of sorbet on a cookie disk. Sprinkle a thin layer of sugar on top of the crème brûlées and caramelize the sugar with a butane torch. Place a brûlée on each plate. Unmold the macadamia nut cakes and place one on each plate. Place a pineapple chip between each item. Garnish with a chocolate stick and diced pineapples, strawberries and mint and serve.

CHEF'S NOTES

- The pineapple chips can be made a few days ahead and stored in an airtight container.

Neapolitan Macaroons with Fresh Fruit, Champagne Gelée and Vanilla Foam

Chef Mellisa K. Root
Serves 8

Chocolate Ice Cream:
960 milliliters half-and-half
115 grams Valrhona cocoa powder
1 vanilla bean, split lengthwise
160 grams egg yolks
170 grams sugar
115 grams Valrhona dark chocolate, chopped

Vanilla Ice Cream:
960 milliliters half-and-half
2 vanilla beans, split lengthwise
210 milliliters egg yolks
284 grams sugar

Strawberry Ice Cream:
455 grams fresh hulled and chopped strawberries
255 grams sugar
960 milliliters half-and-half
210 milliliters egg yolks
120 grams raspberry puree

Champagne Gelée:
Fruits of choice (berries, seedless grapes, apricots, etc.)
24 grams gelatin, bloomed
200 grams sugar
1 liter champagne

Macaroons:
200 grams confectioners' sugar
200 grams almond flour
66 grams fresh egg white
Desired color or colors
160 grams granulated sugar
54 grams water
66 grams frozen egg white

Vanilla Foam:
1/2 liter fat-free milk
50 grams sugar
1 vanilla bean
5 grams lecithin

To Make the Chocolate Ice Cream:
- Heat the half-and-half, cocoa and vanilla bean until bubbles form around the edges of the pan. In a medium bowl, whisk together the yolks and sugar until light and fluffy. Temper the hot half-and-half into the egg mixture. Pour the mixture back into the pan and cook, stirring, until it reaches 85°C. Pour the mixture through a fine-mesh sieve and into a bowl with the chocolate. Burr mix the mixture and cool. Refrigerate overnight. Process according to the manufacturer's instructions for your ice-cream machine.

To Make the Vanilla Ice Cream:
- Heat the half-and-half and vanilla bean until bubbles form around the edge of the pan. In a medium bowl, whisk together the yolks and sugar until light and fluffy. Temper the hot half-and-half into the egg mixture. Pour the mixture back into the pan and cook, stirring, until it reaches 85°C. Pour the mixture through a fine-mesh sieve. Refrigerate overnight. Process according to the manufacturer's instructions for your ice-cream machine.

To Make the Strawberry Ice Cream:
- Place the strawberries in a saucepan with 115 grams of the sugar and cook until the mixture starts to thicken, about 10 minutes. Set aside to cool.
- Heat the half-and-half until bubbles form around the edges of the pan. In a medium bowl, whisk together the yolks and the remaining 140 grams sugar until light and fluffy. Temper in the hot half-and-half. Pour the mixture back into the pan and cook, stirring, until it reaches 85°C. Pour the mixture through a fine-mesh sieve. Chill the mixture and stir in the cooked strawberries and the raspberry puree. Refrigerate overnight. Process according to the manufacturer's instructions for your ice-cream machine.

To Make the Champagne Gelée:
- Slice a medley of fruits to the same thickness and lay them out artistically on a rimmed baking sheet lined with a Silpat. Combine the gelatin, sugar and a small amount of the champagne in a saucepan. Heat, stirring, just until the sugar and gelatin melt. Add to the rest of the champagne and pour over the berries. Refrigerate until firm. Cut into strips.

To Make the Macaroons:
- In the bowl of an electric mixer, combine the confectioners' sugar, almond flour and fresh egg white and mix with a paddle attachment on speed 1. Beat in color or colors. Set aside.
- Mix the granulated sugar and water together and bring the mixture to 121°C. Whisk the mixture into the frozen egg whites and beat until a medium peaked meringue forms. Fold the meringue into the almond mixture. Transfer to a pastry bag and pipe the batter in circles onto a baking sheet lined with a Silpat. Let the macaroons dry on the Silpat until each forms a dry skin on their surface. Bake at 135°C. for 11 minutes.

To Make the Vanilla Foam:
- Heat the fat-free milk until it is just warm to the touch. Stir in the sugar, vanilla bean and lecithin. Just before serving, burr mix until you have a large amount of foam.

To Finish and Serve:
- Place a scoop of each ice cream on each plate along with macaroons and a piece of the champagne jelée. Spoon some of the vanilla foam onto the jelée. Garnish the plates as desired.

Parfait Sampler

Chef Mellisa K. Root
Serves 8

RASPBERRY SHOOTERS

Raspberry Fool:

200 grams heavy cream

20 grams sugar

100 grams raspberry puree

Chocolate crouquant

Vanilla Cream:

960 milliliters heavy cream

96 grams sugar

2 vanilla beans

3 grams gelatin, bloomed

Berry Gelée:

500 grams red currant puree, strained

500 grams raspberry puree

100 grams sugar

24 grams gelatin, bloomed

Raspberries for garnish

White chocolate sticks for garnish

PINEAPPLE SHOOTERS

Pineapple Curd:

412 grams egg yolks

488 grams light-brown sugar

266 grams pineapple puree

453 grams unsalted butter

5 grams pineapple compound

Pineapple Compote:

300 grams sugar

100 grams unsalted butter

1 fresh golden pineapple, peeled, cored and diced

50 grams dark rum

1 cinnamon stick

Coconut Pastry Cream:

560 milliliters milk

400 milliliters unsweetened coconut milk

336 grams sugar

154 grams cornstarch

225 grams whole eggs

224 grams egg yolks

168 grams unsalted butter

200 grams toasted desiccated coconut

Fresh diced pineapple for garnish

Pineapple leaves for garnish

RASPBERRY SHOOTERS

To Make the Raspberry Fool:

- Whisk the cream until frothy. Slowly whisk in the sugar, whisking until the mixture holds stiff peaks. Gently fold in the puree. Pipe the mixture into the bottom of tall, thin serving glasses or shot glasses. Sprinkle with the crouquant. Refrigerate.

To Make the Vanilla Cream:

- Heat the cream, sugar and vanilla beans together in a saucepan until small bubbles form around the edges of the pan. Remove from the heat and let sit until the vanilla has infused the cream. Stir the bloomed gelatin into the cream, and allow to cool. Shortly before the mixture sets, pour it over the crouquant in the glasses. Refrigerate immediately.

To Make the Berry Gelée:

- Heat a small amount of the current puree in a saucepan and stir in the sugar and gelatin. Stir until smooth. Stir the mixture into the remaining purees. Spoon some of the mixture on top of the set vanilla in the glasses. Garnish each glass with raspberries and a white chocolate stick.

PINEAPPLE SHOOTERS

To Make the Pineapple Curd:

- Whisk together the yolks, sugar and pineapple puree in a microwavable bowl. Microwave the curd until it starts to thicken, stopping and stirring at 1-minute intervals. Continue to microwave at 30-second intervals until the mixture becomes very, very thick. Allow to cool, then whisk in the butter and pineapple compound. Divide between tall, thin serving glasses or shot glasses.

To Make the Pineapple Compote:

- Sprinkle a light layer of the sugar into a hot skillet and allow it to melt. As the sugar begins to caramelize, stir in more sugar with a heat-resistant spatula. When all the sugar is melted and you have a golden-brown caramel, stir in the butter. Stir in the pineapple. Continue to stir until the pan is deglazed. Stir in the rum and cinnamon stick.
- Preheat the oven to 325°F. Place the skillet in the oven and roast the pineapple until it is cooked through. Allow to cool, then spoon into the glasses over the curd.

To Make the Coconut Pastry Cream:

- Heat the milk and coconut milk together in a saucepan until bubbles form around the edges of the pan. In a small bowl, whisk the sugar and cornstarch together. Whisk the sugar mixture into the eggs and yolks. Whisking constantly, very slowly whisk the hot milk into the eggs. Return the mixture to the pan and bring to a full boil; boil for 3 minutes. Transfer the mixture to the bowl of an electric mixer fitted with a paddle attachment. Beat on speed 1 until the mixture is cool. Beat in the butter and coconut. Layer the mixture into the glasses on top of the pineapple compote. Top the parfaits with fresh diced pineapple and pineapple leaves.

CHEF'S NOTES

- Chef Root serves this sampler with Orange Shooters (see page 234) as well.

Pumpkin Spice Cake with Ginger Ice Cream and Brandied Fruit Compote

Chef Jennifer Kopp, CEPC
Serves 4

Pumpkin Spice Cake:

1 1/2 **large** eggs

1/2 **cup** sugar

1/3 **cup** canned pumpkin puree

1/2 **teaspoon** lemon juice

1/2 **teaspoon** vanilla extract

6 **tablespoons** all-purpose flour

1 **teaspoon** cinnamon

1/2 **teaspoon** baking powder

Tuile Cylinders:

1/2 **cup** unsalted butter

1/4 **cup** sugar

1/2 **cup** egg whites, warmed slightly

1/2 **teaspoon** vanilla extract

1 **cup** all-purpose flour

Ginger Ice Cream:

1 1/2 **cups** heavy cream

1 **cup** milk

1/4 **cup** sugar

2 **large** egg yolks

1/2 **teaspoon** ground ginger

1/4 **cup** diced candied ginger pieces

Brandied Fruit Compote:

1/2 **cup** unsweetened apple juice

1/4 **cup** diced dried apricots

1/4 **cup** dried cherries

1/4 **cup** golden raisins

1/4 **cup** dark raisins

2 **tablespoons** brandy

Finish and Serve:

Chocolate curves (optional)

Mint sprigs (optional)

To Make the Pumpkin Spice Cake:

- Preheat the oven to 375°F. In the bowl of an electric mixer, beat the eggs and sugar until fluffy and tripled in volume. Beat in the pumpkin, lemon juice and vanilla. Sift together the flour, cinnamon and baking powder and stir them into the pumpkin mixture.
- Scoop the batter into individual flexible silicone molds and bake until firm and springy, about 15 minutes. Cool completely, then remove the cakes from the molds.

To Make the Tuile Cylinders:

- Preheat the oven to 350°F. Combine the butter and sugar. Slowly beat in the egg whites and vanilla. Add the flour and blend until smooth. Spread the batter onto a baking sheet lined with a Silpat; make rectangles about 5 1/2 inches by 2 inches (use a template if you like). Bake until the batter is white and no longer shiny, about 2 minutes. Cool completely.
- When cooled, return the baking sheet to the oven and bake until the tuiles are golden, about 2 minutes. While still hot, peel them from the mat and wrap them around a small rolling pin or large dowel to form cylinders, pressing firmly at the seams. Let cool.

To Make the Ginger Ice Cream:

- In a saucepan bring the cream, milk and half of the sugar to a boil. In a medium bowl, whisk the yolks with the remaining sugar until smooth. Whisk in the ground ginger. Whisking constantly, slowly whisk the hot cream mixture into the egg yolks. Pour the mixture back into the saucepan and cook, stirring, until slightly thickened. Pour into a bowl and refrigerate until chilled.
- Freeze the chilled mixture in an ice-cream machine according to the manufacturer's directions. Transfer the ice cream to a plastic container and stir in the candied ginger pieces. Freeze until ready to serve.

To Make the Brandied Fruit Compote:

- In a medium saucepan, bring the apple juice to a boil. Add the apricots, cherries, light and dark raisins and simmer until the fruits are soft. Remove from the heat, pour the mixture into a bowl, and stir in the brandy. Cover the bowl with plastic wrap and let the compote steep until ready to serve.

To Finish and Serve:

- Spoon some warm compote into the bottom of each serving bowl. Place the cakes on top. Make quenelles or scoops of ice cream and place one inside each tuile cylinder and place them on top of the cakes. Garnish with chocolate curves and mint and serve.

CHEF'S NOTES

- If you don't have flexible silicone molds, you can also bake the cake batter in a greased and floured regular cake pan. When baked and cooled, cut out individual circles of cake.

Raspberry Financier Cream with Lemon-Scented Cheesecake and Fresh Berries

Chef Mellisa K. Root
Serves 8

Financier Cake:
500 grams unsalted butter
500 grams sugar
500 grams almond flour
6 large eggs
200 grams all-purpose flour
200 grams cornstarch
200 grams heavy cream

Raspberry Jelée:
1,000 grams raspberry puree
200 grams sugar
24 grams gelatin, bloomed

Vanilla Chantilly Cream:
1 liter heavy cream
1 vanilla bean, split, seeds scraped out
100 grams confectioners' sugar

Cheesecake:
3 pounds cream cheese
400 grams sugar
7 large eggs
Zest of 2 lemons
Acetate strips
Raspberry powder
Tempered white chocolate
Fresh raspberries for garnish

Berry Sauce:
150 grams sugar
15 grams cornstarch
250 grams water
250 grams raspberry puree
250 grams strawberry puree

Finish and Serve:
Chocolate garnishes
Other garnishes of choice

To Make the Financier Cake:
- Preheat the oven to 350°F. Cream the butter, sugar and almond flour together. Beat in the eggs one at a time. Alternate additions of the all-purpose flour and cornstarch with additions of the cream. Beat until combined. Pipe the batter into the desired mold and bake until golden brown.

To Make the Raspberry Jelée:
- Heat a small amount of the puree up and stir in the sugar and bloomed gelatin until dissolved. Stir the mixture back into the remaining cold puree. Roll up a tube of acetate, plug one end, and fill the tube with the mixture. Refrigerate until set. Once set, unroll the tube. Slice the molded jelée to the desired length.

To Make the Vanilla Chantilly Cream:
- Combine the heavy cream and vanilla seeds. Beat while slowly adding the sugar. Beat until the mixture forms stiff peaks.

To Make the Cheesecake:
- Beat the cream cheese and sugar together until smooth. Beat in the eggs one at a time. Beat in the zest. Make sure the mixture is lump free. Refrigerate the mixture overnight.
- Preheat the oven to 350°F. Pour the cream cheese mixture into the desired molds and bake in a water bath until it is set. Cool and unmold.
- Dust acetate strips with raspberry powder. Take the tempered white chocolate and spread it on top of the raspberry dust; when the chocolate begins to harden, wrap the strip around the outside of the same mold you used to bake the cheesecakes so that it forms itself to exactly the same size. After your chocolate is completely set, remove the acetate and drop the chocolate ring around a cheesecake. Repeat with the remaining 3 cakes. Top the cakes with fresh raspberries.

To Make the Berry Sauce:
- In a medium saucepan, mix together the sugar and cornstarch; slowly stir in the water. Whisk in the fruit purees. Bring the mixture to a rolling boil and cook, whisking constantly, for 3 minutes. Remove from the heat and cool. Transfer the sauce to a squeeze bottle.

To Finish and Serve:
- Cut the financier into servings. Pipe the chantilly cream on top of the financier and place some of the jelée on top as well. Place a piece of cheesecake on each plate, decorate with berry sauce, and add chocolate garnishes and other garnishes of choice.

Trio of Chocolate: Dark Chocolate Fritter, Milk Chocolate Crème and White Chocolate Coffee Ice Cream

Chef Jennifer Kopp, CEPC
Serves 4

Milk Chocolate Crème:

1 sheet platinum gelatin
3/4 cup milk
1/4 cup heavy cream
3 large egg yolks
3 tablespoons sugar
1/4 teaspoon cinnamon
3/4 cup chopped milk
    couverture chocolate
1/4 teaspoon brandy
1/4 teaspoon vanilla extract

Dark Chocolate Ganache:

1 cup heavy cream
3/4 cup chopped dark couverture
    chocolate

Dark Chocolate Fritters:

2 large eggs
2 tablespoons oil
1/2 cup milk
1 teaspoon vanilla extract
1/2 cup sugar
1 cup all-purpose flour
1/4 cup almond flour
1/4 cup cocoa powder
1/2 teaspoon baking powder
Canola oil for frying
Confectioners' sugar for dusting

Finish and Serve:

Melted chocolate for painting (optional)
Chocolate cake or brownies
    cut into 1 x 2-inch rectangles
Marinated raspberries
Raspberry jellies (optional)
Croquant sticks (optional)

To Make the Milk Chocolate Crème:

- Bloom the gelatin in water and set aside. Meanwhile, bring the milk and cream to a boil. In a medium bowl, whisk together the yolks, sugar and cinnamon. Whisking constantly, slowly pour the hot milk mixture into the yolks. Return egg mixture to saucepan and cook, stirring, until mixture thickens enough to coat the back of a spoon.
- Place the chocolate in a small metal bowl. Pour the hot milk mixture over the chocolate and stir until smooth. While still warm, stir in the gelatin. Cool the mixture, then stir in the brandy and vanilla. Refrigerate until very firm.

To Make the Dark Chocolate Ganache:

- Bring the cream to a boil in a small saucepan. Place the chocolate in a bowl; pour in the hot cream and stir until the mixture is smooth, shiny and somewhat elastic. Cover the bowl with plastic wrap, pressing down on the wrap so that it touches the surface of the ganache. Refrigerate until set.
- Scoop out teaspoon-sized balls of the ganache and freeze them. (You will have ganache left over; it can be served warm as an accompaniment to the dessert, or kept refrigerated for another use.)

To Make the Dark Chocolate Fritters:

- In a bowl, stir together the eggs, oil, milk, vanilla and sugar. Sift the flour, almond flour, cocoa and baking powder together in another bowl. Add the dry ingredients to the egg mixture and blend until smooth. Set the batter aside for 15 minutes.
- In a small, deep saucepan, heat the oil to 350°F. Dip each frozen ball of dark chocolate ganache into the batter and gently drop into the oil. Fry until the fritters float and are evenly browned. Drain on paper towels. Dust with confectioners' sugar and serve warm.

To Finish and Serve:

- Paint a rectangle of melted chocolate on each plate. Place scoops of white chocolate coffee ice cream on crunch disks and place one on each plate. Dip a metal spoon in very hot water and roll quenelles of milk chocolate crème. Set one on top of each chocolate cake (or brownie) rectangle and place on the plates. Place 3 raspberries next to the cake. Add a warm fritter to each plate. Garnish with raspberry jellies and croquant sticks and serve.

CHEF'S NOTES

- Chef Kopp serves this dish with Chocolate Hazelnut Crunch (see page 228) and White Chocolate Coffee Ice Cream (see page 238).
- "Feuilletine" flakes are very thin crushed wafer cookie flakes. You can substitute crushed cornflakes, or crush wafer rolls into small flakes.

Vanilla Bean-Pear Frangipane Tartlets with Stewed Huckleberries

Chef Mellisa K. Root
Serves 8

Pâte Sucrée:

2 egg yolks

1/3 cup heavy cream

1 teaspoon vanilla extract

1 3/4 cups all-purpose flour

1 cup confectioners' sugar

1/2 teaspoon salt

1 cup cold unsalted butter

Poached Pears:

1 cup sugar

1/4 cup lemon juice

Zest from 2 lemons
    removed in long strips

15 pink peppercorns

6 whole cloves

1 whole nutmeg

1/4 teaspoon salt

1 vanilla bean

4 pears, peeled and cored

Frangipane:

1 cup sugar

3/4 cup unsalted butter,
    at room temperature

1 cup almond flour

1/4 teaspoon salt

2 large eggs

2 large egg whites

1 teaspoon vanilla bean paste

Stewed Huckleberries:

1 cup pureed huckleberries

1/3 cup maple syrup

1 teaspoon cinnamon

1 teaspoon ground cardamom

1/2 teaspoon lemon juice

1/4 teaspoon salt

1 1/2 cups whole huckleberries

Tuile Cookies:

1/2 cup confectioners' sugar

1/2 cup all-purpose flour

1/2 cup egg whites

1/2 cup melted unsalted butter

Finish and Serve:

Sugar-glazed pear slices (optional)

To Make the Pâte Sucrée:

- Beat together the yolks, cream and vanilla. In another bowl, mix the flour, confectioners' sugar and salt. Grate the cold butter into the flour mixture and toss. Pour in the egg mixture and blend until the dough comes together. Refrigerate until chilled.

To Make the Poached Pears:

- Combine all the ingredients except the pears in a saucepan, add 2 cups of water, and bring to a boil. Add the pears and simmer for 5 minutes. Remove from the heat and allow pears to cool in the poaching liquid.

To Make the Frangipane:

- In a food processor, pulse the sugar and butter together. Add the almond flour and salt and pulse. Add the eggs one at a time and pulse until combined. Add the whites and vanilla paste and pulse until the mixture is smooth.

To Make the Stewed Huckleberries:

- Heat the pureed huckleberries, maple syrup, cinnamon, cardamom, lemon juice and salt. When the mixture reaches a simmer add the whole huckleberries and cook just until the berries plump up; remove the pan from the heat before the berries burst.

To Make the Tuile Cookies:

- Preheat the oven to 350°F. Combine the sugar and flour. Beat in the egg whites. Slowly beat in the melted butter. Cover a baking sheet with a Silpat and spread the batter in the desired shape on the Silpat (use a stencil if you like). Bake until golden brown. Shape while still warm if desired.

To Finish and Serve:

- Preheat the oven to 350°F. Roll the pâte sucrée dough out; cut circles of the dough to line individual tart pans. Spoon a layer of frangipane in the bottom of each. Slice the poached pears and place the slices on top of the frangipane. Bake until the tarts are browned, 20 to 25 minutes. Serve the tarts with ice cream, huckleberries and tuiles; garnish with sugar-glazed pear slices if desired.

CHEF'S NOTES

- Chef Root serves this dish with Ginger Rum Ice Cream (see page 232).

Warm Chocolate Cake with Pistachio Semifreddo, Raspberries and Orange Caramel Sauce

Chef Jennifer Kopp, CEPC
Serves 4

Ganache:

1 cup heavy cream

1 3/4 cups chopped dark couverture chocolate

Pistachio Semifreddo:

2 large egg yolks

2 tablespoons sugar

2 tablespoons pistachio paste

1/2 teaspoon vanilla extract

1 tablespoon brandy

1 cup heavy cream

1 cup ground pistachios for coating, or as needed

Orange Caramel Sauce:

2/3 cup sugar

1 teaspoon lemon juice

1/2 vanilla bean, seeds scraped out

2/3 cup orange juice without pulp

Warm Chocolate Cakes:

2 large eggs

1/2 cup chopped dark couverture chocolate

1/4 cup unsalted butter

6 tablespoons confectioners' sugar, plus more for dusting the cakes

1/4 cup cake flour

Butter and granulated sugar for preparing the molds

Finish and Serve:

12 raspberries

To Make the Ganache:

- Bring the cream to a boil in a small saucepan. Place the chocolate in a medium bowl; pour in the hot cream and stir until the mixture is smooth, shiny and somewhat elastic. Cover the bowl with plastic wrap, pressing down on the wrap so that it touches the surface of the ganache. Refrigerate until set.
- Scoop out four tablespoon-sized balls of the ganache and freeze them; the frozen balls will be used to fill the chocolate cakes. (You will have ganache left over; it can be served warm as an accompaniment to the dessert, or kept refrigerated for another use.)

To Make the Pistachio Semifreddo:

- In the top of a double boiler set over simmering water, combine the yolks and sugar and whisk until fluffy and tripled in volume. Remove from the heat and cool to room temperature. Stir in pistachio paste, vanilla and brandy.
- In the bowl of an electric mixer, whip the cream to stiff peaks. Fold the cream into the egg mixture. Line a terrine mold with plastic wrap and pour the mixture into it. Level the top and freeze until solid.
- Invert the terrine onto a plate and remove the plastic wrap. Coat the semifreddo in the ground pistachios. Cover again with plastic and return the semifreddo to the freezer until ready to serve.

To Make the Orange Caramel Sauce:

- In a saucepan, heat the sugar and lemon juice together until the sugar melts and turns a light amber color. Remove from the heat and stir in the vanilla bean and seeds. Stir in the orange juice. Stir until the mixture is smooth. Cool the sauce; if it is too thick, stir more orange juice in until it reaches the desired consistency.

To Make the Warm Chocolate Cakes:

- Preheat the oven to 400°F. In the bowl of an electric mixer, whip the eggs until foamy. In the top of a double boiler set over simmering water, combine the chocolate and butter and cook, stirring occasionally, until melted and smooth. Slowly whisk the mixture into the bowl with the eggs. Stir in the confectioners' sugar and flour.
- Butter and sugar individual flexible silicone molds. Scoop the batter into the molds. Insert one frozen piece of ganache into each cake, pressing down gently so that each is covered with batter on all sides. Bake until cake is firm, approximately 10 minutes. Remove from the oven, let sit for 2 minutes, then invert the molds onto a parchment-lined sheet pan. Dust the cakes with confectioners' sugar and serve immediately for a molten center.

To Finish and Serve:

- Slice the pistachio semifreddo and place a slice on each plate. Place 3 raspberries on each plate and drizzle orange caramel sauce over the raspberries. Add the warm chocolate cake, garnish each plate with a tuile triangle, and serve.

CHEF'S NOTES

- Chef Kopp serves this dish with Tuiles (see page 237)
- If you do not have a flexible silicone mold, you can bake the cakes in buttered and sugared ceramic dishes or muffin pans.

Apple Compote

Chef Michael Matarazzo
Serves 4

1 tablespoon vegetable oil

1 Granny Smith apple, peeled and finely diced

2 tablespoons sugar

2 tablespoons apple juice

1 cinnamon stick

1/2 star anise pod

Pinch freshly grated nutmeg

- In a small sauté pan, heat the oil over medium heat. Add the apple and sauté until golden brown. Add the sugar and cook until melted. Add the apple juice, cinnamon stick, star anise and nutmeg and simmer until the mixture is very thick and the apples are soft. Remove from the heat and hold at room temperature until ready to serve.

CHEF'S NOTES

- Chef Matarazzo serves this dish with Carpaccio of Pig Ears, Hog Jowl Cobbler, and Blueberry and Apple Compotes (see page 76).

Apple Halves

Chef Michael Matarazzo
Serves 4

2 lady apples, peeled

2 tablespoons clarified butter

2 tablespoons unsalted butter

1 tablespoon honey

2 tablespoons granulated sugar

2 teaspoons cinnamon

2 fresh sage leaves

2 sprigs fresh thyme

2 tablespoons apple brandy

- Cut the apples in half and use a melon baller to scoop out the core and seeds from each half.
- Put the clarified butter and whole butter in a small sauté pan and cook over high heat until the mixture just begins to smoke. Place the apple halves cut-side down and cook until caramelized. Tilt the pan and pour off excess fat. Return to the heat and add the honey, sugar, cinnamon, sage and thyme. Cook until the liquid becomes thick and golden brown. Add the brandy and simmer until you have a thick syrup. Remove the pan from the heat; keep the apples in the syrup until ready to use.

CHEF'S NOTES

- Chef Matarazzo serves this dish with Carpaccio of Pig Ears, Hog Jowl Cobbler, and Blueberry and Apple Compotes (see page 76).

Balsamic Sauce

Chef Edward G. Leonard, CMC
Serves 4

2 tablespoons olive oil

4 chicken wings, chopped into
    small pieces

4 cipollini onions, diced

1/2 cup red wine

2 tablespoons aged balsamic vinegar

1/2 cup veal jus

1 cup chicken stock

1 teaspoon cold unsalted butter

Pinch ground cloves

Kosher salt

- Heat a medium stainless-steel saucepan over medium-high heat. Add the oil; when the oil begins to smoke, add the chopped chicken wings and diced onions. Cook, stirring occasionally, until evenly browned. Deglaze the pan with the wine and balsamic. Simmer until the liquid is reduce by two-thirds. Add the jus and stock and simmer until reduced by half. Strain the sauce through a fine-mesh sieve into another stainless-steel saucepan. Cover with plastic and reserve until serving.
- When ready to serve, bring the sauce to a simmer over medium heat. Whisk in the butter and cloves. Season to taste with salt and serve warm.

CHEF'S NOTES

- Chef Leonard serves this sauce with Roasted Organic Chicken Breast, Confit of Leg, Roasted Salsify and Carrots with Balsamic Sauce (see page 170).

Blueberry Compote and Sauce

Chef Michael Matarazzo
Serves 4

1 cup blueberries

2 tablespoons sugar

- In a small saucepan, combine the blueberries and sugar and place over medium heat. Using a wooden spoon, gently crush the blueberries to release some of their juices. Adjust the heat and simmer gently until the blueberries begin to fall apart, about 15 minutes. Strain the blueberries, reserving the liquid. Place the blueberries in a bowl and set aside.
- Pour the blueberry liquid into a small saucepan and simmer gently until it is a very thick syrup. Set aside.

CHEF'S NOTES

- Chef Matarazzo serves this dish with Carpaccio of Pig Ears, Hog Jowl Cobbler, and Blueberry and Apple Compotes (see page 76).

Braised Collard Greens

Chef Drew Garms
Serves 4

2 bunches collard greens

1/4 cup diced bacon

1/4 cup diced onion

1 quart ham hock stock (or rich chicken stock)

1 tablespoon sugar

2 tablespoons cider vinegar, plus more to taste

1 teaspoon red pepper flakes

Dash Tabasco sauce

1 tablespoon rich pork jus or veal jus

2 tablespoons unsalted butter

Salt and freshly ground pepper

- Thoroughly clean the greens; this may require more that one rinsing. Discard stems.
- In medium pot, cook the bacon until it renders its fat. Add the onion and cook in the bacon fat until translucent. Add the greens to the pot and stir until wilted. Add the stock, sugar, vinegar, pepper flakes and Tabasco. Cover and simmer gently until the greens are very tender, about 3 hours.
- Strain, reserving the greens and liquid separately. Place the liquid in a saucepan and simmer until reduced to a syrup. Remove the saucepan from the heat and whisk in pork jus and butter. Toss the greens in the liquid and season with salt and pepper; stir in more vinegar if needed.

CHEF'S NOTES

- Chef Garms serves this dish with Pan-Roasted Pork Lion with Twice-Cooked Pork Shank (see page 142).

Braised Sauerkraut

Chef Michael Matarazzo
Serves 4

2 **teaspoons** olive oil
1/4 **cup** finely diced apple
  wood-smoked bacon
1/4 **cup** finely diced onion
1/2 **cup** dry white wine
2 **cups** chicken stock
1 **pound** sauerkraut, drained and rinsed
Sachet made with 2 tablespoons caraway
  seeds, 1 bay leaf, 5 allspice berries
  and 4 sprigs fresh thyme
6 **whole slices** apple
  wood-smoked bacon
1 **cup** cold unsalted butter, diced

- Preheat the oven to 325°F. Heat the olive oil in a rondeau. Add the diced bacon and cook slowly until it has rendered its fat and is crispy. Add the diced onion and cook until translucent. Add the white wine, stock, sauerkraut and sachet and bring to a simmer. Lay the whole bacon slices across the sauerkraut, cover the pan with a piece of buttered parchment paper and then with foil. Bake in the oven until the sauerkraut is very tender, about 1 hour.
- Remove and discard the sachet. Strain the excess liquid from the pan into a clean heavy bottom saucepan. Simmer until the liquid thickens. Remove from the heat and stir in the butter a little at a time until the sauce is creamy and emulsified. Fold the butter sauce back into the cooked sauerkraut.

CHEF'S NOTES

- Chef Matarazzo serves this dish with Kielbasa-Stuffed Pork Loin with Braised Sauerkraut, Brussels Sprout and Chestnut Sauté and Crispy Potatoes (see page 128).

Braised Sweetbread and Cipollini Tartin

Chef Edward G. Leonard, CMC
Serves 4

1 **pound** veal sweetbreads,
  soaked in milk for 24 hours
Milk as needed
1 **cup** all-purpose flour
1/2 **teaspoon** ground mace
Kosher salt and fresh cracked pepper
2 **tablespoons** clarified butter
1/4 **cup** diced onion
1/4 **cup** diced carrot
1/4 **cup** diced celery
2 **cloves** garlic, sliced
1/4 **cup** brandy
2 **cups** veal stock
1/2 **sprig** fresh rosemary
1 **teaspoon** unsalted butter
8 cipollini onions,
  peeled and thinly sliced
1 **sheet** puff pastry

- Drain the sweetbreads. Place the sweetbreads in a stainless-steel saucepan and cover with more milk by 1 inch. Place over medium heat. Once the milk begins to simmer, remove the pan from heat and remove the sweetbreads. Once the sweetbreads are cool enough to handle, remove and discard all connective tissue and break the sweetbreads into medium pieces.
- Preheat the oven to 325°F. In a small mixing bowl, combine the flour, mace and a pinch of each salt and pepper. Place a medium rondeau over medium heat and heat the clarified butter for 2 minutes. Dust the sweetbreads with the seasoned flour and add to the rondeau. Cook the sweetbreads until they are lightly browned on all sides. Remove the sweetbreads from the pan and add the onion, carrot, celery and garlic. Continue to cook, stirring often, until the vegetables are lightly caramelized. Add the sweetbreads back to the pan and deglaze with the brandy. Add the stock and rosemary and bring to a simmer. Cover the pan and place in the oven for 20 minutes. Remove the pan from the oven; remove the sweetbreads. Strain the cooking liquid through a fine sieve and add back to the sweetbreads. Season with salt and pepper and allow to cool.
- Place a small sauté over medium heat and melt the butter. Add the sliced onions, season with salt and pepper and cook, stirring often, until the onions are caramelized. Remove from the heat and set aside.
- Grease 4 individual tart molds and fill each with an equal portion of the braised sweetbreads. Top the sweetbreads with the caramelized onions. Using a round cutter the same size as the top of the tart molds, cut 4 rounds of puff pastry. Place a circle of pastry on top of each tart and refrigerate for 30 minutes.
- Preheat the oven to 400°F. Bake the tarts until the pastry is golden brown, about 10 minutes. Invert onto serving plates.

CHEF'S NOTES

- Chef Leonard serves this dish with Moussaka of Veal with Tomato Gravy and braised sweetbread and cipollini tartin (see page 138).

Cabbage and Chanterelles

Chef Edward G. Leonard, CMC
Serves 4

2 tablespoons olive oil
1/2 cup diced smoked bacon
1/2 onion, finely diced
1 garlic clove, sliced
1/2 pound chanterelle mushrooms,
    cleaned and quartered
1 head savoy cabbage, thinly sliced
2 cups chicken stock
Leaves from 2 sprigs fresh thyme,
    chopped
1 tablespoon cold unsalted butter
Kosher salt and freshly cracked pepper

- Place a medium saucepan over medium-low heat. Add the olive oil and bacon and cook, stirring frequently, until the bacon is crisp. Add the onion and garlic and continue to cook until the onion becomes translucent. Add the chanterelles and cook for an additional 2 minutes. Add the cabbage and cook, stirring often, 2 minutes more. Add the stock and bring to a simmer. Simmer until the cabbage is soft and almost all of the stock has evaporated, about 20 minutes.
- Just before serving, reheat the cabbage and chanterelles. Stir in the thyme and cold butter until incorporated. Season with salt and pepper.

CHEF'S NOTES

- Chef Leonard serves this dish with Braised Pig Cheek, Confit of Pig Feet Croquette, Yukon Puree and Serrano Ham Crisp (see page 116).

Carrot and Truffle Soufflé

Chef Edward G. Leonard, CMC
Serves 4

1/4 cup heavy cream
1/4 cup milk
1/4 cup carrot puree
1 tablespoon truffle juice
1 tablespoon minced truffle
1 tablespoon carrot juice
1 tablespoon grated Parmigiano-
    Reggiano
2 tablespoons all-purpose flour
Kosher salt and freshly ground pepper
2 large egg whites, whipped to stiff
    peaks
2 tablespoons unsalted butter, melted

- Preheat the oven to 400°F. In a medium bowl, whisk together the cream, milk, carrot puree, truffle juice, minced truffle, carrot juice, cheese and 1 teaspoon of the flour until all ingredients are incorporated. Season with salt and pepper. Gently fold in the whipped egg whites in 2 batches. Prepare 4 small soufflé dishes by brushing the insides with the melted butter and dusting with the remaining flour. Divide the soufflé mixture evenly between the 4 ramekins and bake until puffed and cooked through, 10 to 15 minutes. Keep warm until serving.

CHEF'S NOTES

- Chef Leonard serves this dish with Roasted Veal Loin, Marrow and Parmesan Sauce, Eggplant and Veal Rib Quenelles and Soufflé of Carrot and Truffle (see page 172).

Carrot Puree

Chef Edward G. Leonard, CMC
Serves 4

6 ounces carrot, peeled and diced
2 cups orange juice
1 sprig fresh thyme
Kosher salt

- Place the carrot, orange juice and thyme in a small stainless-steel saucepan and simmer over medium heat until the carrots are very tender. Drain the carrots, reserving the cooking liquid. Discard the thyme. Place the carrots in the container of a high-speed blender and puree until smooth, adding cooking liquid as necessary to form a smooth, thick puree. Season the mixture with salt.

CHEF'S NOTES

- Chef Leonard serves this dish with Mini Club Sandwiches with Mozzarella, Dried Tomatoes, Quail Eggs and Vegetable Purees (see page 92).

Celery Root Puree

Chef Edward G. Leonard, CMC
Serves 4

6 ounces celery root, peeled and diced
2 ounces potato, peeled and diced
2 cups milk
Kosher salt

- Place the celery root, potato and milk in a stainless-steel saucepan and simmer over medium heat until the vegetables are tender. Drain the vegetables, reserving the cooking liquid. Place the vegetables in the container of a high-speed blender and puree until smooth, adding cooking liquid as needed to form a smooth, thick puree. Season the mixture with salt.

CHEF'S NOTES
- Chef Leonard serves this dish with Mini Club Sandwiches with Mozzarella, Dried Tomatoes, Quail Eggs and Vegetable Purees (see page 92).

Chocolate Hazelnut Crunch

Chef Jennifer Kopp, CEPC
Serves 4

1/3 cup chopped milk chocolate
1/3 cup praline paste
1 3/4 cups feuilletine or
    crushed cornflakes

- In the top of a double boiler set over simmering water, combine the chocolate and praline paste. Cook, stirring occasionally, until melted. Remove from the heat.
- Place the feuilletine in a bowl, drizzle with the chocolate mixture and toss until thoroughly coated. Roll the mixture out between sheets of parchment paper until it is about 1/4-inch thick. Refrigerate until set. Using a 1 3/4-inch round cutter, cut out disks.

CHEF'S NOTES
- Chef Kopp serves this with Trio of Chocolate: Dark Chocolate Fritter, Milk Chocolate Crème, and White Chocolate Coffee Ice Cream (see page 218).

Chocolate Sauce

Chef Mellisa K. Root
Serves 8

233 grams chocolate (64%)
177 milliliters heavy cream
89 milliliters corn syrup
30 milliliters vegetable oil
15 grams sugar
60 milliliters cold milk

- Place the chocolate in a large bowl. Combine the cream, corn syrup, oil and sugar and bring to a simmer. Pour over the chocolate and burr mix. Stir in the cold milk and refrigerate.

CHEF'S NOTES
- Chef Root serves this sauce with Lemon Extravaganza (see page 206).

Chorizo Potato Bar

Chef Jonathan P. Moosmiller, CEC
Serves 4

250 grams cooked and riced Yukon
    gold potatoes
50 grams cornstarch
1 large egg
1 large egg yolk
113 grams chorizo, finely diced
40 grams heavy cream
40 grams clarified butter, melted
2 egg whites
Kosher salt

- In a medium bowl, combine the cooked potato and cornstarch and mix well to form a paste. Add the egg, egg yolk and chorizo and mix well. Add the cream and clarified butter and mix again. In a separate bowl, beat the egg whites until they hold soft peaks. Using a rubber spatula, fold the egg whites into the potato mixture in two stages. Season the mixture to taste with kosher salt.
- Preheat the oven to 300°F. Prepare a shallow baking dish by spraying it with cooking spray and then lining it with parchment paper. Scrape the potato mixture into the prepared dish and use a small spatula to spread it evenly. Bake until set, about 15 minutes.
- Once the mixture has set remove the dish from the oven and place on the counter; cool for 30 minutes. Gently remove the cooled potato mixture from the dish and place it on a cutting board. Using a sharp knife, cut out the desired shape and reserve at room temperature until serving.

CHEF'S NOTES
- Chef Moosmiller serves this dish with Pork and Clam Duo (see page 150).

Cinnamon-Almond Cookies

Chef Jennifer Kopp, CEPC
Serves 4

1 1/4 cups unsalted butter
1/2 cup sugar
2 large eggs
1 teaspoon vanilla extract
2 3/4 cups all-purpose flour
2 teaspoons cinnamon
1/4 cup toasted sliced almonds

- In the bowl of an electric mixer, cream together the butter and sugar. Beat in the eggs and vanilla. Scrape down the sides of the bowl. Add the flour, cinnamon and almonds and mix just until incorporated. Wrap the dough in plastic and refrigerate until chilled.
- Preheat the oven to 350°F. Roll the chilled dough out to a thickness of ¼ inch and cut out circles of dough 2 inches in diameter. Dock the dough circles all over with a fork. Refrigerate until chilled, then bake on parchment-lined baking sheets until lightly golden brown.

CHEF'S NOTES
- Chef Kopp serves this with Chocolate Custard with Coconut Sorbet and Chocolate-Banana Empanadas (see page 200).

Clam Foam

Chef Jonathan P. Moosmiller, CEC
Serves 4

2 tablespoons unsalted butter
3 shallots, thinly sliced
1 ounce thinly sliced celery
1 sprig fresh thyme
2 tablespoons champagne vinegar
2 cups clam broth
1 1/4 cups skim milk
7 grams lecithin granules
Kosher salt

- Place the butter, shallots, celery and thyme in a small stainless-steel saucepan and place over low heat. Cover the pan and cook gently until the shallots and celery are translucent. Add the vinegar and clam broth and bring to a simmer; cook for 2 minutes. Add the milk and lecithin and bring back to a simmer. Once the liquid simmers, remove the pan from the heat and strain the liquid through a fine sieve into a small saucepan. Season with salt, cover, and reserve in a warm place. Just before serving, gently reheat the broth and blend until foamy with a small emersion blender.

CHEF'S NOTES
- Chef Moosmiller serves this dish with Pork and Clam Duo (see page 150).

Corn and Tomato Tart

Chef Edward G. Leonard, CMC
Serves 4

4 ears fresh sweet corn, shucked

1 cup milk

1 cup heavy cream

1 tablespoon honey

5 ounces all-purpose flour

2 ounces melted unsalted butter

3 large eggs

Kosher salt

Extra-virgin olive oil

16 tomato petals

Fresh cracked pepper

1 tablespoon chopped fresh thyme
leaves

- Using a sharp knife, remove the corn kernels from the cobs and reserve the kernels. Cut the cobs into small pieces and place into a stainless-steel saucepan. Add the milk, cream and honey and simmer for 10 minutes. Remove and discard the cobs and add the corn kernels; simmer for 2 minutes more.
- Place the corn and milk mixture in a blender and puree. Strain through a fine-mesh sieve into a mixing bowl and cool. When cooled, add the flour, melted butter, eggs and a pinch of salt and whisk until smooth.
- Place a nonstick skillet over medium heat and heat for 2 minutes. Add a little olive oil. Pour in 1/4 cup of the corn batter and tilt pan so the batter covers the entire surface. Cook until lightly browned on the bottom and then use a spatula to flip the corn crêpe; cook until lightly browned on the other side. Remove the crêpe from the pan and repeat the process until you have 5 crêpes. Reserve any leftover batter for another use.
- Preheat the oven to 300°F. Rub a 3 x 6-inch baking dish with olive oil. Cut all of the crêpes to fit lengthwise inside the baking dish. Place 2 pieces of crêpe in the baking dish and cover with 8 tomato petals. Season with salt and pepper and sprinkle with chopped thyme. Drizzle with olive oil. Place 2 more pieces of crêpe on top and top them with the remaining tomato petals; season again with salt, pepper and thyme and drizzle with olive oil. Place a single layer of crêpe on top, cover the pan with aluminum foil, and bake for 15 minutes. Remove the foil and bake for an additional 5 minutes. Remove from the oven and allow to cool.
- Once cool, remove the tart from the baking dish and cut it into 4 equal portions. Place the tarts onto a greased baking sheet and reheat before serving.

CHEF'S NOTES

- Chef Leonard serves this dish with Baked Sole with Corn and Roma Tomato Tart, Truffle Popcorn and Lobster Ravioli (see page 110).

Cranberry Compote

Chef Chris Desens, CEC
Serves 4

1 cup cranberries

1/4 cup Port

1/4 cup orange juice

1/4 cup sugar

2 tablespoons diced yellow onion

1 tablespoon cider vinegar

- Combine all the ingredients and cook until the cranberries pop and the mixture thickens.

CHEF'S NOTES

- Chef Desens serves this with Madeleine's Fried Turkey (see recipe page 132).

Cranberry Wild Rice

Chef Jonathan P. Moosmiller, CEC
Serves 4

1 tablespoon extra-virgin olive oil
1 garlic clove, minced
1/2 cup dried cranberries
1 cup wild rice
Leaves from 3 sprigs fresh thyme
1 bay leaf
4 1/2 cups chicken stock
Kosher salt and freshly ground pepper

- Place a 1-quart saucepan over medium heat and add the oil and garlic. Cook, stirring frequently, for 3 minutes. Add the dried cranberries and continue to cook 2 minutes more. Add the wild rice and cook, stirring, until the rice is lightly toasted, about 2 minutes. Add the thyme, bay leaf and stock. Simmer until the rice grains are tender and begin to pop open, about 45 minutes. Discard the bay leaf and season the rice with salt and pepper. Check rice before serving to make sure it is very hot and double check the seasoning.

CHEF'S NOTES
- Chef Moosmiller serves this dish with Quail Two Ways with Foie Gras, Cranberry Wild Rice, Haricot Verts and Mushrooms (see page 160).

Fava Beans

Chef Jamie P. Keating, CCC
Serves 4

2 teaspoons olive oil
40 fava beans, blanched and peeled
1/4 cup diced fennel
1 teaspoon chopped fresh rosemary
Kosher salt
Chili powder
1 tablespoon unsalted butter
3 ounces goat cheese

- Heat the olive oil in a small skillet and sauté the fava beans and fennel until softened. Stir in the rosemary, salt and chili powder. Stir in the butter. Serve with goat cheese on top.

CHEF'S NOTES
- Chef Keating serves this dish with Mint Pesto Rack of Lamb and Braised Denver Rib (see page 134).

Frisée Salad

Chef Jamie P. Keating, CCC
Serves 4

1 bunch frisée lettuce
1/4 cup lemon juice
1 teaspoon Dijon mustard
Kosher salt and freshly ground pepper
1/2 cup olive oil

- Cut sprigs of the lettuce and soak in ice water for 20 minutes. Drain and pat dry with paper towels. Place in a large bowl. In another bowl, whisk together the lemon juice and mustard. Slowly whisk in the oil. Season with salt and pepper. Toss the vinaigrette and lettuce together just before serving.

CHEF'S NOTES
- Chef Keating serves this dish with Smoked Salmon Belly and Crab Terrine (see page 182).

Fruit Salsa

Chef Jennifer Kopp, CEPC
Serves 4

Fruit Salsa
Zest of 1 lime, removed in thin strips
3 cups water
1 cup plus 1 teaspoon sugar
1 banana, peeled and diced
3 strawberries, diced
1 tablespoon lime juice
1 teaspoon light rum

- In a small saucepan, combine lime zest and 1 cup of the water and bring to a boil. Drain, discard the water, return the zest to the pan, and boil again with another cup of water. Drain again and return the zest to the pan. Add the remaining cup water and 1 cup of the sugar and bring to a boil. Cook until the lime zest becomes translucent. Drain, cool and set the zest aside.
- When ready to serve, combine the banana, strawberries, lime juice, rum, zest and remaining teaspoon sugar and toss.

CHEF'S NOTES
- Chef Kopp serves this with Chocolate Custard with Coconut Sorbet and Chocolate-Banana Empanadas (see page 200).

Ginger Rum Ice Cream

Chef Mellisa K. Root
Serves 8

2 cups half-and-half
1/4 cup candied ginger
7 egg yolks
1/2 cup brown sugar
1/4 cup dark rum

- Combine the half-and-half and the ginger and bring to a boil. Whisk the yolks and sugar together. Whisking constantly, slowly whisk the hot half-and-half into the eggs. Return the mixture to the saucepan and cook, stirring, until the mixture thickens enough to coat the back of a spoon. Strain the mixture and chill over ice. When cold, freeze in an ice-cream machine according to the manufacturer's instructions, adding the rum half way through freezing.

CHEF'S NOTES
- Chef Root serves this ice cream with Vanilla Bean-Pear Frangipane Tartlets with Stewed Huckleberries (see page 220).

Haricot Verts and Mushrooms

Chef Jonathan P. Moosmiller, CEC
Serves 4

1 pound haricot verts, trimmed
1 tablespoon unsalted butter
1/2 cup honey mushrooms
1 shallot, minced
1 tablespoon snipped chives
Kosher salt and freshly ground pepper

- Bring 1 gallon salted water to a boil over high heat. Add the haricot verts and cook until crisp-tender, about 3 minutes. Drain and shock in an ice-water bath. Drain again and set aside until serving.
- When ready to serve, place a medium sauté pan over medium heat for 2 minutes. Add the butter and cook for 1 minute. Add the mushrooms and cook for 2 minutes. Stir in the minced shallots and blanched haricot verts and cook for 2 minutes. Stir in the chives and season with salt and pepper.

CHEF'S NOTES
- Chef Moosmiller serves this dish with Quail Two Ways with Foie Gras, Cranberry Wild Rice, Haricot Verts and Mushrooms (see page 160).

Marinated Strawberries

Chef Mellisa K. Root
Serves 8

1 quart strawberries, hulled and halved
200 grams sugar
20 grams Grand Marnier
1 vanilla bean
Zest of 1 orange

- Combine all the ingredients and marinate one day. Strain the accumulated liquid into a saucepan and simmer until reduced and syrupy. Coat strawberries in the reduced liquid and reserve.

CHEF'S NOTES
- Chef Root serves this with Lemon Extravaganza (see page 206).

Meringue Cookies

Chef Mellisa K. Root
Serves 8

200 grams sugar
100 grams egg whites
Baked squares of puff pastry
Lemon zest
Chocolate sprigs

- Cook the sugar until it reaches 121°C. Whisk the egg whites until they hold soft peaks. Whisking constantly, slowly whisk in the hot sugar. Beat until the meringue forms stiff peaks. Pipe the meringue onto the puff pastry squares, forming little peaks. Brown the meringue. Garnish each cookie with lemon zest and a chocolate sprig.

CHEF'S NOTES
- Chef Root serves this cookie with Lemon Extravaganza (see page 206).

Parsnip-Potato Puree

Chef Chris Desens, CEC
Serves 4

1 cup peeled, diced Yukon gold potato
4 garlic cloves
1 cup peeled, diced parsnip
3/4 cup heavy cream
Salt and ground white pepper
Nutmeg

- Cook the potato and garlic in salted water until soft; drain and puree in a food mill. Cook the parsnip in the cream until softened; puree, using as much of the cream as needed. Fold in the potatoes and season with salt, white pepper and nutmeg.

CHEF'S NOTES
- Chef Desens serves this with Madeleine's Fried Turkey (see recipe page 132).

Orange Shooters

Chef Mellisa K. Root
Serves 8

Gingerbread:
224 grams unsalted butter
336 grams dark-brown sugar
2 teaspoons baking soda
1 teaspoon salt
3 tablespoons ground ginger
2 teaspoons ground cinnamon
1 teaspoon ground cloves
1 teaspoon ground nutmeg
1/2 teaspoon ground cardamom
4 large eggs
336 grams molasses
448 grams all-purpose flour
336 milliliters hot water
Orange marmalade

Chocolate Creamuex:
1 liter heavy cream
240 grams egg yolks
180 grams sugar
400 grams chocolate (64%)
8 grams gelatin, bloomed

Segmented Oranges:
3 oranges
20 grams sugar
20 grams triple sec
2 sprigs thyme
Chocolate rings for garnish

To Make the Gingerbread:
- Preheat the oven to 335°F. Cream together the butter, sugar, baking soda, salt, ginger, cinnamon, cloves, nutmeg and cardamom. Beat in the eggs one at a time. Beat in the molasses. Stir in the flour. Beat in the hot water. Pour the batter into greased muffin cups and bake until a toothpick inserted into the center of the muffins comes out clean. Allow to cool, then crumble the gingerbread and place it in the bottom of tall, thin serving glasses or shot glasses. Top the gingerbread with orange marmalade.

To Make the Chocolate Creamuex:
- Heat the cream in a large saucepan until bubbles form around the edges. Whisk the yolks and the sugar together in a bowl. Whisking constantly, slowly whisk the hot cream into the eggs. Pour the mixture back into the pan and cook, stirring constantly, until the mixture reaches a temperature of 85°C. Strain through a fine-mesh sieve into a bowl with the chocolate and mix with a burr mixer. Stir in the bloomed gelatin. Pour the mixture over the marmalade in the glasses and refrigerate until set.

To Make the Segmented Oranges:
- Segment the oranges and toss them with the sugar, triple sec and thyme. Macerate the mixture for 4 hours. Place in the glasses on top of the chocolate creamuex and garnish each glass with a chocolate ring.

CHEF'S NOTES
- Chef Kopp serves this with her Parfait Sampler (see page 212).

Poached Clams

Chef Jonathan P. Moosmiller, CEC
Serves 4

4 tablespoons unsalted butter
1 ounce brunoise of chorizo
1 ounce brunoise of onion
1 ounce brunoise of peeled celery
1 ounce brunoise of carrot
20 manila clams, purged
Leaves from 2 sprigs fresh
    thyme, chopped
3 ounces white wine
Kosher salt

- Place a small stainless-steel saucepan over medium-low heat and add 1 tablespoon of the butter and the chorizo. Cook until the chorizo releases some of its fat and begins to crisp. Add the onion, celery and carrot and continue to cook, stirring often, until the vegetables have softened. Add the clams, thyme and wine. Cover the pan and cook until all of the clams have opened.
- Remove the clams from the pan. Remove the clam meat from each shell and set them aside; discard the shells. Strain the liquid the clams cooked in and simmer until it is reduced to just 1 tablespoon of liquid. Whisk in the remaining 3 tablespoons butter and remove from the heat; reserve until serving.
- To serve, place the clam meats into the pan with the reduced liquid and butter mixture and heat over very low heat just until warm.

CHEF'S NOTES
- Chef Moosmiller serves this dish with Pork and Clam Duo (see page 150).

Polenta

Chef Jamie P. Keating, CCC
Serves 4

1 cup milk
3/4 ounce butter
1 teaspoon kosher salt
1 teaspoon ground white pepper
Nutmeg
1/2 cup semolina
1 large egg
1/2 cup heavy cream
1 ounce grated Parmesan

- Preheat the oven to 325°F. Spray 4 round metal molds with cooking spray and place them on a sheet pan covered with parchment.
- In a saucepan, combine the milk, butter, salt, pepper and nutmeg and bring just to a simmer. Slowly stir in the semolina and cook, stirring constantly. Beat the egg and cream together and stir them into the semolina mixture. Immediately remove from the heat and stir in half the Parmesan. Pour the mixture into the prepared molds and top with the remaining cheese. Just prior to serving, bake for 15 minutes.

CHEF'S NOTES
- Chef Keating serves this dish with Mint Pesto Rack of Lamb and Braised Denver Rib (see page 134).

Potato Disks

Chef Edward G. Leonard, CMC
Serves 4

4 Yukon gold potatoes, peeled
2 cups chicken stock
1 tablespoon unsalted butter
2 sprigs fresh thyme
Kosher salt

- Cut the potatoes into 16 slices, each 1/4-inch thick. Take a 1 1/2-inch round cutter and cut out disks from the slices. Discard the potato scraps or save for another use.
- Place the potato disks in a medium saucepan and add the stock, butter and thyme. Cover the potatoes with a parchment-paper lid and place over medium heat. Bring to a simmer, adjust heat, and cook until the potatoes are just tender. Remove from the heat and allow the potatoes to cool in the liquid. Gently reheat the potatoes in their liquid before serving; drain, season lightly with salt, and divide between plates.

CHEF'S NOTES
- Chef Leonard serves this with Roasted Pork Loin with Chorizo Crisp, Clam Butter Sauce, Potato and Pork Rillettes (see page 162).

Ragout

Chef Timothy R. Prefontaine, CSC
Serves 4

Duck fat
2 tablespoons finely diced onion
2 tablespoons thinly sliced celery
2 tablespoons paysanne carrots
1 tablespoon minced shallot
1 teaspoon minced garlic
1/4 cup diced roasted tomato
1/4 cup Madeira
1/4 cup duck jus
1 cup baby arugula leaves
1 cup white beans, soaked overnight
    and cooked until tender in
    chicken stock
Duck confit from 1 leg and thigh
Salt and freshly ground pepper

- Heat a little duck fat over medium-high heat and sauté the onion, celery and carrot for 1 minute. Add the shallot and garlic and cook 1 more minute. Add the tomato and cook for 3 minutes. Deglaze the pan with the Madeira and add duck jus. When the liquid has reduced, fold in the arugula, beans and confit. Season with salt and pepper and set aside.

CHEF'S NOTES
- Chef Prefontaine serves this dish with Roulade of Duck with Foie Gras and Pistachio, Ragout of White Beans and Duck Confit, Broccolini and Natural Jus (see page 174).

Potato Sponge

Chef Timothy R. Prefontaine, CSC
Serves 4

1 pound warm, cooked, riced potatoes

1 ounce cornstarch

1 ounce all-purpose flour

1 pound whole eggs

8 ounces melted unsalted butter, plus
more for brushing on the sponge

1 teaspoon chopped fresh rosemary

1 teaspoon chopped fresh thyme leaves

1 tablespoon chopped parsley

Salt and freshly ground pepper

2 cups warm whipped seasoned
potatoes (sautéed bruniose of carrot,
celery, red onion and rutabaga
folded in)

- In a stainless-steel bowl, mix together the warm potatoes, cornstarch and flour. Slowly whisk in the eggs, then whisk in the melted butter. Stir in the rosemary, thyme and parsley, season with salt and pepper, and strain the mixture through a china cap.
- Preheat the oven to 325°F. Line a half sheet pan with a Silpat. Pour the potato mixture onto the Silpat and spread until it about 1/4-inch thick. Bake for 11 minutes. Cool the potatoes slightly on the pan, then transfer them to a cutting board and cut the sheet into three equal pieces. Lay one piece down and brush with melted butter; spread with half the warm whipped potato mixture. Top with another piece of the baked potato sheet, brush with more butter and spread the rest of the whipped potato mixture on top. Cover with the last piece of baked potatoes and brush lightly with butter. Cover loosely with a piece of plastic wrap and weight down by gently placing 3 half sheet pans on top. Refrigerate for about 2 hours.
- Cut the potato sponge into the desired shapes. To serve, place portions on a double-panned half sheet pan and reheat in a 325°F. oven for about 10 minutes.

CHEF'S NOTES

- Chef Prefontaine serves this dish with Olive-Brined Lamb Loin with Sun-Dried Red Pepper and Herb Crust, Potato Sponge, Braised Lamb Neck and Shallot Marmalade (see page 140).

Roasted Salsify and Carrots

Chef Edward G. Leonard, CMC
Serves 4

12 pieces salsify, cut into sections 1/2
inch in diameter and 2 1/2 inches
long, peeled and blanched

12 carrots, cut into sections 1/2 inch in
diameter and 2 1/2 inches long,
peeled and blanched

1 tablespoon unsalted butter, melted

1 tablespoon extra-virgin olive oil

Leaves from 1 sprig fresh
thyme, chopped

Kosher salt and freshly
cracked black pepper

- Place the blanched salsify and carrots in a medium bowl. Add the melted butter, oil and thyme. Toss gently; season with salt and pepper and toss again. Transfer the vegetables to a baking sheet and set aside until serving.
- To serve, place the baking sheet into a preheated 350°F. oven and bake until the vegetable are lightly browned and heated through, about 10 minutes.

CHEF'S NOTES

- Chef Leonard serves this dish with Roasted Organic Chicken Breast, Confit of Leg, Roasted Salsify and Carrots with Balsamic Sauce (see page 170).

Serrano Ham Crisps

Chef Edward G. Leonard, CMC
Serves 4

4 thin slices Serrano ham

- Preheat the oven to 250°F. Place the ham slices on a baking sheet lined with a Silpat and bake until crisp, about 1 hour. (This may be done up to 2 days ahead of time). Store the crisps in an airtight container.

CHEF'S NOTES

- Chef Leonard serves this dish with Braised Pig Cheek, Confit of Pig Feet Croquette, Yukon Puree and Serrano Ham Crisp (see page 116).

Shallot Marmalade

Chef Timothy R. Prefontaine, CSC
Serves 4

2 teaspoons olive oil
8 ounces shallots, thinly sliced
1 tablespoon sugar
2 tablespoons red wine
2 tablespoons red-wine vinegar
2 tablespoons lamb stock or brown
veal stock
1/2 teaspoon chopped thyme
Salt and freshly ground pepper
2 tablespoons unsalted butter

- Heat the olive oil over medium-low heat. Add the shallots and cook until well caramelized. Add the sugar and cook an additional 2 minutes. Add the wine and vinegar and cook until reduced; add the stock and thyme and reduce again. Season with salt and pepper and whisk in the butter. Keep warm until serving

CHEF'S NOTES

- Chef Prefontaine serves this dish with Olive-Brined Lamb Loin with Sun-Dried Red Pepper and Herb Crust, Potato Sponge, Braised Lamb Neck and Shallot Marmalade (see page 140).

Spinach

Chef Jonathan P. Moosmiller, CEC
Serves 4

1/4 cup extra-virgin olive oil
2 garlic cloves, sliced
1 pound spinach, stems removed and
discarded, leaves rinsed well
Juice of 1 lemon
Kosher salt

- Place a large sauté pan over medium-high heat and allow to heat for 2 minutes. Add the oil and garlic and cook until the garlic is soft, about 2 minutes. Add the spinach and continue to cook, stirring often, until the spinach is wilted. Season with lemon juice and salt. Reserve in a warm place until serving.

CHEF'S NOTES

- Chef Moosmiller serves this dish with Pork and Clam Duo (see page 150).

Tuiles

Chef Jennifer Kopp, CEPC
Serves 4

1/2 cup unsalted butter
1/4 cup sugar
1/2 cup egg whites, warmed slightly
1/2 teaspoon vanilla extract
1 cup all-purpose flour
Cinnamon for dusting

- Preheat the oven to 350°F. Combine the butter and sugar. Slowly beat in the egg whites and vanilla. Add the flour and blend until smooth. Spread the batter onto a baking sheet lined with a Silpat, making triangles about 3/4 inch wide at the base and 6 inches tall (use a template if you like). Sprinkle a pinch of cinnamon on top of each cookie. Bake until the batter is white and no longer shiny, about 2 minutes. Cool completely.
- When cooled, return the baking sheet to the oven and bake until the tuiles are golden, about 2 minutes. While still hot, peel them from the mat and set aside on a flat surface to cool.

CHEF'S NOTES

- Chef Kopp serves this with Warm Chocolate Cake with Pistachio Semifreddo, Raspberries and Orange Caramel Sauce (see page 222).

White Chocolate Coffee Ice Cream

Chef Jennifer Kopp, CEPC
Serves 4

1 cup heavy cream
1/2 cup milk
1/4 cup sugar plus 1/3 cup sugar
1 1/2 cups coffee beans
3 cups half-and-half
4 large eggs
1 1/4 cups chopped white chocolate

- In a saucepan, bring the heavy cream, milk and 1/4 cup of the sugar to a boil. Pour into a mixing bowl and add the coffee beans. Cover the bowl with plastic wrap and let sit for 45 minutes to infuse.
- In a separate saucepan, bring the half-and-half to a boil. In a medium bowl, whisk the eggs with the remaining 1/3 cup sugar until smooth. Whisking constantly, slowly pour the hot half-and-half into the eggs. Return the mixture to the saucepan and cook, stirring, until it thickens enough to coat the back of a spoon. Pour into a mixing bowl and stir in the white chocolate.
- Pour the cream and coffee bean mixture through a fine-mesh sieve to strain out the coffee beans. Discard the beans. Stir the coffee-flavored cream mixture into the white chocolate mixture. Pour the entire mixture through a fine-mesh sieve and refrigerate until chilled. Freeze according to the manufacturer's instructions for your ice-cream maker. Transfer the ice cream to a plastic container and freeze until ready to serve.

CHEF'S NOTES

- Chef Kopp serves this with Trio of Chocolate: Dark Chocolate Fritter, Milk Chocolate Crème and White Chocolate Coffee Ice Cream (see page 218).

Yukon Potato Puree

Chef Edward G. Leonard, CMC
Serves 4

1 pound Yukon gold potatoes, peeled and quartered
1/4 cup kosher salt
1/2 cup unsalted butter, softened
1 cup heavy cream
1 ounce white truffle, minced
2 tablespoons white truffle oil
Fine sea salt and freshly ground pepper

- Place the potatoes in a pot and cover with cold water by 3 inches. Add the kosher salt and bring to a boil over high heat. Reduce the heat and simmer until the potatoes are fork tender.
- Drain the potatoes and return them to the pot. Place over medium heat and stir constantly until all excess water has evaporated from the potatoes, 3 to 5 minutes. Rice the potatoes into a medium bowl and stir in the butter, cream, truffle, and truffle oil. Season to taste with salt and pepper. Cover with plastic wrap and place in a warm place until serving.

CHEF'S NOTES

- Chef Leonard serves this dish with Braised Pig Cheek, Confit of Pig Feet Croquette, Yukon Puree and Serrano Ham Crisp (see page 116).

Acidulated Water: Water with lemon juice or other acid added, intended to keep raw fruit or vegetables from discoloring.

Adobo Sauce: Seasoning paste used in Mexican cuisine made with ground chiles, herbs and vinegar.

Albumin: Clarifying protein found in egg whites, leeks, blood, and connective tissue.
- Soluble in cold liquid.
- It congeals when heated and traps impurities.

A la Minute: At the last minute, just before service.

Au Jus: Served with unthickened pan juices, often with the addition of stock or other flavorings.

Barding: Wrapping meats with thin slices of fat or fatty meats, like bacon, before cooking.

Bechamel: Basic white sauce.

Beurre Manié: A 60/40 mix of whole butter and flour used as a liaison.

Bird Chiles: Slender, straight, chiles, bitingly hot and resembling the arbol.

Blanch: To immerse food briefly in boiling water, either to help loosen the skin or to precook briefly to set color and flavor.

Bouquet Garni: Little bundles of herbs and spices, usually wrapped in cheesecloth.
• Classic combination – parsley, peppercorns, thyme, and bay leaves.

Braise: To cook a seared product in a tightly covered pan with varying amounts of a flavorful liquid for a lengthy period of time.
- Best for tough cuts of meat.
- Usually completed in the oven.
- Braised vegetables are usually not seared.

Bread: To coat with bread or cracker crumbs before cooking, usually after first dipping food into beaten egg or other liquid so crumbs will adhere.

Brine: A salt solution. Also the act of soaking a product in a salt solution.

Brunoise: To dice vegetable minutely, or the resulting diced vegetable mixture.

Capon: Castrated and fattened rooster.

Carryover Cooking: The cooking that takes place after a product is removed from the oven.
- Remove roasts from the oven at least 5 degrees below the desired temperature.

Chard: A member of the beet family that produces large leaves and thick stalks.

Chèvre: Goat's milk cheese.

Chiffonade: To finely cut greens to produce thin strips.

Chinois: A metal, conical strainer with fine-mesh. Sometimes known as a "China cap."

Concasser: To chop roughly – often used to describe a rough chop of blanched, peeled, and seeded tomatoes.

Confit: Meats cooked and preserved in fat. Fruits preserved in sugar or liquor.

Consommé: Clarified stock that has been fortified with lean ground meat and additional mirepoix and bouquet garni.

Coral: The roe of lobster or other crustaceans.

Court-Bouillon: A poaching liquid that contains water, an acid (wine, citrus, vinegar), aromatics and other flavorings.
- Acids help flavor and coagulate the proteins of the products being poached.

Cube: To cut into small cubes (about 1/2 inch). In meats, to tenderize by pounding with a special tool that imprints a checkered pattern on the surface, breaking tough fibers to increase tenderness.

Darne: A thick slice of a large raw fish.

Dash: A very small amount, less than 1/8 teaspoon.

Deglaze: To dissolve and pick up the flavorful bits left on the bottom of a pan after cooking.
- Acids like wine work best because they help extract flavor.
- Stock, water or other liquids can also be used.

Demi-glace: "Half glaze" — a brown sauce reduction.

Depouillage: To skim the impurities off the top of a stock, soup or sauce.

Dredge: To coat or cover food lightly but completely with flour, sugar, or other fine substance.

Emulsion: A mixture of one liquid with another with which it cannot normally combine smoothly.

Farce: Stuffing or forcemeat.

Fat: Generic term for butter, margarine, lard or vegetable shortening; also the rendered drippings of meat or fowl.

Fines Herbes: A fine mixture of fresh herbs used to season meats, fish and sauces.

Foie Gras: Fattened goose or duck liver.

Fry: To cook in hot fat — pan-frying in a skillet (very little fat) or deep-frying in a heavy pan (food immersed in fat).

Fumet: White stock with other flavorings added, simmered and reduced by 50%.

Galanga: A root that is a relative of ginger, used in Thai cuisine — sometimes spelled galangal.

Glacé: Brown stock reduced by 85% to 90%.

Grill: To cook on a rack over direct heat - gas, electricity, or charcoal; to broil on a grill.

Herbs: Leaves of plants used either fresh or dry.
- When substituting dry for fresh, use 1/3 the amount.

Hydrogenation: A process in which extra hydrogen atoms are pumped into unsaturated fat.

Jus Lie: Pan juices thickened with a slurry.

Julienne: Matchstick pieces of vegetables, fruits or cooked meats.

Kohlrabi: Root vegetable that resembles a turnip but has a more delicate flavor.

Larding: Threading strips of fat into a piece of meat before cooking.
- Larding needle – hollow needle

Liaison: Thickening or binding agent used in the preparation of a soup or sauce.

Liaison Finale: Finishing or enriching agent added to soups or sauces at the end of the cooking process.

Madeira: Fortified wine, either sweet or dry, from the Portuguese island of Madeira.

Maillard Reaction: When natural sugars and proteins react to heat by caramelizing-browning and forming a crust.

Mandoline: A slicer with adjustable blades.

Marinade: A flavorful liquid used to tenderize and flavor products.
- Usually includes an acid, oil, herbs and spices

Mirepoix: Rough cut flavorful vegetables–traditionally carrots, onions, celery and sometimes leeks.

Monder: To blanch, peel and seed tomatoes.

Monter au Beurre: To swirl small chunks of cold, whole butter into a sauce at the end of the cooking process.

Nage: A light sauce created from a court bouillon.

Napper: To lightly coat with a sauce or to cook a sauce until it coats the back of a spoon.

Parboil: To boil until partially cooked; remainder of cooking is done by another method.

Purée: To sieve or whirl food into a smooth, thick mixture.

Quenelle: A dumpling made of meat, poultry or fish. It also refers to the basic quenelle shape — An oval formed by using 2 spoons that have been moistened in water.

Ragout: A rich stew.

Reduction: The result of boiling down liquids in order to concentrate flavors.

Remouillage: Second, weaker extraction made from the remnants of a stock.
- Half the water, half the cook time
- Used to start another stock

Render: To liquefy the fat from a meat product over low heat.
- Product should be diced or scored.

Resting: Letting a roast rest for 5 to 15 minutes after cooking.
- Equalizes internal pressure so juices can be re-absorbed
- Allows for carryover cooking

Roast: Oven-cook foods in an uncovered pan to produce a well-browned product with a moist interior.
- Dry cooking method
- Best for tender cuts of meat

Rondeau: Heavy pan with straight sides that are less than the width of the base. It is commonly used for braising.

Roux: A cooked combination of fat and flour used to thicken sauces and soups.

Sabayon: A mixture of egg yolks and an acid whisked over hot water just until the yolks start to thicken.

Sambal: A chile paste, often with garlic, salt, sugar and other spices, used in Asian cuisine.

Sauternes: A fruity, sweet white wine from the Bordeaux region.

Scald: To heat milk just below the boiling point (tiny bubbles appear around the edge of the pan when it has reached the proper temperature).

Sear: To brown meat quickly either in a hot pan with very little oil or in a hot oven.

Shock: To stop the cooking process by plunging a food in ice water.

Simmer: To cook in liquid over low heat just below the boiling point (bubbles form slowly and burst before reaching the surface).

Singer: To dust with flour after sautéing or roasting – flour mixes with the fat to create a quick roux.

Skim: To remove fat or scum from the surface of a liquid with a spoon or ladel.

Slurry: 50/50 mixture of cold liquid and refined starch – most often arrowroot or cornstarch.

Smoke Point: The temperature at which oils begin to smoke, burn and/or break down.

Spices: Buds, fruits, flowers, bark, berries, seeds and roots of plants and trees, used as seasonings.

Star Anise: the brown, fragrant pod of a Chinese evergreen used as a spice.

Steam: To cook in water vapors, on a rack or in a steam basket, in a covered pan above boiling water.

Steep: To infuse in liquid.

Stew: To cook a product barely covered in a flavorful liquid until the product is tender.
- Good for tough, small cuts of meat.
- Usually completed on top of the stove.
- Stewed vegetables are usually not seared.

Stir: Using a spoon or a whisk in a broad, circular motion, to mix ingredients without beating or to prevent them from sticking.

Sweat: To cook slowly over medium/low heat without browning.
- Good for flavor extraction.
- Moisture development encouraged.

Tamarind Concentrate: A sour-flavored paste made from the the pod of a tropical tree.

Texture: The structural quality of a food—roughness, smoothness, graininess, or creaminess.

Truss: Tie products prior to cooking.
- Helps maintain a products shape.
- Ensures even cooking.

Tuile: A thin, crisp, curved wafer.

Turmeric: The root of a musky-smelling tropical plant, used as a spice — usually used in powdered form.

Whip: To beat rapidly with a wire whisk, or electric mixer, incorporating air to lighten a mixture and increase its volume.

Whisk: To beat with a wire whisk until blended and smooth.

Whitewash: 50/50 mixture of cold liquid and flour.

Zest: Outer colored peel of citrus fruits. Also, the act of removing this outer peel.

MAIN PLATE — SEAFOOD

SALAD

SAUCES & SIDES

SPONSORS ■

American Culinary Federation Sponsors

Specials thanks to our sponsors for their continued support.

American Culinary Federation

The Beef Checkoff

Blodgett

Chef Revival

Club Managers Association
of America

Fortessa

Friedr. Dick

KitchenAid

Kraft Foodservice

Tyson Food Service

Uncle Ben's

Unilever

Westchester Country Club